IRON MAN
AND
PHILOSOPHY

The Blackwell Philosophy and Pop Culture Series

Series Editor: William Irwin

IRON MAN
AND
PHILOSOPHY
FACING THE STARK REALITY

Edited by
Mark D. White

WILEY

John Wiley & Sons, Inc.

Published by John Wiley & Sons, Inc., Hoboken, New Jersey
Published simultaneously in Canada

For general information about our other products and services, please contact our Customer Care Department within the United States at (800) 762-2974, outside the United States at (317) 572-3993 or fax (317) 572-4002.

Wiley also publishes its books in a variety of electronic formats. Some content that appears in print may not be available in electronic books. For more information about Wiley products, visit our web site at www.wiley.com.

Library of Congress Cataloging-in-Publication Data:

Iron Man and philosophy: facing the Stark reality / edited by Mark D. White
p.cm.
Includes index.
ISBN 978-0-470-48218-6 (pbk.)
1. Iron Man (Motion picture) I. White, Mark D., date.
PN1997.2.I76I76 2010
791.43'72—dc22
2009031396

Printed in the United States of America

10 9 8 7 6 5 4 3 2 1

CONTENTS

IRON INTRODUCTIONS AND ARMORED ACKNOWLEDGMENTS

Strange how much I owe to my life-giving transistors! They not only power my Iron Man armor, but they keep my injured heart beating so that Tony Stark can remain alive! My very existence is hanging by an electric cord!

Well, enough philosophy for now! If I know my women, and nobody knows them better than Tony Stark . . .

—*Tales of Suspense* #53, May 1964

Well, that may be enough philosophy for Tony Stark, but it's definitely not enough for the contributors to the book you're holding, not to mention its humble editor. For nearly forty years, comics buffs—and more recently, movie fans—have thrilled to the adventures of the armored avenger Iron Man and the romantic and business exploits of the man behind the mask, Tony Stark. But compared to other celebrated superheroes, Iron Man looks like a straightforward character.

1

Tony's not a deeply tortured soul like Batman or a perennial outcast like each of Uncanny X-Men, and he's not a front for a harsh portrayal of abuse of power like the characters of *Watchmen*. He's a guy in a shiny metal suit who fights bad guys—so what can philosophers possibly say about him?

As it turns out, plenty! A certain webslinger we know is fond of saying that with great power comes great responsibility, and Iron Man certainly wields great power—but does he show great responsibility? Does he behave ethically, and does he reason philosophically? Is there a downside to the tremendous technological advances that form Iron Man's incredible armor? And is his true superpower the armor of Iron Man or the intelligence of Tony Stark? Speaking of whom, Tony Stark is infamous for his playboy persona or, to put it more bluntly, his alcoholic womanizing. So how do these character flaws reflect on Iron Man the hero? Despite the glitz, glamour, and gleaming armor, is tragedy actually the defining aspect of Tony Stark's life?

As you read this book, I hope you come to agree—if you didn't already—that even the most "normal" of superheroes can inspire fascinating philosophical questions. Stan Lee may not have realized it at the time, but when he took a brilliant, handsome, and wealthy weapons manufacturer and turned his life upside down, he created a character with enough inner and outer turmoil to inspire stories like "Demon in a Bottle," "Armor Wars," and "The Mask in the Iron Man" (just to name a few). And Iron Man has *more* than enough depth to inspire philosophers like us—and that includes you, dear readers—to think about power, responsibility, intelligence, virtue, technology, and just what it must feel like to soar into the sky with jet-powered boots. (I'm still waiting for the last one—someday!)

•   •   •

For shepherding this book through with ease and grace, I want to thank Connie "Pepper" Santisteban and Eric "Happy" Nelson at Wiley; none of the books in the Blackwell Philosophy and Pop Culture Series—or our love triangle, so essential to the plot—would be possible without them. Heartfelt thanks go out to Robert "Yinsen" Arp, who helped get this ball rolling in the first place (and happily avoided the fate of his namesake). As always, I could not do this without the support and assistance of my copilot, series editor Bill "Rhodey" Irwin (could *War Machine and Philosophy* be next?). And finally, I thank all my fellow Avengers (as it happens, no West Coast ones—go figure) who contributed chapters to this book—I never could have defeated the evil Dr. Deadline without you!

For the years of Iron Man stories that inspired all of us involved with this book, we thank the creators, starting with Stan Lee, Larry Lieber, Don Heck, and Jack Kirby and continuing on with David Michelinie, Bob Layton, Denny O'Neil, Joe Quesada, Warren Ellis, Daniel and Charles Knauf, and Matt Fraction. Let us not forget the folks who gave ol' Shellhead even more worldwide exposure through the *Iron Man* films: Jon Favreau, Robert Downey Jr., and Gwyneth Paltrow, plus their costars, screenwriters, crew, and producers.

And thank you, Tony Stark. As the song goes, you get knocked down, but you get up again—they're never gonna keep you down. And as long as they don't, we'll be there, reading the comics, watching the movies, and thinking about the philosophy.

PART ONE

THE NUTS AND BOLTS OF TONY STARK

THE STARK MADNESS
OF TECHNOLOGY

George A. Dunn

For me, it was the jet boots.

Not that I didn't also covet that incredible array of weapons built into Tony Stark's armor—the repulsor rays, missile launchers, pulse beams, and flamethrowers—but it was those jet boots that really got me salivating. To my preadolescent mind, it was Tony's marvelous ability to lift himself off the ground and soar through the clouds that made him a bona fide *superhero* and not just some hotshot engineer outfitted with an admittedly awesome arsenal of weapons. After all, the prefix "super" comes from a Latin word meaning "above," so to watch a real superhero in action you should need to crane your neck and look up in the sky.

But the jet boots were also emblematic of what to my mind was the most glorious thing about Tony's way of being a superhero. Unlike, say, Reed Richards of the Fantastic Four, Tony wasn't simply someone who happened to be a superhero in addition to being a hotshot engineer. He was a superhero *because* of those jet boots and the enviable power they gave him, which is to say that it was his extraordinary engineering prowess that allowed him to make himself super, without having to wait around for gamma rays or a radioactive spider bite. Consequently—and best of all, to my way of thinking—you didn't even need to be Tony to wield his remarkable superpowers (at least until recently, when Extremis transformed him into a full-fledged technological artifact in his own right). All you needed was access to Stark technology. In principle, anyone could become the Iron Man. Of course, as the memorable "Armor Wars" story line drove home with a vengeance—and by "vengeance," I mean Tony Stark in a murderous rage—you would be ill-advised to use that technology without the permission of its creator.[1] On the other hand, you might get to be one of the lucky few, like James "Rhodey" Rhodes, "Happy" Hogan, or, more recently, Pepper Potts, all of whom Tony has authorized at one time to don some version of his Iron Man armor and take flight.

And the upshot to all this was that while I might have missed my chance to be born on Krypton, the prospect of flying with those gleaming red jet boots wasn't entirely beyond the reach of my juvenile imagination and its superheroic aspirations.

"A Heart of Gold and an Appearance to Match"

The enduring appeal of Iron Man owes a great deal to how Tony Stark personifies the spectacular promise of technology to turn our dreams into reality, a promise that has stoked a fire in the bellies of countless men and women in the modern era, not only in preadolescent boys with airborne imaginations. Occasionally, the promised marvels fail to materialize. While my youthful hopes shone brightly for the day when ads for genuine jet boots appeared in the comic book pages right next to the ones pitching Amazing Live Sea-Monkeys and X-Ray Specs, I've learned that this isn't likely to happen any time soon. Decades of trials with jet-powered apparatuses have established that the human body isn't aerodynamically suited for this type of flight, except in the zero-gravity conditions of outer space. (The Sea-Monkeys were a big disappointment, too.)

But in all probability, the appeal of Iron Man owes just as much to the way his gleaming golden armor bathes him in the glory of a mythical past, a romantic world of medieval knights-errant, often graced with superhuman abilities, invincible in battle against an endless succession of menaces that threaten the peace of their kingdoms. Consider Stan Lee's account of how he first came up with the inspiration for Iron Man:

> I thought, *Well, what if a guy had a suit of armor, but it was a modern suit of armor—not like years ago in the days of King Arthur—and what if that suit of armor made him as strong as any Super Hero?* I wasn't thinking robot at all; I was thinking armor, a man wearing twentieth century armor that would give him great power.[2]

Medieval knights often ruled over a kingdom of their own or were pledged to the service of some honorable and righteous lord who commissioned their noble exploits and invested them with the authority to act on his behalf. Tony Stark certainly fits that bill, as does Iron Man in his guise as Tony's most recognizable "employee." Like a feudal knight, Tony reigns over a powerful kingdom—an industrial kingdom, in his case—that owes its prosperity to his wisdom and foresight. Most important, as one of Tony's female companions once described his Iron Man alter ego, "he has a heart of gold and an appearance to match his golden deeds."[3] He is the very essence of chivalry—noble, generous, and courageous; a perfect gentleman; skilled in the arts of war; and a formidable fighter for justice.

In short, Tony epitomizes not only the dream of technology enhancing human powers far beyond the limits of our natural endowments but also the possibility of the noble chivalric ideal surviving into the technological era, despite all of the other transformations the human condition is bound to undergo, transformations perhaps more profound than we can currently foresee. He's a sublime anachronism, an inspired amalgam of past and future at their best. And, to the extent we can persuade ourselves that this hybrid really is a portent of things to come, the future looks as bright as the fire spitting from the heels of Iron Man's jet boots.

These days, however, when I think about knights, I often recall the words of a seventeenth-century philosopher named René Descartes (1596–1650). In his *Discourse on Method*, Descartes offered an assessment of the education he received at one of the top schools in Europe, judging almost the entire curriculum to have been a colossal waste of his time. His appraisal of the value of the literature he was required to read concludes with his remark that "fables make us imagine many things as possible that are not" and even the authors of "histories" are guilty on occasion of "altering or exaggerating the importance of matters in order to make them more worthy of being read" and "at any rate, will almost always omit the baser and less notable events." Consequently, "those who regulate their conduct by the examples they draw from these works are liable to fall into the excesses of the knights-errant of our tales of chivalry, and to conceive plans beyond their powers."[4] Could Tony Stark, a character in a modern-day fable, mislead us into thinking that impossible things are really possible? (I'm not just talking about the jet boots, by the way.)

"Masters of Nature"

No doubt, you've heard the old wisecrack about the philosopher's boots being firmly planted in the clouds. Clearly, this droll image of thinkers traipsing around the stratosphere is meant to belittle philosophy as a lot of rarefied nonsense with little or no relevance for life as it is lived by the rest of us here on the ground. But couldn't we interpret it instead as an acknowledgment that philosophers—some of them, at least—might have something in common with high-flying superheroes like Iron Man?

Descartes was the sort of philosopher who enjoyed pondering the perennial questions of what was then known as "first philosophy"—the existence of God, the nature of the soul, and other lofty matters—whenever he could squeeze in a short break from his main preoccupations, such as inventing analytical geometry, working out the law of refraction in optics, and offering some of the first mathematical descriptions of the behavior of light.[5] While these may seem like fairly modest accomplishments compared to the invention of a lightweight exoskeleton that doubles as a high-tech weapons arsenal, the truth is that neither Stark Industries nor the Iron Man armor could have gotten off the ground without Descartes' pioneering contributions to science and mathematics. But Descartes was a forerunner of Iron Man in another, even more important, respect. In addition to helping shepherd into being the experimental, mathematics-based methods that launched the scientific revolution, he was among the first to promote the idea of using these new scientific methods to equip human beings with wonderful new abilities, in addition to significantly enhancing our existing ones.

Consider his research in optics, undertaken for the expressed purpose of enhancing the power of the human eye. "All the management of our lives depends on the senses," he wrote in the opening line of his essay the *Optics*, "and since sight is the noblest and most comprehensive of our senses, inventions that serve to increase its power are undoubtedly among the most useful there can be."[6] To tackle the problem of designing superior optical instruments, he offered a definition of light, analyses of the human eye and the phenomenon of vision, a formulation of the law of refraction, a discussion of lenses for "perfecting vision" and correcting the "faults of the eye," and, finally, directions for constructing a machine that could manufacture those lenses. By contemporary standards, the results may not be all that impressive, paling in comparison to the fantastic sensory enhancement Tony Stark enjoys due to his Iron Man armor. But it's a start and, most important, an indispensable foundation for greater inventions to come.

It's Not All in the Hardware

Still, from another perspective, Descartes was an even more stupendous inventor than even the illustrious Tony Stark, despite the fact that the most earth-shattering products of his ingenuity, his new methods in mathematics and natural science, didn't contain a speck of "hardware." As a number of recent philosophers have argued, we would be hugely mistaken to think that the essence of technology consists of hardware. The "most obvious, massive, and impressive example" of technology may be the machine, argued the French philosopher and social theorist Jacques Ellul (1912–1994), but the essence of technology (or *technique*, as he called it) is something less tangible, "the totality of methods rationally arrived at and having absolute efficiency (for a given state of development) in every field of human activity."[7] Wrapped in that thicket of words is a simple and cogent insight: what makes our technological civilization possible is not our *tools* but rather the *rules* that tell us how to construct and use them. In the "starkest" terms, the essence of technology lies not in the Iron Man armor and arsenal but in the know-how that created and that operates them. At bottom, argued Ellul, technology is a set of proven methods to get the job done—whatever it may be— in the most efficient way possible. Machine technology is simply an external embodiment of those methods, kind of like their "exoskeleton."

Descartes was a vigorous proponent of yoking science to a tried-and-true method. Patterned after "the procedures in the mechanical crafts," the rules of his method required every scientific question to be framed as a search for some unknown quantity in a mathematical equation. Because mathematics was, in his opinion, what made the procedures of first-rate craftsmen so reliable, translating scientific problems that weren't ostensibly about numbers and figures into ones that were seemed like a surefire way to find solutions that would be not only rigorous but, just as important, useful for the invention of new devices to expand human powers. One measure of Descartes' success is that three centuries later, when young Tony Stark was enrolled at MIT, the curriculum he studied was imbued from top to bottom with Cartesian zeal for mathematics. Although Descartes' private use of his method produced little technological hardware, it wouldn't be at all off the mark to call him one of the chief engineers of the "software"—the intangible directives and protocols—that has directed the assembly of our modern technological civilization.

Descartes' vision of what a technologically oriented science could accomplish extended far beyond the manufacture of machines to make better lenses. He expected nothing short of marvels from the triumphant parade of top-notch scientists and engineers who would follow in his footsteps—or maybe even, as in the case of Tony Stark, blaze a trail up above his footsteps in the sky. Consider Descartes' stunning prediction of how, through his method,

> we could know the power and action of fire, water, air, the stars, the heavens and all the other bodies in our environment, as distinctly as we know the different crafts of our artisans; and we could use this knowledge—as

the artisans use theirs—for all the purposes for which it is appropriate, and thus make ourselves, as it were, the lords and masters of nature.[8]

When we understand how nature works, we're in a position to put nature to work for *us*. Then we can, as people often say, "master nature." But when Descartes used the term "master" (*maître*) in the passage we just quoted, he was thinking of something much more specific than simply elevating us to a position of dominion over the rest of nature. To be a master in his century was to be a highly accomplished artisan, someone possessing the knowledge and skill to craft the right raw materials into beautiful and functional artifacts. Using science to become masters of nature suggests that we can eventually turn *all* of nature into a store of raw materials to be refashioned however we like.

If you're thinking that Descartes is beginning to sound like Tony Stark's own personal publicist, heralding his technological prowess centuries in advance, then just wait until you hear this. Descartes believed that we could eventually come to understand the natural world every bit as well as an artisan understands his machines because *nature is in fact nothing other than an incredibly intricate machine*. The only real difference is that the operations of artifacts are for the most part performed by mechanisms that are large enough to be easily perceivable by the senses—as indeed must be the case if they are capable of being manufactured by human beings. The effects produced by nature, in contrast, almost always depend on structures that are so minute that they completely elude our senses.[9]

This simply means that as our machines come to be composed of more intricate and miniaturized parts, they increasingly approximate the designs used by nature itself. And that's exactly where Stark technology has been heading from the beginning. It was microtransistors that made the Iron Man armor possible when the character was first introduced in March 1963 in the pages of *Tales of Suspense* #39. Ever since, Tony's passion has been miniaturization, with every upgrade of his armor requiring circuitry of progressively more minute components, shrinking over time to microscopic dimensions.[10] Tunneling ever deeper into the nano-regions of reality, manipulating structures that lie far below the threshold of detection by our unaided senses, Stark technology has long been advancing on the ability to create an entirely synthetic nature, new and improved, built to human specifications.

The Heroism of Generosity

But what should those specifications be? When it comes to guidance on how best to use our technological power, that avatar of mathematical precision Descartes became curiously vague. In the end, his counsel came down to extolling a virtue and prescribing a maxim. The virtue is *generosity*, one of the chief virtues that traditionally defined the practice and ideals of the knight in shining armor. The mark of a generous person, according to Descartes, is that he never swerves from his constant "volition to undertake and execute all the things he judges best."[11] That sounds like a pretty admirable trait, but it does leave us wondering what exactly Descartes' generous knight would judge to be best. What if someone—a villain like Norman Osborn, for instance—judges it best to use the technological power at his disposal to achieve world dominion and turn superheroes into outlaws (and vice versa)?[12] In that case, Descartes might refer us to his maxim: We should abide by "the law that obliges us to do all in power to secure the general welfare of mankind."[13] Of course, it's the line between concern for the general welfare and preoccupation with private gain that has always divided the heroes from the villains in the comic book universe, so Descartes' maxim will undoubtedly have a familiar ring to many of us. But while taking the side of the general good may be a fine maxim for a hero, it doesn't yet tell us what really is best for ourselves and others.

At one time there was a general consensus among philosophers that we could discover what was best for human beings by looking to the nature of our species and, more specifically, to the things that we all naturally require in order to survive and flourish. Basic needs like health and safety must be met, but most philosophers agreed that human happiness also depended on satisfying our so-called higher needs for such goods as friendship, aesthetic enjoyment, and intellectual understanding. Our need for these things is so deeply embedded in our nature—or, as people say nowadays, they're so hardwired into our brains—that they've usually been thought to provide a stable yardstick for judging what really does and doesn't contribute to "the general welfare of mankind." But what if our technology were to advance to the point where we could refashion not only our natural environment but even human nature itself, including the human brain and nervous system? What could guide our decisions then?

When Descartes was describing how to design a machine to grind better lenses, his aim was the enhancement of human powers, specifically, our ability to see clearly and distinctly things that are very small or a great distance away. Descartes' lenses are elementary prosthetic devices, designed to supplement and remedy the defects of the senses with which we were born. Tony's Iron Man armor, with its assortment of sophisticated sensory and motility enhancing devices, may seem leagues beyond Descartes' lenses, but they're still essentially the same type of thing. Jet boots are also prosthetic devices, albeit extraordinarily cool ones. But in this day and age, when so many of us not only wear glasses but also walk around with cell phones and mp3 players fastened semipermanently to our ears, we're no longer impressed by the *idea* of prosthetic enhancement, even as we continue to marvel at some of the forms it can take, such as synthetic exoskeletons or implanted neural stimulators.

"The Body Is Wrong"

However, in the critically acclaimed "Extremis" story line, Warren Ellis's 2004 reboot of the *Iron Man* comic, a new technological threshold was crossed, as Tony faced a threat to his life that could be countered only by the most radical technological means.[14] In the past, Tony's life was saved by a magnetic chest plate, a prosthetic device that kept the shrapnel in his chest from reaching his heart. But in "Extremis," only a top-to-bottom redesign of his very physiology holds out any hope of saving him.

"Extremis" features a flashback to Iron Man's origins in Afghanistan, in which Tony tells Dr. Ho Yinsen, with whom he was held captive by Afghan guerrillas, that "adapting machines to man and making us great" have always been the goals of his research.[15] It was with Yinsen's help that Tony built the first primitive prototype of his Iron Man armor with a lifesaving magnetic chest plate, a textbook case of constructing a machine adapted to human needs. Now fast-forward to the present: once again mortally wounded, but this time in battle with a terrorist possessing superpowers acquired through biotechnology, Tony turns to the experimental serum Extremis, both to save his life and to give himself a fighting chance against his foe: the same two ends his armor served in Afghanistan.

But listen to Maya Hansen, the designer of the Extremis technology, as she explains how it works, and ask yourself whether you think that what it does should also be described as "adapting machines to man":

> It's a bio-electronics package, fitted into a few billion graphic nanotubes and suspended in a carrier fluid. . . .

It hacks the body's repair center—the part of the brain that keeps a complete blueprint of the human body. . . . The normal human blueprint is being replaced with the Extremis blueprint, you see? The brain is being told the body is wrong. . . . Extremis uses the nutrients and body mass to grow new organs. Better ones.[16]

Extremis uses bioelectric robots to rebuild Tony's body, including his nervous system, from the inside out: healing his injuries, making him stronger than ever before, and equipping him with a broad spectrum of new abilities. He now stores the undersheath of his Iron Man armor in the hollows of his bones, "wired directly into my brain," and can make it emerge at will. He can direct the other components of his armor at a distance by using brain impulses to manipulate a "vectored repulsor field," allowing him to suit up with the speed and effortlessness of thought. The operating systems of his armor are similarly linked directly to his brain. To top it off, he's jacked into every electronics system in the world—every satellite, cell phone, and computer network—making him an information security expert's nightmare.

Yet enviable as these powers may be, we can't help but wonder whether this overhaul of Tony's physiology is really an extension of his program of "adapting machines to man" or more a case of adapting a man to the machines: specifically, adapting Tony to his technological milieu by transforming him into another technological artifact. And once we begin redesigning human beings to make them interface more efficiently with our artificially constructed technological environment, don't we become like cogs in a giant machine that has commandeered *us*, rather than vice versa?

The twentieth-century philosopher Martin Heidegger (1889–1976) expressed a similar set of concerns about the direction our technological civilization was heading in a famous essay titled "The Question Concerning Technology."[17]

For Heidegger, technology isn't simply a set of hyperefficient means to achieving our goals, whatever they may happen to be. Even more essentially, technology is a way of understanding and interpreting the world, in which the whole of nature is approached as "standing-reserve," a store of raw materials and energy waiting to be extracted, stored, shifted around, transformed, and controlled (ostensibly, at least) by human beings. But as this technological worldview becomes so dominant that it crowds out every other way of interpreting the world, Heidegger thought that we would come "to the brink of a precipitous fall." Having trained ourselves to view *everything* as "standing-reserve" from which energy can be extracted to be reconfigured for our use, the denizen of modern technological civilization is bound to reach "the point where he himself will have to be taken as standing-reserve."[18] And that's precisely what Extremis does when it commandeers the brain, tells it "the body is wrong," and uses the body's existing mass as a "standing-reserve" from which a new enhanced human organism can be constructed.

And so we return to our earlier problem. When human nature itself becomes "standing-reserve," one last frontier of the natural world for us to technologically master and modify, then our old-fashioned conceptions of human flourishing automatically become outdated and can no longer offer any guidance for determining "the general welfare of mankind."

"How Many Have Drawn Blood with My Sword?"

But maybe the obsolescence of those antique standards is good news, and we're completely free to use our power however we choose, free as a bird or at least free as a man with jet boots, unchained from the human nature we inherited from the past of our species, with nothing to prevent us from forging whatever ersatz nature suits our fancy. Then again, however, maybe that sense of freedom is an illusion. We often speak of how the human race has gained unprecedented freedom and power through the technological conquest of nature, but that language is somewhat misleading inasmuch as it implies that technology empowers us all equally. As we all know, it's those who possess or control access to the new technology—corporations like Stark Industries and the governments of rich nations—who are most empowered, often at the expense of those who lack access. This is not to deny that the powerful might have benign intentions, but, on the other hand, they might not.

The earliest *Iron Man* comics were bursting with optimism about how a courageous and well-intentioned hero like Tony Stark, armed with cutting-edge technology, could vanquish the many foes of freedom in the world. But by the mid-eighties, it had become clear to Tony that he had unleashed forces he couldn't control. Unable to prevent the dissemination of his Iron Man armor designs to villains like Spymaster and Obadiah Stane (Iron Monger), Tony faced the sickening realization that the very technologies he designed to make the world safer were actually being used to put it at graver risk than it ever would have been without them. Of particular interest is Stane, a sort of dark doppelganger of Tony. Like Tony, he's a powerful tycoon and weapons mogul, although his corporate intrigues are not in the service of old-fashioned chivalric virtues such as generosity but rather the newfangled capitalist virtue of greed instead. Suddenly, Tony's archenemy is no longer a communist in another country intent on destroying our way of life but a ruthless domestic capitalist who ends up possessing much of Tony's technology and none of his ideals.

All of this was a prelude to "Armor Wars," one of the most celebrated *Iron Man* story lines of all time. By that time, Tony was no longer a cold war munitions manufacturer. In a minor revision to his history, we're told that he supplied the U.S. military with weapons during the Vietnam era but only because he was "eager to end an unsavory war." Since then, he's been "dedicating himself to the positive aspects of life through his brilliance and business acumen and his courageous secret life as the heroic Avenger called Iron Man." But when he discovers that despite his precautions, his armor technology has fallen into the hands of a host of villains— including Force, Stilt Man, the Raiders, the Controller, the Crimson Dynamo, and the Mauler—he exclaims in horror, "How many have drawn blood with my sword?" Feeling responsible for every murder committed with the aid of his technology and needing to redeem himself, the golden knight goes on the offensive to confiscate or disable all of the armor made from his designs, using whatever means prove necessary.[19] Hanging in the balance is whether he was deluded to pride himself on being such an unalloyed force for goodness.

The course of events in "Armor Wars" doesn't give Tony much cause for reassurance. In fact, Tony's zeal to regain exclusive control of his technology yields nothing but grief on several fronts for himself and others. He almost destroys his own company, sullies the reputation of Iron Man so thoroughly that Stark Industries must "fire" him as a corporate spokesman, finds himself pitted against Captain America and the U.S. government, and nearly provokes an international incident as a result of a deadly battle with the Gremlin, a Russian scientist whose Titanium Man armor makes him a target in Tony's crusade. Powering up his jet boots to escape the Gremlin's crushing embrace, Tony inadvertently ignites his adversary's titanium armor and kills him in the blazing inferno.[20] Oh, my beloved jet boots! Those emblems of freedom have become nightmarish instruments of death.

Jet Boots and Clay Feet

"Armor Wars" illustrates what contemporary philosopher John Gray has called "the chaotic drift of new technologies," their tendency to proliferate into new applications that their designers neither intended nor foresaw, even coming to serve ends that their designers may find downright abhorrent.[21] This suggests a reason our modern relationship to technology can never be as simple and straightforward as the medieval knight's relationship to his sword, a tractable tool that is so perfectly obedient to the will of the expert swordsman that it feels more like an extension of his own arm than an independent entity. The swordsman's art depends on a highly specialized set of skills acquired only in the course of a long apprenticeship, but the power of modern technology consists of stores of information that can travel around the world with the push of a button. To master his sword, the knight need only train his body and mind, but to "master" modern technology in a way that would ensure that it is used solely for benign ends, we would need to rein in the proliferation of knowledge—or, if that proves impossible, to eradicate greed and the lust for power from the human heart.

No doubt, top scientists are at work on these problems as we speak, but to the extent that they succeed, we may find that instead of extending our freedom as originally promised, technology has engineered it away. Certainly, one lesson of "Armor Wars" is that among the casualties of the struggle to master technology may be some of the high ideals we once believed technology ought to serve. In any case, it seems unlikely that either the flow of information or the evil imaginations of the human heart will ever cease. Consequently, wrote Gray, "If anything about the present century is certain, it is that the power conferred on 'humanity' by new technologies will be used to commit atrocious crimes against it."[22] Not even the genius of Tony Stark can shield us against that.

For me it was the jet boots, as I'm sure it was for a lot of boys who shared my fascination with the freedom and power that technology seemed to confer. But Iron Man's devoted fans didn't consist only of boys. Discussing the early years of the *Iron Man* comic, Stan Lee recalled, "We later learned that, of all our Super Heroes, Iron Man got the most fan mail from females." Our hero's wealth and glamorous lifestyle undoubtedly accounted for some of this volume of mail, but Lee believed that it was also because "he had that weak heart and was a tragic figure."[23] The tragic nature of Iron Man was, in fact, as much a part of Lee's original conception of the character as his aura of being a knight in shining armor. Indeed, as we're first being introduced to Tony Stark in the issue of *Tales of Suspense* that gave Iron Man to the world, we're offered glimpses of his life in a series of panels that show him adored by beautiful women who swoon over him as "the dreamiest thing this side of Rock Hudson." But at the same time, we're alerted that "this man who seems so fortunate, who's envied by millions—is soon destined to become the most tragic figure on earth!"[24]

I must confess that the crippled and vulnerable heart beneath the armor never struck me as the most salient aspect of Iron Man, at least not until many years later when, like many other observers of modern civilization, I began to suspect that our technological prowess engendered as many problems as it solved. It was then that I realized those gleaming jet boots really hid feet of clay.

NOTES

1. *Iron Man*, vol. 1, #225–232 (1987–1988), collected in trade paperback in 2007.

2. Quoted in Andy Mangels, *Iron Man: Beneath the Armor* (New York: Del Rey, 2008), p. 4.

3. *Tales of Suspense* #40 (April 1963).

4. René Descartes, *Philosophical Writings*, vol. I, trans. John Cottington, Robert Stoothoff, and Dougald Murdoch (Cambridge, UK: Cambridge University Press, 1985), p. 114.

5. The Cartesian coordinates, the x and y axes we all used when graphing equations in high school algebra, are named after him.

6. Descartes, *Philosophical Writings*, p. 152.

7. Jacques Ellul, *The Technological Society*, trans. John Wilkinson (New York: Vintage Books, 1967), pp. xxv, 3.

8. Descartes, *Philosophical Writings*, pp. 142–143.

9. Ibid., p. 288.

10. See the chapter "The Literal Making of a Superhero" by Travis Rieder in this volume for more on miniaturization and nanotechonology and their ethical implications.

11. René Descartes, *The Passions of the Soul*, trans. Stephen H. Voss (Indianapolis: Hackett, 1989), p. 104.

12. If that sounds preposterous, see the "Dark Reign" story line introduced in the aftermath of "Secret Invasion" in Marvel Comics titles starting in December 2008, and especially the "World's Most Wanted" story line in *Iron Man*, vol. 5, #8–19 (2009).

13. Descartes, *Philosophical Writings*, p. 142.

14. *Iron Man*, vol. 4, #1–6 (2005–2006), collected in trade paperback in 2007. This story also contains an update of Iron Man's origin story, elements of which were incorporated into the 2008 *Iron Man* film. For instance, Iron Man's *original* origin story from *Tales of Suspense* #39 (March 1963) was set in Vietnam during the height of the cold war, but Ellis relocated the action to a more contemporary hot spot, Afghanistan.

15. *Iron Man*, vol. 4, #5 (January 2006).

16. Ibid., vol. 4, #3 (April 2004).

17. Included in Martin Heidegger, *The Question Concerning Technology and Other Essays*, trans. William Lovitt (New York: Harper & Row, 1977), pp. 3–35.

18. Ibid., p. 27.

19. *Iron Man*, vol. 1, #225 (December 1987).

20. Ibid., vol. 1, #229 (April 1988). See the chapter "Can Iron Man Atone for Tony Stark's Wrongs?" by Christopher Robichaud in this volume for more on Tony's action to reclaim his stolen technology in "Armor Wars."

21. John Gray, *Straw Dogs: Thoughts on Humans and Other Animals* (New York: Farrar, Straus and Giroux, 2007), p. 177.

22. Ibid., p. 14.

23. Quoted in Mangels, *Iron Man: Beneath the Armor*, p. 8.

24. *Tales of Suspense* #39 (March 1963).

THE TECHNOLOGICAL SUBVERSION OF TECHNOLOGY: TONY STARK, HEIDEGGER, AND THE SUBJECT OF RESISTANCE

Rocco Gangle

Got to Get Away: Engineering Escape

Early in the 2008 film *Iron Man*, Tony Stark constructs the prototype for what will later become the Iron Man armor. Returning from a demonstration of Stark Industries' powerful new Jericho weapon in Afghanistan's Kunar Province, Stark is captured by members of a nefarious political group called the Ten Rings and held prisoner in their desert cave. The leader of the Ten Rings demands that Stark build them a replica of the Jericho weapon using materials the group has stolen from the U.S. military. The Ten Rings intends to use Stark's knowledge and technical skills for its own political ends, and its members are willing to torture Stark in order to get him to do what they want. Because they have Tony Stark completely in their power, it would appear that the Ten Rings equally controls Stark's capacities as a scientist and an engineer. Despite himself, Stark seems to have become a kind of instrument or tool in the hands of the Ten Rings.

Placed in this difficult situation, Stark doesn't seem to have many options: if he does what the Ten Rings demands, he assists an evil and destructive political group, but if he doesn't follow its orders, he dies. Stark, however, thinks of a third option: he uses the materials given to him by the Ten Rings against its members in order to escape the cave without doing what they ask. Taking advantage of their relative ignorance of the very science and engineering knowledge they need him for, Stark disguises his blueprints for the armor that will enable his escape from the cave as the weapon his captors want. With the helpful cooperation of his fellow prisoner Yinsen, who is also a scientist and an engineer, Stark is able, even under the watchful eyes of the Ten Rings, to design and build the very armor that makes his escape from the cave possible.

Tony Stark's escape from the cave in Afghanistan clearly depends on the power of technology. It is the technology of the armor that defeats the Ten Rings, and it is technology that subsequently transforms Tony Stark the man into Iron Man the hero. Technology certainly has its benefits, but it also has its problems, as our philosophical investigation will reveal.

What Makes It Tick? Questioning Technology with Stark and Heidegger

The German philosopher Martin Heidegger (1889–1976) thought that the question of technology was perhaps the most important philosophical question of our time. Worried about the destructive and dehumanizing potential of modern technology, Heidegger believed that only by coming to understand technology thoughtfully would human beings avoid being swept away in history by its overwhelming power. Heidegger called into question the everyday understanding of technology that sees it as nothing more than a means to an end, fully within human control. Although this everyday understanding of technology is not wrong, according to Heidegger, it fails to penetrate deeply enough into what is really at stake.

So, what is the essence or inner meaning of technology? Of course, we all know what technology is; it surrounds us everywhere. Nothing is more familiar to us than computer screens and cell phones, automobiles and refrigerators, electric lights and indoor plumbing. We know, even without ever really thinking about it, that all of these things are technological. But, on the other hand, it is difficult to say exactly what *makes* these things technological. Is technology itself merely a simple property of certain objects? Or does it involve a unique and complex history that has linked social and political organization, economic production, and everyday life in our modern world? If we find ourselves living our lives primarily within a technological world, shouldn't we try to understand as much as possible about the specific character of that world? We can't fully know ourselves without knowing the kind of world we inhabit. So our everyday understanding of technology would seem to conceal a deeper problem. Without addressing this deeper problem, we can't get a good handle on what we—or Iron Man—are all about.

The word "technology" derives from two Greek terms: *technê* and *logos*. *Technê* refers to an art or a craft, a "knowing-how" to do or make something. *Logos* is the source of our word "logic," among others. It refers to the power of human language to represent and know things. Technology binds together scientific knowledge and economic power in a practical context. As a scientist, on the one hand, and an engineer and a businessman, on the other, Tony Stark is a perfect figure of technology: he is both a man of science and a man of action.

We Can Build You: The Causes of Iron Man

To get at the real essence of technology, Heidegger considered it in terms of the philosophical problem of *causality*. How exactly does one thing make another thing happen? How does something come to be? In particular, Heidegger linked technology to a philosophical tradition that goes back to Aristotle (384–322 B.C.E.) and that distinguishes four kinds of causes: material (what something is made of), formal (the shape or definition of a thing), efficient (what makes or produces the thing), and final (the end or purpose of a thing).[1] These four types of cause are useful insofar as they apply to almost anything we might consider. They give us four different ways of looking at something and trying to explain it: in terms of its *matter*, its *form*, its *source*, and its *purpose*.

Various aspects of a thing come to light when we consider it in these different ways. If, for example, we analyze the Iron Man armor in terms of these four kinds of cause, we might see it like this:

Material cause: a high-strength metal alloy
Formal cause: the blueprints for the armor, its design and shape
Efficient cause: Tony Stark and his computer assistant Jarvis
Final cause: the transformation of Tony Stark into a powerful hero

All of these causes work together to bring Iron Man into being. Each of them is necessary in its own way. Try to imagine

Iron Man existing without one of them—you'll see that it just doesn't work.

In general, the four types of cause are what make any given thing come into existence in the world. In his discussion of technology, Heidegger interpreted these four types of cause in terms of a kind of *responsibility*: "The four causes are the ways, all belonging at once to each other, of being responsible for something else."[2] This causal responsibility is what philosophers call *ontological*; it concerns the very being or essence of things as related to a common world of meaning. As Heidegger put it, "The four ways of being responsible bring something into appearance. They let it come forth into presencing."[3] In particular, it is important to realize that final causes, or purposes, are essential aspects of all technologically produced objects. The Iron Man armor, for instance, is not merely a complex arrangement of matter and energy; it is what it is because it was designed for a specific reason. Because it was built with this purpose in mind, the Iron Man armor carries with it a particular meaning.

In this way, Heidegger emphasized that technological causes don't only produce material effects within the world; they also allow new kinds of meaning and experience to emerge for human beings. For this reason, technology should be understood as essentially creative, or poetic. Technology makes or reveals a certain kind of world, a technological world with its own models of being and truth. Heidegger said, "Technology is a mode of revealing. Technology comes to presence in the realm where revealing and unconcealment take place, where *aletheia*, truth, happens."[4] In other words, technology should be understood as more than simply a powerful tool for doing what we want *within* the world we already have. It also calls into being and shapes the human world itself in a particular way. Technology for Heidegger is a way of being that in the modern world has become *our* way of being.

Look Out Beyond! The Dangers
of Technology

Heidegger was especially concerned with the dangers of modern technology, in which the power to create is linked to the mathematical knowledge and control of nature. It is precisely this kind of *technê* that Tony Stark has mastered as a scientist and an engineer. According to Heidegger, in the world of modern technology nature tends to be transformed into nothing more than a kind of supply zone of power. Everything in nature appears as a mere "standing-reserve" of energy and possible use.[5] Instead of nature itself, we see only "natural resources." This is true even of people, as the contemporary phrase "human resources" suggests. Instead of working in and with nature, nature is controlled or "challenged" by human beings: "The revealing that rules in modern technology is a challenging, which puts to nature the unreasonable demand that it supply energy which can be extracted and stored as such."[6] Heidegger emphasized that in such a development, humans are never fully in control. The history of technology happens *to* us as much as it is caused *by* us. Perhaps our technological world determines who we are even more than we determine what it is.

In this way, for Heidegger the technological world runs the risk of converting everything—including human beings themselves—into mere material for spreading the logic of blind power "standing-reserve" everywhere. Heidegger suggested that the essence of technology is such that it tends of its own accord to do so, almost like a kind of world cancer. And sadly, any attempt to stop or cure this cancer seems inevitably to reproduce its logic. Technological solutions (such as cars or refrigerators) often give rise to new and unforeseen problems (such as pollution and global warming). These new problems then demand scientific and technological solutions of their own. In this respect, the modern world sometimes resembles a man trying frantically to escape from quicksand who tends through his own movements to sink still farther down.

Yet despite all this, Heidegger insisted that the modern, scientific form of technology is also related to a new historical possibility for human freedom. This is because technology forces us to ask about the relationship of human beings to *Being* itself, or essence, in a new way: "it is technology itself that makes the demand on us to think in another way what is usually understood by 'essence.'"[7] In other words, the power of technology to create and sustain a new kind of world makes us think about the world itself differently. In particular, thinking about the essence of the technological world forces us to rethink the essence of human beings in that world. In his influential book *Being and Time*, Heidegger developed a conception of human existence that contrasts individual responsibility with the thoughtless conformity of mass media and technological production.[8] And Tony Stark's use of technology in building, wearing, and wielding the Iron Man armor actually shows us a way that the power of technology can be harnessed to human individuality and ethically accountable action such that the worst tendencies of technology itself are resisted.

Suiting Up: Making Power Responsible

Once Tony Stark escapes from the cave of the Ten Rings, having witnessed the deaths of U.S. soldiers caused by Stark Industries' own weapons, he feels challenged and humbled by the courage of his fellow captive Yinsen. Stark reflects on his complicity in the destruction he has seen and thereby faces a new dilemma. Should he return to his previous life as a self-indulgent and largely conscienceless playboy? Or should he reorient his life around what he has learned through his traumatic experience in the desert? Stark's experience in the cave-prison in Kunar Province taught him something: it is wrong to contribute to the research and development of weapons technology without at the same time taking responsibility for how such weapons are actually used.

Tony Stark experiences a kind of conversion in the Afghanistan desert; his whole way of looking at the world and himself changes. As a major contributor and innovator within the American military-industrial complex, Stark comes to realize that the power of technologically advanced weaponry must be called into question on the basis of human values and individual ethical decisions. As Stark explains publicly in the press conference he holds shortly after his escape, "I saw young Americans killed by the very weapons I created to defend them and protect them, and I saw that I had become part of a system that is comfortable with zero accountability." To a journalist's surprised question, "What happened over there?" Stark replies, "I had my eyes opened. I came to realize that I have more to offer this world than just making things to blow up."

Stark realizes that his company lacks a sense of accountability for its own actions. If Stark Industries is producing weapons that are eventually used to kill people, then Stark Industries finds itself implicated in the system of causal relations that is ultimately responsible for those deaths. To participate consciously in such a system of production is to be at least partially accountable for its real effects.[9] This means that by designing and building weapons without attending to how they are actually used, Stark Industries has been evading its responsibilities—as has Stark himself. His existence, Heidegger would say, has been *inauthentic*. Tony Stark wants to remedy this situation.

Yet the economic and material power of Stark Industries is only one piece of a much larger economic and political world of defense contracting, diplomacy, and war making, a world far more extensive and powerful than any individual human being. How could one person—even someone with the resources and capabilities of Tony Stark—hope to resist such a system effectively? Just as in his escape from the Afghanistan cave, here, too, Stark's special suit of technological armor provides the answer. In this case, though, instead of being the response to a pressing *individual* need, Stark's donning the armor results from a carefully thought out decision, a resolution on his part to live and act in an ethically responsible and accountable way *for the sake of others.*

Philosophers give the name *subjectivity* to the kinds of experiences and causes that are involved in conscious, responsible action. When we choose to do one thing rather than another or when we experience the anxiety and necessity of making our own decisions, we are *subjects* in this philosophical sense. Subjectivity implies not only the power to act but, more important, the ability to define yourself through what you do. To be a subject is to be able, at least in part, to create who you are. Indeed, we can't help it; we *have to* create ourselves through our projects and choices. The possibility of accepting our inevitable responsibility for such choices and projects opens up what Heidegger calls *authentic* existence.

Heidegger's philosophy shows us how certain aspects of modern technology, such as its tendency to reduce human beings to mere "human resources" and its logic of power without responsibility, must be resisted if we are to live authentically. In this light, Tony Stark's escape from the Ten Rings and his construction of the Iron Man armor show us a way to use technology subversively. Stark's actions demonstrate how the negative tendencies of technological power may be transformed from within technology itself. When Tony Stark becomes Iron Man, he uses technology specifically to avoid the irresponsibility of Stark Industries' complicity in military-industrial destruction. If Heidegger was right that such destructive tendencies are somehow caught up in the very essence of modern technology, then Tony Stark/Iron Man may be said to use technology to resist technology itself by injecting subjectivity into what would otherwise be a merely blind and self-perpetuating process.

This Means You: Deciding to Become Iron Man

What happens to Tony Stark when he chooses to become Iron Man? In one sense, he doesn't change at all. Even when wearing the technological suit of armor, he is still, of course, the same man. But in another sense, at least, he is changed tremendously: as Iron Man, Tony Stark wields the power of a small army. Yet the use of that power is entirely the responsibility of a single individual, Tony Stark himself. As a kind of "one-man army," Iron Man appears as the synthesis of technological military might and individual ethical conscience.

We see this idea conveyed clearly in the first film at the moment that Tony Stark walks in on his friend Colonel James "Rhodey" Rhodes discussing with a group of soldiers whether manned aircraft or unmanned drones make better strategic weapons. Rhodes asks, "The future of air combat: is it manned or unmanned? I'll tell you: in my experience no unmanned aerial vehicle will ever trump a pilot's instinct, his insight—that ability to look into a situation beyond the obvious and discern its outcome—or a pilot's judgment." Tony enters just then and offers a possibility none of those present had considered: "Why not a pilot *without* the plane?" With the help of the Iron Man armor, this is in effect what Tony Stark himself becomes, a technological man who is not merely *using* technology but who manifests technological power *in person*. The phrase "a pilot without the plane" captures precisely how Iron Man manages to unite technology and authentic responsibility. Tony Stark becomes *one* with the Iron Man suit. There isn't the same gap or difference between Tony Stark the human being and the

Iron Man armor that there is, for instance, between a person typing at a computer and the computer itself or between a pilot and a plane.

When Tony Stark puts on the armor, he creates something new: Iron Man. Yet this creation is nothing other than what Stark himself becomes. Sure, Tony Stark is *inside* the armor. But in an important sense he also *becomes* the armor, and it is by becoming the armor that Tony Stark becomes Iron Man. This particular transformation becomes possible only because of the technological essence of the armor. So if the armor is essentially a kind of technology, then it is by becoming technological that Tony Stark becomes Iron Man.

With his transformation into Iron Man, not only does Tony Stark the individual become powerful, but the system of military technology represented by Stark Industries becomes responsible. Tony Stark's scientific and engineering genius had been instrumental in developing the weaponry sold by Stark Industries. So in some sense Stark himself was already implicated in the military developments those weapons made possible. But by using his technological knowledge to create a suit of armor that he then *becomes*, Stark puts himself in a situation where he is directly responsible and accountable for the use of his scientific knowledge and expertise. His knowledge does not simply become an external product that is then used by others for their own purposes. It stays with him as he lives and acts. The capabilities of the suit become Tony Stark's own. Once he has mastered the technology, Stark doesn't say, "The suit can fly," but rather, "Yeah, *I* can fly."

The Face Shield Is a Mirror: Iron Man and You

Tony Stark reconstructs himself technologically as Iron Man, a symbol of justice and power. Stark's decision and self-transformation represent a more general ethical and political possibility, that of critical practice *from within* systems of technological domination and control. As Iron Man, Tony Stark shows us how technology can be more than just a tool or an instrument. It can become part of who we are; it can magnify our potential. And at the same time, Tony Stark's transformation into Iron Man reveals how such use of technology calls all of us to greater accountability for the social, economic, scientific, and historical processes we already participate in and contribute to.

The enormous forces of history in the world can feel overwhelming. What can a single person do in the face of such overpowering obstacles? Tony Stark's decision to become Iron Man stands as one model of how such forces may be appropriated and used to resist their own worst tendencies. Any such appropriation depends finally on the responsible actions of creative and courageous individuals. Power itself is no guarantee of goodness, but without power it is difficult to imagine how the good could ever possibly prevail. Trying to find ways to use the power of science and technology responsibly raises questions and demands we must all face in today's world. It is a question of the human futures we choose to create, both individually and collectively. Tony Stark used his knowledge and skills to become Iron Man. What will *you* become?

NOTES

1. See Aristotle, *Physics*, book II, part 3, available at http://classics.mit.edu/Aristotle/physics.2.ii.html.

2. Martin Heidegger, "The Question Concerning Technology," in David Farrell Krell, ed., *Basic Writings* (San Francisco: HarperCollins, 1993), p. 314.

3. Ibid., p. 316.

4. Ibid., p. 319.

5. Ibid., p. 322.

6. Ibid., p. 320.

7. Ibid., p. 335.

8. Martin Heidegger, *Being and Time: A Translation of Sein und Zeit*, trans. Joan Stambaugh (Albany: State University of New York Press, 1996).

9. For more on Tony's moral responsibility (or lack thereof), see the chapters by Christopher Robichaud ("Can Iron Man Atone for Tony Stark's Wrongs?") and Mark D. White ("Did Iron Man Kill Captain America?") in this volume.

THE LITERAL MAKING
OF A SUPERHERO

Travis N. Rieder

In 2008's *Iron Man* film, Tony Stark, the genius CEO of Stark Enterprises, does something truly unique among comic-book superheroes: he intentionally *creates* his superhero alter ego and *becomes* Iron Man by virtue of nothing more than his intelligence and advanced technology. After a nasty imprisonment by terrorists and a wake-up call concerning the use of his weapons, Tony trades in a carefree playboy lifestyle for the more responsible role of peacekeeper (which is not to say that he gave up *all* of his bad habits!).

Believe it or not, it may soon be possible, through advances in cutting-edge science and technology, to replicate something similar to Tony's creation, which gives Iron Man a certain degree of "realism." But should we? Is that a path we should explore? Or is it a road we dare not take? Addressing these questions will require deep thinking about superheroes, nanotechnology, and some pretty serious philosophy.

Iron Man as Realistic? Have You *Seen* This Movie?!

So, why in the world should we think that Iron Man, as a character, is even *kind of* realistic? After all, he's a superhero who can fly, dogfight with jets, face down an entire armed militia, and perform many other amazing feats. Why should we think this is anything but fantastical? To be sure, the scare quotes around "realism" are important: I am not claiming that we should expect Iron Man to come about exactly as depicted in the comic books, cartoons, or films. Instead, I think there is a unique feature of Iron Man that makes him a more realistic superhero than most others: Iron Man is the product of technological creation, and he is fantastic only in degree, not in kind.

This means Iron Man does not require that the world be different from what we think it is. We don't need a world in which genetic mutations could allow a person to read minds or heal quickly (as with the X-Men), or a world in which exposure to gamma rays could result in special abilities (as with the Incredible Hulk). We don't even need to imagine someone spending a lifetime training in the martial arts and criminology in order to fight crime (as with Batman). All Iron Man needs in order to exist is technology that is more advanced than today's by a significant degree. We would need advances in robotics, computing, materials manufacturing, and possibly even artificial intelligence (depending on how seriously we take Tony's computer, Jarvis, as a component of the superhero). But none of this requires that we live in an alternate universe. In short, it would require only an incremental advance in technology to develop a fully mechanized body-armor suit that would provide its wearer with phenomenal strength, near-invincibility to small-arms fire, and access to advanced weaponry. This is what I call the "realism" of Iron Man.

But are such advances forthcoming? While technology moves forward all the time, is there any reason to think that we are living in a world in which the incredible intricacies of the Iron Man armor might be rendered possible? If we look to the field of nanotechnology, the answer is yes.

Really Cool Toys: Nanotechnology and the Making of a Hero

Nanotechnology is a very young field at the intersection of many disciplines, including (but not limited to) engineering, physics, chemistry, biology, and medicine.[1] At the most general level, nanotechnology involves manipulating matter at the level of the incredibly small: 1 to 100 *billionths* of a meter, or nanometers.[2] At this level, scientists are working not with mass compounds, but rather with individual molecules and atoms, which has many technological benefits. Although the complicated details need not concern us here, it is helpful to note the two most prominent benefits. First, scientists and technologists are developing tools for what we can call *precision engineering*, or constructing materials with extreme accuracy. Second, and more common, by working at the nanoscale, we are able to unlock unique properties of various materials—properties that occur only at this very small range. These are the features of nanotechnology that promise truly outstanding innovations in science and technology.

So let's turn to the (literal) making of a superhero: what technological innovations might aid a real-life Tony Stark in developing armor relatively similar to Iron Man's? Although certainly not exhaustive, I will suggest here three major roadblocks to the creation of Iron Man today, and how nanotechnology is not only potentially capable of solving each problem but also how nanotechnologists are *in fact* currently working in just these directions.

The first and most obvious difficulty with the creation of anything remotely similar to Tony Stark's Iron Man is its incredible intricacy. Feel free to take a break, pop in your DVD of our metallic hero, and fast-forward to the development scenes in Tony's workshop in which he's working out the kinks involved in his precision design. And then fast-forward again to the scenes in which Tony is being transformed into Iron Man, as the thousands upon thousands of interlocking pieces come together in exactly the right way. Of course, such precision is not possible now.

The second, and related, difficulty is a roadblock in computing technology. Computers are advancing at an amazing rate, with new models being made obsolete within years, if not months, of their creation. Related to our increasing ability to work at ever smaller scales, we are able to fit more and more transistors on a microchip, which translates into faster processing; and we are able to encode memory on smaller spaces, which has led to ever-expanding hard drives. Yet there is a natural barrier eventually—one that technologists and futurists have been well aware of for years—because we can miniaturize only up to the point at which we can no longer work with natural materials. Once we've reached the limits of our tools, we simply cannot make things smaller and therefore cannot make computers, at their current size, more powerful.

Finally, a major problem with the development of something like Iron Man has to do with his seeming invulnerability: how could it ever be possible to armor an individual person so well that he was virtually impervious to normal munitions? Well, okay, so we could do that by putting him behind a thirty-foot concrete barrier—which won't be much help when fighting alongside the Avengers! So how could we armor someone that well while leaving him or her mobile, agile, and possibly even able to fly?

Nanotechnology offers potential solutions to each of these problems. The first two issues that are raised essentially concern problems of scale: if we are to be able to construct something relevantly similar to Iron Man, then we must develop the ability to work at a very small scale. This is true in terms of precision engineering parts, as well as in the realm of electronics and computing. But miniaturization is exactly the trend in technology today, especially in nanotechnology. One key to unlocking the most amazing and unpredictable technologies of tomorrow lies in our ever-expanding ability to manipulate matter at the level of individual atoms and molecules. Although this process is still in its infancy—we're simply not very good at it yet, and building anything in this way requires perfect conditions and lots of time—we will get better. And when we do, then issues of precision will not be issues at all.

This leaves only the issue of material strength. Will nanotechnology be of any help here? The answer: it most certainly will. Remember those "novel properties" that I mentioned occurring at the nanoscale? Well, it just so happens that one of them is—yes, you guessed it—phenomenal strength. In fact, one of the most highly anticipated developments in nanotechnology concerns perfecting our use of "carbon nanotubes," which are superstrong rolls of graphene sheets. These tubes are estimated to be close to a hundred times the strength of steel, while weighing only one-sixth as much! Yes, if I needed to build a body-armor suit that would allow me to take on supervillains and global terrorists, this is what I would want it made of. (Size 42 chest, please.)

In sum, Iron Man is different from other superheroes, because he is *made* by Tony Stark, and there is nothing physically impossible about his construction. Furthermore, many of the areas of research that would be required in order to develop Iron Man are already under way, including research specifically into military battle suits (!) at MIT's Institute for Soldier Nanotechnologies.[3] The world of Iron Man may be our world in the not-so-distant future, which makes it ripe for philosophical discussion of a very particular kind.

Iron Man, This Is Nanoethics; Nanoethics, Meet Iron Man

Constructing an Iron Man provides us with an entertaining, thorough, and detailed case study in *nanoethics*, which considers the societal and moral implications of nanotechnology.[4] As in other applied ethics fields, the primary tools are case studies, stories that inspire the reader to think critically about an ethical problem.

Using Iron Man as a case study raises the following question: should we invite Iron Man's world to be our own? Our ever-increasing technological capabilities imply that we may someday be able to construct something relevantly similar to Iron Man, as shown by MIT's research into battle suits. If our research priorities are taking us down a road that leads to a world like the comics, should we be concerned? Should we hope to live to see it or lobby against the technology and funding that would make it possible? In short: is the "realism" of Iron Man totally cool, really quite horrifying, or something in between?

The Iron Man case study in nanoethics raises the issue of technological catastrophes and our duty to try to avoid them. This issue is of particular importance now, as humans have only relatively recently developed technology that is capable of causing destruction on a truly global scale. Whereas technology was once a moral issue for relatively local reasons—it may cause harm to particular people or disrupt families or cultures—advances in modern technology over the last century or so are capable of threatening the lives of countless millions of people worldwide, as well as the health of animals and the environment. Each time such advances are made, there is a looming ethical question concerning whether the potential benefits of the advance outweigh the risks being taken. And this is precisely the question that Iron Man puts to nanotechnology, specifically in its military applications.

So, do the potential benefits of Iron Man–inspired military battle suits outweigh the risks involved? Is that even the right question to be asking? How do we go about making decisions that are likely to affect so many people? In an effort to answer these kinds of questions, various thinkers have put forward two rival candidates for decision-making procedures: cost-benefit analysis and the precautionary principle.

Cost-benefit analysis, in its simplest form, is a theory of decision making that advises actions or policies that will maximize expected net benefits—that is to say, those actions or policies that will bring about the greatest benefit, with the least cost, in the most likely cases. Most of us engage in such analysis regularly, and we may even think that we *ought to* engage in such reasoning; it has even seemed to many people to define *rational* decision making.[5] If this is correct, then the rational thing to do in light of Iron Man–style case studies is to evaluate the potential harms involved (abuses of power, Iron Man suits falling into the wrong hands—you get the idea) and estimate the probability of them occurring. We then do the same for potential benefits (such as real-life superheroes, and . . . uh . . . I'm sure there are others!) and compare the two. If, given the probabilities involved, a particular act or policy seems likely to bring about significantly more benefits than costs, this counts in its favor. And if this expected benefit/cost balance is the highest among all plausible options, then this fact may count *decisively* in its favor.

Cost-benefit analysis—at least, in the simple form represented here—has therefore only one question for our Iron Man case study: is this technology likely to bring about more benefits than costs? In answering, one is likely to point out that technology virtually always carries risks, and that inaction in the face of risk would have precluded many of today's most useful advances. Furthermore, if the potential consequences of a certain technology are genuinely terrible, then we should hope that *we* (referring to the virtuous "we," of course) obtain the technology before our enemies do. Such reasoning is likely to make technological pursuit seem warranted under cost-benefit reasoning for most reasonable estimates of likelihood. Although various Iron Man exploits may raise awareness of the ways in which the technology can go wrong, such risks do not speak decisively against nanotechnological and battle suit–related development.

Certainly, it is possible to muddy the waters here and alter our simple analysis in order to make it more realistic. One way this might be done is by arguing that cost-benefit analysis, while helpful, is simply not sufficient for demonstrating that we ought to pursue some course of action. This line of thought is followed by the contemporary philosopher David Schmidtz, who claimed that although satisfying cost-benefit analysis is *necessary* for demonstrating the acceptability of some course of action, it may well not be *sufficient* for such a demonstration. In other words, even though cost-benefit analysis may count in favor of some course of action, if that action had something else quite wrong with it—say, if it violated certain rights or core principles—then it may still be the case that we should not pursue the action in question. Cost-benefit analysis, under this more moderate formulation, is a minimum standard for correct action, not a criterion of rightness.[6]

Enter the Precautionary Principle

Concerns about cost-benefit analysis remain, however: even if it's a particularly rational method of decision making, and even if we were to take a more moderate line akin to that of Schmidtz, is it the case that satisfying a cost-benefit criterion even *counts in favor* of some action's *morality*? Sometimes, the potential harm is very great (even if it is very unlikely), and a more precautionary approach to action and regulation may hold that cost-benefit analysis is simply the wrong tool for the job, as we have reason to avoid such risks regardless of their probability. This line of thought is called the *precautionary principle*. The precautionary principle is notoriously ill-defined, and many different, mutually exclusive principles go by this name. In this chapter, I will use the term (or sometimes "precautionary mentality") to refer to the position that when the potential dangers of an action or a plan are bad enough, we have reason to avoid them, *even though* it is very unlikely that the dangers will occur. In other words, cost-benefit analysis may recommend the action, because the dangers are so improbable, but the precautionary principle (or mentality) would disagree.

We have reached an age in which we regularly threaten our very existence, and one might think that this fact calls for a more careful way of doing things. Sure, it might be the case that Iron Man is no cause for concern, and that the development of superhero-ish battle suits will be only for the good. But the precautionary principle would remind us that, in the film, Obadiah almost won the battle with Tony, and that if he had, the world would have lived in fear of "Iron Armies" being sold to the highest bidder. In a world where the consequences of our mistakes are *this* bad, we may best be advised to avoid some risks.

This all might seem a bit academic. One particularly understandable reaction to the debate is to ask whether cost-benefit analysts and the more precautionary folks are really disagreeing. Couldn't it be the case that those with a more precautionary mind-set simply perform a different cost-benefit analysis? Perhaps what's actually happening is that both camps look at Iron Man and assign different "badness" ratings to the potential costs and different "goodness" ratings to the benefits. Then, when it comes time to crunch the numbers, each following his or her own estimates, the precautionary folks end up arguing against the Institute for Soldier Technologies, and the cost-benefit analysts claim that we should move forward as planned. But this is not due to different methodologies or different mentalities; rather, it is due to the different values people assign to various outcomes.

Although this is an understandable reaction, those who advocate a precautionary approach to regulating technology would disagree. They claim that some outcomes are *so bad* that something must be done to prevent them, *no matter how unlikely they are.* This mentality is fundamentally different, because no weighting of values or manipulations of calculations could lead them to promote the development of Iron Man or whatever technology is being discussed. A good (and particularly famous) example of this kind of reasoning can be found in computer scientist Bill Joy's article in *Wired* magazine in 2000, in which he argued for relinquishment of all nanotechnological, genetic engineering–related, and advanced robotics research.[7] According to Joy (the CEO and cofounder of Sun Microsystems— obviously no Luddite!), the only way to save humanity from extinction is complete and utter relinquishment of these dangerous technologies, a radical position indeed. While it's true that even if Joy is correct in his pessimistic view of current technology, cost-benefit analysis *could* come to the same conclusion, it could just as well disagree. Joy's precautionary principle, however, recommends relinquishment *regardless* of the particular estimates of costs, benefits, and probabilities used. If nanotechnology in general—or Iron Man technology in particular—poses some particular level of threat, then we would be justified in abandoning it, regardless of its improbability. *This* is the real dispute between cost-benefit analysis and the precautionary principle.

So, That's It? No Solution?

What should we say about the "realism" of Iron Man? Is the fact that Stark's world might be ours in the not-so-distant future exciting or alarming? While I've provided only the bare sketch of some tools for thinking about this problem and nothing like a solution to it, in the interest of full disclosure I will say this: I think the precautionary mentality has something going for it. Not only is it unclear to me that precaution is always irrational, but it is also unclear that rationality always counts in favor of some particular action. It seems at least reasonable to me to suppose that regardless of the rationality of relinquishing particular research programs, it may be *morally required* of us, because we don't have the right to take particular risks. Consider again the power of the technology that we are now able to create. In undertaking certain social experiments, we are putting the global community at risk, even if that risk is, admittedly, very small. Is such an action justifiable? Have the global citizens consented to be put at risk? *Would they* consent to this? Especially given the fact that much of the world's population stands to gain little, if anything, from the First World's technological experimentation, it is unclear why they should agree to being put at risk.

The case is far from clear, however. Perhaps I want to be precautionary in my fear of Obadiah, yet I am willing to risk allowing other nations (which may not be as morally restrained as we are) to develop Iron Man technology first. But doesn't precaution dictate that we take the seriousness of such a risk as a reason to try to be the first in control of Iron Man? This problem and many others make it far from obvious that the precautionary principle solves all of our technology regulation issues. As I hope the case of Iron Man has made clear, however, there is some intuitive plausibility to the claim that when it comes to technology, we are in an era in which it pays to be careful.

NOTES

1. The material presented here can be found in virtually any introductory account of nanoscience and nanotechnology. For an accessible introduction written specifically for nonspecialists, see Mark A. Ratner and Daniel Ratner's *Nanotechnology: A Gentle Introduction to the Next Big Idea* (Upper Saddle River, NJ: Prentice Hall, 2003) and the July 2004 Royal Academy of Science report titled "Nanoscience and Nanotechnologies: Opportunities and Uncertainties."

2. To ensure that your mind is appropriately blown, consider that a human red blood cell is approximately 7,000 nanometers across, and the width of an average human hair is approximately 80,000 nanometers across! This means that if you take some material at the largest end of the nanoscale (100 nm), we could lay 800 of these objects side by side before they even reached the width of a single hair. Now that's small!

3. The Institute for Soldier Nanotechnologies was founded in 2002 with a five-year, $50 million grant. It's now in its second five-year contract and posts regular updates on the status of its research at http://web.mit.edu/isn/index.html.

4. For introductory discussions, see Davis Baird, Alfred Nordmann, and Joachim Schummer, eds., *Discovering the Nanoscale* (Amsterdam: Ios Press, 2005); Fritz Allhoff et al., eds., *Nanoethics: The Ethical and Social Implications of Nanotechnology* (Hoboken, NJ: John Wiley & Sons, 2007); and Fritz Allhoff and Patrick Lin, eds., *Nanotechnology and Society: Current and Emerging Ethical Issues* (New York: Springer, 2008).

5. Although this close tie between cost-benefit analysis and rationality has seemed obvious to many, a particularly famous (and particularly entertaining) version of this view can be found in the writings of Harvard law professor Cass R. Sunstein. An interesting example of his position can be found in his *Laws of Fear: Beyond the Precautionary Principle* (Cambridge, UK: Cambridge University Press, 2005).

6. For more on Schmidtz's defense and modification of cost-benefit analysis, see his paper "A Place for Cost-Benefit Analysis,"*Philosophical Issues* 11 (2001): 148–171.

7. The article appeared in *Wired*, issue 8.04 (April 2000). While there is widespread disagreement as to the soundness of Joy's predictions concerning future technology, his standing as a brilliant scientist and an all-around clear thinker demands that it be taken seriously.

PART TWO

WEARING THE ARMOR RESPONSIBLY

CAN IRON MAN ATONE FOR TONY STARK'S WRONGS?

Christopher Robichaud

As a genius superhero, a wealthy industrialist, a high-ranking government official—and, lest we forget, a man of considerable talent in having a good time—Tony Stark is seen as a paragon of American achievement and excellence. But there's a private side to him, too, and it betrays a haunted man.[1] On closer examination, Stark's party-boy lifestyle reveals dispositions that border dangerously on self-destruction.[2] His techno-geek savvy finds him much better at, and much more interested in, building gadgets than personal relationships—just ask Pepper Potts (among others). And his career in and out of his high-tech armor is a checkered one, at best. Whether it's following the trail of shady arms deals done by Stark Industries, controlling the damage caused when Iron Man technology falls into the hands of villains, or confronting the national crisis of Captain America being assassinated under his watch, Tony Stark often finds himself trying to right the wrongs that he, inadvertently or not, helped bring about.[3]

Indeed, his ongoing campaign to address both the circumstances and the guilt stemming from his perceived failings is arguably the main motivation behind Stark's exploits as Iron Man. No doubt, this is what makes him such a fascinating character in the Marvel Universe. So, are personal atonement and public redress achievable? Or are they outside the grasp of the invincible Iron Man?

Distinctions with a Difference

Let's begin to answer these questions by looking at some issues surrounding moral responsibility. There is a difference between causal and moral responsibility. We're causally responsible for an event when we in some way contribute to bringing it about. But that's not enough for us to be morally responsible for it. Suppose Obadiah Stane, aka the Iron Monger, somehow manages to reprogram the Iron Man suit to be under his control, but only once Tony puts it on and activates it. Unaware of this, Tony dons the suit and is then forced by Stane to attack the S.H.I.E.L.D. flying helicarrier. If this happens, Tony will be causally responsible, at least in part, for attacking S.H.I.E.L.D. headquarters. It's his body in the armor, after all, and if he hadn't gotten into the armor, S.H.I.E.L.D. wouldn't have been attacked. But Stark isn't *morally* responsible for his actions. He didn't know that Stane had tampered with the Iron Man suit, and once he was in it, he wasn't in control of his actions. Blame therefore falls squarely on the shoulders of the Iron Monger.

Notice that there are two features of the case, either of which is sufficient to absolve Tony Stark from moral blame for attacking S.H.I.E.L.D.[4] One is that he was ignorant of Stane's tampering. Had he known what the Iron Monger had done and nevertheless gotten into the suit, then even though Stane would've controlled Tony's actions from that point onward, we still would be warranted in holding Tony partially blameworthy for the attack, because he knowingly put himself in the thrall of a villain. The other feature exonerating him from moral responsibility is that he wasn't in control of his actions. We're not morally responsible for things that we do against our will. If we learned that Stark could've brought the Iron Man suit under his sway but freely chose not to, then we would again be warranted in concluding that he shares moral blame for the attack on S.H.I.E.L.D., even if he donned the suit without knowing what Stane had done.

To Act or Not to Act, That Is the Question

Distinguishing between causal and moral responsibility opens the door to another important distinction, that between actions and omissions. There's an obvious difference between doing something and not doing something. But can both be causes? Philosophers are split on this. If Iron Man punches the Crimson Dynamo during a street fight and sends him hurtling into a building, then it's clear that Iron Man's *action* was a cause of the Crimson Dynamo hitting the building. But suppose instead that the Crimson Dynamo is charging Iron Man. He overshoots his mark, though, and sails past Iron Man, crashing into a building. Iron Man does nothing in this case but stand still. Was this *omission* by Iron Man a cause of the Crimson Dynamo's hitting the building? On the one hand, if Iron Man had stepped into his path, the Crimson Dynamo presumably wouldn't have hit the building. And that seems sufficient to establish that Iron's Man's omission is a cause. On the other hand, once we allow that omissions are causes, it turns out that we're causally involved in a lot of things that we don't typically think we are. Just looking at this example, it sounds at least a little weird to claim that Iron Man *caused* the Crimson Dynamo to hit the building merely by standing still.

Deciding whether actions and omissions are both causes is important when it comes to moral responsibility. Most people think that we can be morally responsible for omissions. If, for example, Iron Man can easily save a child from a burning building but for some reason chooses not to, then he's morally responsible for that child's death. But did he *cause* the child's death? This question concerns us because it seems that a person is morally responsible for something only if she's causally responsible for it. All this amounts to saying is that if we didn't play some part in bringing about an event, then we aren't morally responsible for it. But if we agree that moral responsibility requires causal responsibility, then whether Iron Man is morally responsible for the child's death will depend in part on whether he's causally responsible for it, and that's going to depend on whether omissions can be causes.

Let's take a stand on these controversial matters by agreeing that moral responsibility requires causal responsibility, and that omissions can be causes. Certainly, there's more to be said about this, but we've already put enough on the table to feel comfortable that neither of these assumptions is absurd, nor are their alternatives vastly more attractive.[5]

Time to Claim Responsibility

So far, we've seen that a person is morally responsible for an action or an omission only if that action or omission is a cause, it's brought about freely, and it's done knowingly. It's important to have these conditions in place, because it allows us to look at some things that Tony Stark clearly *feels* that he's morally responsible for, and ask whether he really is.

Let's focus for the moment on the question of whether he's blameworthy for the shady dealings of Stark Industries. As we see in the first *Iron Man* film, Tony undergoes something akin to a religious experience while being held by his captors. There, with the help of fellow captive Yinsen, he learns that rather than being a true American patriot, he's helming a company that's responsible for putting dangerous weapons into the hands of some very bad people. He also learns that outside the confines of his country, he's viewed as a mass murderer of the first order. Tony's escape as Iron Man gives him a change of heart—almost literally!—that sets him on a course to right the wrongs that Stark Industries has helped bring about, to correct its mission along the way, and to improve his personal life as well. Tony is motivated by guilt, which he feels in virtue of thinking that he's to blame for the suffering and death that have occurred as a result of the proliferation of Stark Industries' weapons.

But is he in fact morally responsible? We might be tempted to conclude that he isn't. It's Obadiah Stane, not Tony, who's morally responsible for selling Stark Industries' weapons to radical fringe groups. Sure, Tony was too busy drinking, gambling, carousing, and playing in his garage to properly attend to Stane's practices, but this lack of oversight on his part—this omission—at best establishes only that he, like Obadiah, was causally responsible for how Stark Industries' weapons were distributed. He's not morally responsible, though, because he was ignorant of what Stane was doing, and ignorance excuses a person from moral responsibility. Once Tony finds out what Obadiah is up to, he tries to stop it. But until he finds out, he can't be held blameworthy for the shady dealings of his company.

Nice as this might sound for Tony, a closer examination of the situation doesn't put him so easily in the clear. It's true that ignorance excuses us from moral responsibility, but only if that ignorance is itself reasonable and not a failing—not willful or negligent. Suppose the Mandarin knew ahead of time that as part of the mental mastery it would take to use his deadly rings, he'd render himself psychotic and thereby become incapable of understanding the harm he'd cause others. If that were the case, then we would rightly be unmoved by someone claiming that the Mandarin isn't morally responsible for what he now does because he lacks the mental faculties needed to appropriately value life. Because his current ignorance is willful, he is, in fact, morally responsible for his actions.

Similarly, Tony can use ignorance as an excuse only if his ignorance of Stark Industries' weapons sales wasn't willful or negligent. We need to consider whether he would've uncovered Stane's plans long before he actually did, if he had devoted a little more care to running his company and a little less time to his playboy lifestyle. Because Tony's a genius, it seems fair to say that even Stane's clever subterfuge wouldn't have gone unnoticed for long. So Tony's ignorance is negligent, and, as such, it doesn't exonerate him from moral responsibility. Given that we've already decided that his lack of oversight was a cause of the weapons sales, and given that there's no reason to think that Tony isn't making his choices freely, we can conclude that the factors needed for moral responsibility are present, and thus he is not exonerated from moral culpability.

Blame and Wrongdoing

Does it follow that Tony Stark is morally blameworthy for the proliferation of Stark Industries' weapons? Not necessarily. After all, we have yet to look at whether Tony's lack of oversight was in fact wrong, and it may seem that he will be blameworthy only if it was. But, perhaps surprisingly, things are more complicated than that. We can be morally culpable for doing things that aren't wrong, just as we can do something that is good without deserving moral praise. No doubt this seems odd, but consider the following. Suppose the Controller, in his ongoing attempts to create an army of minions, tries to control a man with his slave discs. Unbeknownst to the Controller, though, this man has terminal brain cancer.

And strangely enough, the Controller's attempts to psychically control him end up curing him of his cancer and render him immune to the Controller's further attempts.

Did the Controller do something wrong? Perhaps not. This man would've died of brain cancer if the Controller had not tried to enslave him. He failed and, in the process, cured the man! Not only doesn't it seem like it was the wrong thing to do, it seems like it was the right thing to do. But does this mean that we need to praise the Controller or, at the minimum, conclude that he's not blameworthy? No, and that's because he had thoroughly malicious intentions behind his action, and it's the intention that matters when it comes to moral responsibility. In this case, the Controller is blameworthy even though he did the right thing, or at least not the wrong thing. And if this seems difficult to accept, it's worth pointing out that we often have no problem acknowledging that a person can sometimes be blameless in doing the wrong thing. Someone might, for example, unwittingly or otherwise accidentally do something with terrible consequences.

But even though a person can be morally blameworthy for doing something that isn't wrong, in the case we're considering, it seems right that Tony Stark's lack of oversight of his company was wrong. It led to great pain and suffering. And so, barring any compelling reasons to think otherwise, we ought to judge him morally blameworthy for this wrongful omission.

Sometimes "I'm Sorry" Just Isn't Enough

It's worth asking at this point: so what? What does being morally blameworthy amount to? Let's consult the contemporary philosopher T. M. Scanlon, who offered a detailed account of blame and blameworthiness.[6] For Scanlon, concluding that someone is blameworthy and actually blaming them are different things, and they have different conditions of appropriateness. To judge that a person is blameworthy is to judge that her actions are guided by attitudes that compromise a fundamental moral relationship she bears to the moral community. It's to judge, in other words, that her actions stem from attitudes that impair an important moral relationship she bears to the rest of us. Now to blame her is to judge her blameworthy *and* to modify one's own attitudes toward her in a way that reflects this impaired relationship.

Furthermore, Scanlon thought that even if a person is rightfully blameworthy, it doesn't follow that all of us are equally warranted in blaming her. The appropriateness of directing blame at a person is determined not only by the accuracy of the judgment that she's blameworthy but also by our proximity to the wrong done. If I wrong you, all persons are equally warranted, with the right evidence, to judge me blameworthy. But you're more warranted in blaming me—in adopting that specific mental attitude toward me—than is someone who barely knows either of us and is entirely unaffected by the wrong done.

So, according to Scanlon's account, the people most directly affected by the illicit weapons sales of Stark Industries are the ones most warranted in blaming Tony for the causal role his wrongful negligence played in those sales. They aren't Americans, it turns out, but rather are families in the far reaches of the developing world. What, then, should Tony Stark do? He already feels guilt over his role in causing harm to these people. Given that they rightfully blame him, it seems that he should do whatever it takes to repair the moral relationship he bears to them.

Clearly, Tony must act in a way that invites forgiveness. The question is, though, what exactly must Tony do to invite such forgiveness? Feeling guilty doesn't seem to be enough. But neither does genuinely understanding what he has done, feeling guilty over it, and publicly owning up to it by making an apology. Tony doesn't do that, as we know, but it doesn't seem that it would have been enough even if he had. Why not? Perhaps it's because some wrongs are so harmful that it takes more than genuine acknowledgment of guilt to warrant forgiveness.[7] As I write this, the daily news details a seemingly never-ending account of wrongful, blameworthy actions performed by some business executives that have caused serious harm to many people. A lot of us are warranted in blaming them. And popular opinion is that genuine contrition by these executives, although welcome, is not sufficient to warrant forgiveness. But then what more is required of them? What more is required of Tony Stark? Is his decision to become Iron Man what he should do as part of his attempts to seek forgiveness?

Atonement Ain't Easy

Most people aren't as talented and connected as Tony Stark is. In addition to expressing contrition, the only thing they can do to warrant forgiveness is submit to the justice system and accept punishment for any legal wrongdoing. Indeed, according to some views of punishment, the very point of it is restorative: the aim of punishment is to facilitate the restoration of a wrongdoer's standing in the moral community.[8] And we might think that Tony's uniqueness doesn't exempt him from going this legal route in the pursuit of atonement. His negligence as CEO of Stark Industries put dangerous weapons into dangerous hands, hands that were a threat not only to people on the other side of the world, but to everyone. Tony never even seems to consider handing himself over to the authorities in order for the justice system to determine whether he bears any legal culpability for his negligence. And when he reveals himself publicly to be Iron Man, he doesn't offer an apology for what he's done in the past. The closest he comes to that—in the film, at least—is during his first press conference after returning from Afghanistan. It may very well be, then, that even in light of all the good Tony does as Iron Man, he still has not acted in a way that warrants forgiveness from those he has harmed.

Putting that aside, it's worth exploring the extent to which his professed agenda as Iron Man might put him on the path to forgiveness. Tony clearly feels that he has to somehow "right the wrongs" Stark Industries has done, and that the best way he can do that is as Iron Man. But what does righting wrongs amount to? We're all taught as children that we can't undo what's already been done. For all that the Iron Man suit allows Tony to accomplish, it'll never allow him to bring Yinsen or his family back. They died due to Raza and his terrorist group's pursuit of local dominance, something that was made possible only through their possession of Stark Industries' weapons. So if wrongs can't be undone, what does "righting" them look like?

Tony seems to think that at the very minimum, it involves stopping things from getting worse. He uses the Iron Man armor to crush Raza's terrorist group and to start the long process of collecting rogue weapons. In this case, is it enough to "stop the bleeding"? Probably not. It's reasonable to think that it also involves putting a lot of good back into the world, in addition to stopping the harms one has caused. But we have to be careful. Atonement can't *require* that Tony, on balance, do more good as Iron Man than the harms he did previously, because it may not be possible for Iron Man to do enough good without further negative ramifications.

The Guilt Never Goes Away

We've focused on one particular omission of Tony's—his negligence in running Stark Industries—to investigate whether he's morally responsible for it, what that means, and what atonement for it might look like. But as we know, there is *a lot* that Tony Stark feels guilty about and feels the need to set right. Is he morally responsible for the Iron Man technology being stolen? Does Captain America's death rest on his shoulders? Although we can't answer these questions now, the distinctions we've looked at and the reasoning we've gone through will help us whenever we want to evaluate the vast array of things Tony Stark wrestles with, now and down the road.[9] His guilt sometimes might be misplaced and sometimes not, and the requirements for his atonement will likely be dependent on the circumstances. For the moment, perhaps we can take comfort in the fact that Tony Stark is constantly examining his actions and their moral standing. The Iron Man armor is one of the most powerful weapons in the world, and it's good to know that the man inside it, while flawed, is nevertheless reflective and interested in accounting for his mistakes. Those are qualities we would all do well to emulate.

NOTES

1. It's no surprise that a recent Iron Man story line was titled "The Five Nightmares" (*Iron Man*, vol. 5, #1–6, 2008).

2. For instance, the "Demon in a Bottle" story line (*Iron Man*, vol. 1, #120–128, 1979) makes Tony's struggles with alcohol explicit. (See the chapter by Ron Novy titled "Fate at the Bottom of a Bottle: Alcohol and Tony Stark" in this volume for more on this important aspect of Tony's character.)

3. These story lines are found in the film *Iron Man* (2008), in the "Armor Wars" story line (*Iron Man*, vol. 1, #225–232, 1987–1988), and in numerous Marvel titles starting with *Captain America*, vol. 5, #25 (April 2007), respectively.

4. For a more detailed discussion of the kind of reasons that can rightly be used to excuse one from moral responsibility, see Denis Thompson's *Political Ethics and Public Office* (Cambridge, MA: Harvard University Press, 1987), pp. 40–65.

5. A good starting place for further reading on this subject can be found in Andrew Eshleman's "Moral Responsibility," in the *Stanford Encyclopedia of Philosophy*, http://plato.stanford.edu/archives/fall2008/entries/moral-responsibility.

6. See his *Moral Dimensions* (Cambridge, MA: Harvard University Press, 2008), chap. 4.

7. People who believe in unconditional forgiveness will disagree with this, but most of us don't endorse unconditional forgiveness.

8. For an interesting development of this view, see Christopher Bennett's *The Apology Ritual* (Cambridge, UK: Cambridge University Press, 2008).

9. See the chapter by Mark D. White titled "Did Iron Man Kill Captain America?" in this volume for more on Tony's responsibility for Cap's death.

DID IRON MAN KILL
CAPTAIN AMERICA?

Mark D. White

Sometimes It Sucks to Be Tony Stark

Tony Stark, also known as the "Invincible" Iron Man, may be riding high at the box office these days, but in the Marvel Comics Universe, it's a much different story. Several years ago, after a tragic disaster in Stamford, Connecticut, involving young, inexperienced heroes, Tony joined and eventually led the U.S. government's efforts to register all superheroes. The superhero community split down the middle, with his longtime friend, ally, and idol Captain America leading the resistance in what became known as the "Civil War." The conflict ended with Captain America's surrender and, soon thereafter, his assassination while in custody (which was not directly related to the dispute over registration). Tony was made director of S.H.I.E.L.D. (an international spy agency) and head of the Fifty State Initiative, which placed registered superheroes in every state in the United States.[1]

But the fun didn't last. Soon, the Hulk returned from the planet that Tony and other heroes had banished him to. The green guy proceeded to destroy a New York City still recovering from the Civil War, only to find itself in the midst of "World War Hulk."[2] After that party ended, it was revealed that the shape-shifting Skrulls, members of an imperialistic alien race with long-standing grievances with humanity (and with Tony Stark in particular—what, you're surprised?), had been hiding on Earth for years, having taken the forms of heroes and civilians they abducted. Once this "Secret Invasion" became much less of a secret, heroes and villains joined forces to battle the Skrulls, which culminated in the death of a founding Avenger, the Wasp.[3] In the end, Tony Stark was blamed for it all and fired as head of S.H.I.E.L.D.—only to be replaced by Norman Osborn, the former Green Goblin and the head of the Thunderbolts, who killed the Skrull leader—and quickly became "America's Most Wanted" fugitive.[4] It's official: it sucks to be Tony Stark.

Through all of this, Iron Man was a tremendously unpopular figure within both the Marvel Universe and the fan community. Captain America's former sidekick (and eventual successor) Bucky Barnes blamed him for the death of Steve Rogers; She-Hulk took him to task for exiling her cousin the Hulk to another planet; Hank Pym (Ant-Man, Giant-Man, Yellowjacket, now the new Wasp) held him res-ponsible for the death of Hank's ex-wife, the (original) Wasp; Goliath's nephew Tom Foster blamed him for Goliath's death at the hands of a clone of Thor; Thor, of course, blamed him for stealing Thor's DNA and cloning him; and all of the heroes who opposed registration (such as the post–Civil War New Avengers) blamed him for driving them underground. Many vocal fans compared Tony Stark to Hitler and anxiously awaited his comeuppance. (Happy now?)

But does he deserve all of the hate and blame? Does Tony really bear responsibility for all of the fallout from these events? Why did he do it anyway? In tackling these questions, I'll focus on *Civil War*, because this series contains the most extensive discussion of Tony's rationale for his actions, and because the registration act can be seen as the beginning of Tony's problems (at least, this latest batch of them!).

What If He Had Just Stayed Home and Polished His Armor?

Before we start to look at Tony Stark's responsibility for everything that's happened in the aftermath of the Civil War, let's review a little Marvel history. Several years ago, a run-in between the young superhero group New Warriors and the villain Nitro ended with the deaths of hundreds of people (including many children) in Stamford. Soon afterward, the U.S. government moved forward with the Superhuman Registration Act (SHRA), which had already been in the works due to previous superhero-related disasters (including the Hulk's rampage in Las Vegas, which motivated his off-planet exile). After initial reservations and attempts to dissuade Congress and the president from this path, Tony Stark got onboard with it and soon became the figurehead for the movement. Some heroes immediately registered, and he threatened to imprison those who didn't, then eventually enlisted super-villains in the effort to round them up.

Tony often argued that the SHRA was a foregone conclusion: in the middle of the Civil War, he told Cap, "It was coming anyway. I always thought it was inevitable, though I did try to delay it. But after Stamford there was no stopping it."[5] After Cap's assassination, Tony tells his corpse, "I knew that I would be put in the position of taking charge of things. Because if not me, who? Who else was there? No one. So I sucked it up. I did what you do. I committed."[6] At the very end of the *Civil War* series, he told Miriam Sharpe, the mother of a Stamford victim and subsequently a strong advocate for registration, that "the superhero community just found the greatest friend they'll ever have. Do you really think I'd let anyone else guard my friends' secret identities?"[7] In fact, Tony started out fighting the SHRA, calling it "the enemy" and arguing to Congress that heroes saved many more lives and much more property than they'd ever destroyed. Of course, Tony will be Tony—he secretly paid the Titanium Man to start a fight with Spider-Man to try to make a case against the SHRA (guess how well *that* worked). But after he saw that the SHRA was inevitable, he switched his strategy to take charge of it himself.[8]

One could say that Tony was merely trying to make the best of a bad situation. He is, as he (all too) often tells us, a futurist; he can predict what's going to happen, and he tries to make it better. If we take him at his word and acknowledge that he has the intellect and the means to do what it takes, then we may think it irresponsible of him *not* to do whatever he could to help people, which, in this case, meant commandeering the registration movement before someone else got his or her hands on it (corrupt politicians, Doctor Doom, Norman Osborn—*oops*). Most ethical theories recognize some duty or obligation to help others in need, especially if one is particularly placed and equipped to do so (for example, a doctor who witnesses someone having a heart attack). In such cases, standing by and doing nothing might be seen as unethical or wrong. Whatever your opinion of what Tony actually did, you can't say that he stood by and did nothing.

If we grant that Tony felt something had to be done, we can still ask why he felt *he* had to be the one to do it. ("Can you imagine some C-plus-average public-sector schlub in the Department of Redundancy Department riding herd on people like Cap?" he asked Happy Hogan.[9]) For one, Tony felt that he was the only person qualified to do it—do *you* know any other futurists? Tony recognizes that there are other smart (even smarter) people in the Marvel Universe—Reed

Richards, for example, or Henry Pym—but they are technicians, not "big thinkers." As the Mad Thinker told Reed Richards after seeing his social dynamics equations predicting the outcome of the Civil War, "Stark doesn't have the mind to appreciate the subtleties of your equations. But he does have the gut instincts of a futurist and the political sense to know that his actions would make him reviled among his former friends in the superhero community. And he's man enough to do what needs to be done."[10] Plus, he is the only person we're aware of who knew that the SHRA was coming, due to his close government contacts as former secretary of defense and (then) head of the Avengers. He did tell others about it (namely, the Illuminati), but they were split on what to do. Tony felt that action had to be taken, and, as he told Cap, no one else was stepping up—what's a proactive guy supposed to do? He acted. If he hadn't acted, and things went wrong, we'd be blaming him now anyway.

Tragic Dilemmas, the Superhero's Stock in Trade

Basically, Tony saw no alternative to cooperating with the government in pushing registration; it was the least bad option.[11] As he leads Daredevil into the Negative Zone prison, Stark tells him that "the only other option is a complete ban on all superheroes."[12] Iron Man made a pragmatic decision; he compared the alternatives (given the situation at hand and the information he had) and decided that the best course of action was to spearhead registration. In an ideal world, in which heroes were always responsible and the public never feared them, the SHRA would not be necessary. But Tony knows from personal experience how heroes, despite the best of intentions, can screw up.

Tony has lost control of his technology a number of times. It's been stolen by the supervillain community ("Armor

Wars"); it's been appropriated by his own government ("The Best Defense"); and the armor has even become sentient ("The Mask in the Iron Man").[13] In fact, immediately before the Stamford incident, the son of Professor Yinsen—the man who helped Tony build the first Iron Man armor—takes control of Tony's mind (and thereby his armor) and forces him to kill several hundred people. After the threat is dealt with, Tony's mentor Sal Kennedy tells him, "You know none of this was your fault. Not legally, not ethically, not morally. You said it yourself—the armor is like a gun. It was Yinsen's son that aimed it and pulled the trigger." Tony answers, "Every superhero is a potential gun . . . and the last time I checked, guns required registration."[14] And what's more, U.S. defense secretary Jack Kooning told Tony that if it weren't for the Stamford tragedy, the poster boy for the SHRA would be Iron Man, based on the incident with Yinsen's son, rather than the New Warriors.[15]

Stark also cites his problems with alcohol when defending his role in the SHRA to Captain America: "You know how dangerous a drunk is behind the wheel of a car? Imagine one piloting the world's most sophisticated battle armor." Then he accuses Cap of being idealistic: "See, that's the problem here. It's why you can't see things from my perspective. Because it's predicated on the premise that superheroes make mistakes. And you're Captain America. You don't make mistakes. . . . If everyone were like you, we wouldn't need registration. But they're not."[16] Tony is uniquely positioned to acknowledge the fallibility, the humanity, of even the most superhuman heroes; as Happy tells him, "You, my friend, are the only cape in the bunch that's both one of us and one of them. Who else can see both sides the way you do? Who else can make sure things are fair?"[17] Although Captain America has witnessed the heinous evil that men can do, he always chooses to see the best in people; while Tony is no less hopeful, he *is* more realistic and therefore chooses to prepare for the worst.

Some philosophers would say that Tony faces a *tragic dilemma*, a choice between horrible options that nonetheless must be made and from which "it is impossible to emerge with clean hands."[18] The most a person can do is choose the least bad option; that is what Tony does, and he has to live with the outcome. Despite his glamorous image—the shiny cars, the fancy clothes, the beautiful women—Tony's life has been a series of tragic dilemmas from the day he builds the first makeshift armor to keep his heart beating. Soon thereafter, he falls in love with his assistant, Pepper Potts, but bemoans—in almost *every* early story—that he can never reveal his love for her or allow her to love him, because of the dangerous life he leads and the precarious state of his heart.[19] The choice is either to stop being Iron Man or to deny his love for Pepper; there is no third way. Either choice involves enormous cost to him, to Pepper, or to the people he has pledged to protect as Iron Man. As he says to his fellow Avengers on disassembling the team after a series of trage-dies, "I am in one of those positions where there is no way to do anything without letting someone down."[20]

Deciding what role he will play in the battle over regis-tration is similarly a tragic dilemma for Tony. After Captain America's funeral, Tony is visited by a mysterious stranger (presumably, Uatu the Watcher, grand Peeping Tom of the Marvel Universe), and Tony reaffirms to him the inevitability of registration and his position that "one of us had to be on the inside. Running the show. Why couldn't Steve see that?" The stranger replies, "Perhaps because, for all his virtues . . . Steve Rogers was never a pragmatist. He was not one to be comfortable with the lesser of two evils." Tony simply says, "But it isn't an evil . . . it's a burden."[21] He knows that car-rying this burden will come at enormous cost to himself and others (more on that later), but the alternative also has tre-mendous costs: operating as an outlaw and letting someone else run registration and control his friends' identities and fates.

Neither option is "good," but Tony decides that supporting and spearheading registration is the least bad option.

At least, until Captain America dies.

So, *Did* Tony Kill Cap?

Bucky Barnes and Hank Pym, and presumably much of the superhero and civilian community (not to mention comics fans), blame Tony Stark for the death of Captain America. But *is* he responsible? Again, let's review. After the Civil War ends with Captain America's surrender, he is taken into S.H.I.E.L.D. custody and assassinated on the way to his arraignment. Although it initially appears that a sniper (the villain Crossbones) fired the kill shot, it is revealed (to readers) soon afterward that he was actually killed by a gunshot from his longtime love Sharon Carter, whose mind is being controlled by Cap's enemies the Red Skull and Dr. Faustus.[22]

While the assassination itself apparently has no connection to the Civil War or the registration act, it is true that had Cap not been in custody, his enemies may not have had the opportunity to assassinate him. And true, he might not have been in custody if Iron Man had not headed the registration effort so effectively. It would seem that as a result of Tony's actions, the dominos were set up just right to place Cap in front of the mind-controlled Sharon Carter's gun. But is it that simple?

No, for several reasons. First, all of the "ifs" and "might haves" and "maybes" don't add up to responsibility, which needs (at least) a clear chain of causation. Did Tony do anything that directly led to Cap's death? Did he pull the trigger? No. Did he push Cap in front of the gun? No. Did he manipulate Sharon to shoot him? No. What he did was set a chain of events in motion, none of which led directly to Cap's death. Indeed, there were many other causes more directly related to the death (namely, Carter's firing the gun, Dr. Faustus's manipulation of Sharon Carter, Red Skull's orders to Faustus, and so on).

Second, even if we could make a case that Tony's action did inadvertently set up the circumstances under which Cap was killed, did he *knowingly* do it? Could Tony reasonably foresee that his actions would lead to Cap's death? We already acknowledged that he knew there would be costs— he claims he foresaw the war, after all—but he couldn't foresee any particular deaths. If I see a truck coming and push you in front of it, then I'm responsible for what happens to you. If I push you *out* of the way of the truck but accidentally push you into an open manhole, most people would say that I'm not responsible for that—I made a good faith effort to help you but didn't foresee the later harm.[23]

Third, the example of the truck suggests another general moral principle: we are responsible for the negative consequences of bad acts but not of good acts, whether we foresee those consequences or not. I pushed you out of the way of the truck—a good thing—which inadvertently put you in a position to fall down the manhole: undoubtedly a bad thing, but one I would not be held responsible for. At times we've all acted ethically but with bad results, and some friend will always say, "Hey, you did the right thing," or "You had no choice, you had to do it, it's not your fault." But if you do something wrong, and someone gets hurt, you are usually held responsible, even if you didn't foresee it. Suppose Pepper Potts discovers that a Stark Industries employee is embezzling money from the company to pay for his mother's surgery. If she tells Tony the truth about it, and he fires the employee, Pepper may feel sorry for him—but she shouldn't feel responsible, because she did the right thing by telling the truth (and the employee was doing wrong). But if Pepper lies to Tony or covers up the theft, and another employee is mistakenly fired because of it, Pepper would feel responsible and rightly so: it wouldn't have happened if not for her deception.

So, if we want to blame Iron Man for the death of Captain America, we would have to show that Tony did something wrong *and* that it directly led to Cap's death. As we saw, many think Tony was wrong in taking charge of registration, but it's difficult to see how that directly contributed to Cap's assassination, other than putting him in the wrong place at the wrong time.[24] The link is even more tenuous if we try to blame Tony for the Skrull secret invasion, which presumably was made easier by the distrust of heroes—and among heroes—that was bred during the Civil War, and for the subsequent death of the Wasp. Each of these is further removed from Tony's original actions, and more outside events contributed to each one, weakening the claims of Tony's moral responsibility.

Why, Tony, Why?

Let's get back to whether Tony was wrong to support registration. Some moral traditions, such as Kantian deontology or Aristotelian virtue ethics, take motivation to be the true barometer of a person's moral character.[25] In other words, doing good things is not enough to be a moral person; you also have to do them for the right reasons. Also, as long as you act for the right reasons, it does not always matter whether your actions go as planned ("it's the thought that counts"). So, was Tony's support of registration an act of selfless heroic sacrifice, a reflection of devotion to justice and the law? Or was it merely an exercise in self-serving egoism on the part of a megalomaniacal control freak bent on world domination? Or did the two coincide—was the right thing to do in general also the thing Tony wanted to do?

One good (if not conclusive) way to tell if someone is properly motivated to act morally is to ask whether they sacrifice their own interests to do so. (This is not necessary to prove moral motivation, but it helps!) Throughout the Civil

War story line, people mention the sacrifices Tony made to support registration, most notably the respect of many of his fellow heroes (as even the Mad Thinker recognized). At one point Miriam Sharpe thanks Tony for all of the pro-registration heroes' efforts, saying, "I hate how much it's cost you personally. I never would have asked if I'd known your lives would get torn apart like this," to which Tony replies, "There's no shame in making enemies if it means making people safer."[26] Even reporter Sally Floyd, no great admirer of Tony's, says after it's all over, "You sacrificed your status as a friend, colleague and hero for the greater good of this country. You alone understood the ramifications of such a course of action."[27] Since he disregarded the personal costs of his actions in favor of (what he perceived as) the good consequences for all, Tony's motivation appears sincerely moral.

Perhaps Tony's greatest loss is that of his idol, colleague, and friend Captain America. As Tony said to Cap's corpse, "To do what I needed to do to win this quickly—I knew that meant you and I would probably never speak again. Or be friends again. Or partners again. I told myself I was okay with it because I knew it was right and I—I knew it was saving lives. . . . I was willing to get in bed with people we despise to get this done. And I knew the world favors the underdog and that I would be the bad guy. I knew this and I said I was okay with it."[28] After all this, he ends by saying, "It wasn't worth it," referring to Cap's death. But in the big picture, I think it's fair to say that Tony still believes his actions were right, even though he regrets some of the consequences.

Let's look at this from the other angle: did Tony have anything to gain personally from the SHRA? At one point, Peter Parker hears a news report about no-bid contracts going to Stark Enterprises (and Fantastic Four Inc.) to build the Negative Zone prison and other projects resulting from registration, and later, when he sees Tony, Peter directly questions his motivations (questions that Tony deftly dodges).[29]

Working with reporter Ben Urich, Peter also hacks into the computers at Tony Stark's accounting firm and discovers massive revenue flows two days before the SHRA was announced.[30] But does Tony need to manipulate the entire superhero community into a self-destructive battle simply to make money? Ask yourself this: would he have done the same thing if the potential for profit were not there? We can never know (well, unless a writer chooses to explore it further in the future), but given Tony's record of heroism—and the uncertainty of profit going into the whole mess—I think it's safe to give Tony the benefit of the doubt.[31]

More Props for Tony

Am I being too generous to ol' Shellhead? Tony's not perfect, by any means, but come on—I don't think anybody can seriously doubt Tony's heroism. In fact, during the same period that the boldness of his decision making and the degree of his authority increased, so did the risks he took, the sacrifices he made to save lives, and the responsibility he carried on his armored shoulders. For instance, in "Execute Program," Tony ends the remote manipulation of his mind and his various armors by blasting his heart with ten thousand volts, killing himself (and therefore the conduit through which his armors were controlled). After Tony is revived, Secretary Kooning—always the sweetheart—says, "The only thing that I can't believe is that a guy as narcissistic as Tony Stark would kill himself to save someone else."[32] And after the Civil War, Tony defeats a giant genetically engineered neoplastic tumor, a cancer consuming the entire S.H.I.E.L.D. helicarrier, by shedding his armor and letting it envelop him, trusting his Extremis-boosted immune system to fight it off.[33] Finally, once Norman Osborn takes his old job following the Skrull invasion, Tony protects the database of his friends' secret identities—the one in his head—by becoming a fugitive, fighting to stay one step ahead of Osborn, all the while gradually *lobotomizing* himself, potentially destroying the very intelligence that is the source of all he has built over the course of his life to safeguard his friends' lives.[34]

If that's not enough, let's give Tony the final word on his motivations as a hero, taken from his statement to the world while flying up to face the Incredibly pissed-off Hulk on his return to Earth (and before the Hulk just *crushes* him):

> This is Tony Stark. Iron Man. Director of S.H.I.E.L.D. And yes, I fired the Hulk into space. So if you need to blame someone for his return . . . blame me. But everything I've done . . . everything I'll do today . . . everything I'll ever do . . . I do to protect this world. Someone once told me that with great power comes great responsibility. . . . When I put on this armor, I took on more power than any human was ever intended to have . . . and maybe more responsibility than my heart can truly bear. But today . . . I will do my job. I will protect you . . . no matter what it takes.[35]

The Hero's Responsibility

Again, while preparing to face the Hulk, Tony thinks to himself, "Some people avoid hard choices. As a CEO, as an Avenger, as director of S.H.I.E.L.D., as a recovering alcoholic, I make them on a daily basis. Some days, it's as simple as not having a drink. On others, millions of lives hang in the balance. I do what I think best. What I think is right. I make no apologies for that. But I do make one promise: that I'll face the consequences. I make the decision . . . and I pay the price."[36]

The nature of a tragic dilemma is that you choose the action that you judge best or right. You may regret that you had to make such a choice, and you may regret the consequences of that choice, but should you regret the choice you made? The point is that you have to make a choice, as Tony explained when trying to convince the Sentry to help control the Hulk: "Every day I choose between courses of action that could affect millions, even billions of lives. With stakes that high, how dare I decide? But at this point, doing nothing is a decision in and of itself."[37] Tony's words prove that he understands the nature of tragic dilemmas and the responsibility that comes with them. After all, he's been making them his entire career in the golden armor. Tony will have to live with his decisions, which is the most any of us can do in such circumstances. That, in and of itself, is very heroic.

NOTES

1. See *Civil War* #1–7 (2006–2007; 2007 trade paperback) and subsequent Marvel story lines.

2. *World War Hulk* #1–5 (2007–2008; 2008 trade paperback).

3. *Secret Invasion* #1–8 (2008–2009; 2009 trade paperback).

4. "World's Most Wanted," in *Iron Man*, vol. 5, #8–19 (2009).

5. *Iron Man/Captain America: Casualties of War* (February 2007), reprinted in *Civil War: Iron Man* (2007). See also *New Avengers: Illuminati* (one-shot, May 2006, reprinted in *The Road to Civil War*, 2007), after he shows the rest of the Illuminati an early draft of the SHRA: "I'm telling you: this is happening. Right now. House of M, Nick Fury's Secret War, the 198, the attack on Avengers Mansion . . . it's all come to this. An environment of fear has been created where this can not only exist but will pass."

6. *Civil War: The Confession* (May 2007), reprinted in *Civil War: Iron Man*.

7. *Civil War* #7 (January 2007).

8. *Amazing Spider-Man* #529–531 (2006), included in *The Road to Civil War*. Of course, not everything Tony did was simply going along with the flow, making sure things worked better than they would have without him; other times he was much more proactive. After all, Tony (together with Mr. Fantastic, Dr. Strange, and Black Bolt) tricked the Hulk into a spaceship and shot him through space to a faraway planet, where he was enslaved before fighting his way to eventually rule the planet. Then he came back, madder than hell, and started "World War Hulk" to exact revenge on his captors. (*That's* karma for you.)

9. *Iron Man*, vol. 4, #13 (December 2006), reprinted in *Civil War: Iron Man*.

10. *Fantastic Four* #542 (March 2007), reprinted in *Civil War: Fantastic Four* (2007).

11. Reed Richards called it "the lesser [*sic*] of thirty-one evils. Each more horrible than the next" (ibid.). We get the point, Reed, thank you.

12. *Civil War* #5 (November 2006). Oddly, Daredevil wasn't convinced, calling Tony "Judas." (That *had* to hurt.)

13. For references and more details on these story lines, see the chapters in this volume by Christopher Robichaud ("Can Iron Man Atone for Tony Stark's Wrongs?") and Stephanie and Brett Patterson ("'I Have a Good Life': Iron Man and the Avenger School of Virtue").

14. See "Execute Program" (*Iron Man*, vol. 4, #7–12, 2006; 2007 trade paperback); the quote is from #12, November 2006.

15. *Iron Man*, vol. 4, #13 (December 2006).

16. *Iron Man/Captain America: Casualties of War* (February 2007).

17. *Iron Man*, vol. 4, #13 (December 2006). (Tony responds, "You're the only guy I ever met who can make me feel like a moron.")

18. Rosalind Hursthouse, *On Virtue Ethics* (Oxford, UK: Oxford University Press, 1999), p. 71. See chap. 3 in Hursthouse's book for a discussion of irresolvable dilemmas (ones in which the "right" action is indeterminate), and pp. 71–77 on tragic dilemmas in particular. The closest analogue in Kantian deontology is the case of a conflict of obligations; on this, see Roger J. Sullivan, *Immanuel Kant's Moral Theory* (Cambridge, UK: Cambridge University Press, 1989), pp. 72–75. Utilitarians don't recognize irresolvable or tragic dilemmas, because either one option generates more "good," or two options generate equal amounts of "good," so the utilitarian would be indifferent between them. (See the chapter "Does Tony Stark Use a Moral Compass?" by Sarah Donovan and Nick Richardson in this volume for more on these systems of ethics.) For more on moral dilemmas in general, see Terrance McConnell's "Moral Dilemmas" in the *Stanford Encyclopedia of Philosophy*, http://plato.stanford.edu/entries/moral-dilemmas/.

19. At the end of one early tale, as Tony and Pepper attend to an injured Happy—the third point in the early love triangle—Tony thinks to himself, "Perhaps it's better that Pepper does prefer Happy! I realize now I can never lead a normal life . . . never give up the mission I was meant to fulfill! Not while menaces such as the Unicorn remain to threaten the land I love!" (*Tales of Suspense* #56, August 1964, reprinted in *Essential Iron Man*, vol. 1, 2005). That's right—the Unicorn, armed with his "unicorn power horn." (Hey—do you have a unicorn power horn? No? That's what I thought.)

20. *Avengers Finale* (January 2005), reprinted in *Avengers Disassembled* (2005). See also the chapter "Iron Man's Transcendent Challenge" by Stephen Faller in this volume for a contrasting view of tragic dilemmas.

21. *What If? Civil War* (February 2008).

22. *Captain America*, vol. 5, #25 (April 2007).

23. Another factor involved in responsibility, discussed in Christopher Robichaud's chapter in this volume ("Can Iron Man Atone for Tony Stark's Wrongs?"), is voluntariness, which is not an issue here because Tony was clearly in control with everything he did. That was not the case, however, when Yinsen's son manipulated the armor in "Execute Program."

24. By now, you may have noticed that I haven't discussed the ethics of the registration movement itself. As much as I would have loved to, that's a much larger issue that I can't do justice to here, because I wanted to focus specifically on Tony's role in registration. The general conflict regarding registration is the time-honored choice between liberty and security, and despite all of the snappy bumper stickers out there, it

is never an easy choice. To be precise, it is no choice at all; it is never one or the other, but rather the combination of both that the citizens of a country are comfortable with. (Any political philosophy text or reader should give more insight into this; I suggest Robert M. Stewart's *Readings in Social and Political Philosophy*, 2nd ed. [Oxford: Oxford University Press, 1996].)

25. See the chapter by Donovan and Richardson in this volume for more on motivation and character.

26. *Civil War* #6 (December 2006).

27. *Civil War: Front Line* #11 (April 2007).

28. *Civil War: The Confession* (May 2007).

29. *Amazing Spider-Man* #535 (November 2006), reprinted in *Civil War: Amazing Spider-Man* (2007). This is one of the more blatant allusions in *Civil War* to the War in Iraq initiated during the presidency of George W. Bush; see the *Civil War: Front Line* series (2006–2007) for many more.

30. *Civil War: Front Line* #9 (December 2006).

31. Especially because further investigation by Urich and Sarah Floyd shows that Tony rerouted these profits into charitable organizations that provide assistance to police officers, firefighters, registered heroes, and their families (*Civil War: Front Line* #11, April 2007).

32. *Iron Man*, vol. 4, #12 (November 2006). Ironically, Tony pulls the same trick on the Crimson Dynamo at the beginning of the story, stopping the villain's heart only to revive him seconds later (*Iron Man*, vol. 4, #7, June 2006).

33. Ibid., vol. 4, #18 (July 2007).

34. See "World's Most Wanted," in *Iron Man*, vol. 5, #8–19 (2009).

35. *Iron Man*, vol. 4, #19 (August 2007); the same speech appeared in *World War Hulk* #1 the same month. (But in *Iron Man*, Spider-Man is shown listening, and when he hears Tony repeat his famous "with great power" line, he quips, "Well, whaddaya know. He was listening."

36. *Iron Man*, vol. 4, #19 (August 2007).

37. *World War Hulk* #4 (November 2007). (Why do I have the urge to listen to Rush all of a sudden?)

FATE AT THE BOTTOM OF A BOTTLE: ALCOHOL AND TONY STARK

Ron Novy

For Tony Stark, 1979 is a miserable year. Iron Man causes a chlorine gas leak at the scene of a train wreck, a flying tank knocks Tony's plane out of the sky, and a repulsor blast kills the Carnelian ambassador at the United Nations. Not only that, but Stark is suffering from "designer's block," Captain America replaces Iron Man as chairman of the Avengers, a rival industrialist remotely controls Iron Man's armor, and Jarvis resigns. Oh, and Tony loses controlling interest in Stark International.[1] As they say, it's enough to drive a super-hero to drink.

In the "Demon in a Bottle" story line, Tony Stark confronts his most intimate enemy: alcoholism.[2] We see tumblers, bottles, and snifters with increasing frequency as the story progresses. Tony's judgment becomes impaired: his clumsiness risks the lives of innocent people, he insults his friends, and he shows off classified technology to impress a one-night stand.

Toss in an exploding island, having Blizzard, Melter, and Whiplash cramp a date with Bethany Cabe, and battling Justin Hammer's unitard-wearing private army, and we've recapped most of the action. At the end, as Stark puts it, he must choose between "the drink or the dream."[3] But can an alcoholic really choose to stop drinking (or choose to start, for that matter)?

There are two seemingly incompatible ways of understanding alcoholism. According to the "choice model," a person's dependence is a result of a character flaw that leads to making self-destructive decisions. By contrast, according to the "disease model," alcoholism is an illness and the addict is an innocent victim. Some groups, such as Alcoholics Anonymous, try to have it both ways: the alcoholic is "powerless over alcohol" and yet responsible "to make amends" for harms caused.[4] But to accept one model over another is to reach very different conclusions regarding the person's responsibility for his situation. Under the choice model, the addict is held responsible for his condition, while under the disease model, the person is no more responsible than a kite in the wind. We can't have it both ways—so which is it?

Smart Guy, Bad Choices

In the case of Tony Stark, we're concerned with the responsibility of an alcoholic who continues to drink. We should also note that there is a fair amount of evidence that some of us are genetically predisposed toward alcoholism and addiction. So when we consider a person's responsibility for his alcoholism, we're not interested so much in the genetic or environmental factors that led the person to drink in the first place, but rather in the person's responsibility for continuing to drink, despite the clear evidence that he has a problem.

What does it mean to say that a person is responsible for his alcoholic drinking? At a minimum, responsibility would require that given the option of draining a highball or not, he chooses to drain it, and that no one put a gun to his head and said, "Drink!" Given that taking that drink is a necessary and wholly avoidable step in bringing about his alcoholic condition, he is responsible for his actions and can be praised or blamed accordingly.

Under the choice model of alcoholism, at each and every step of the way Stark could have chosen to do otherwise—with "otherwise" ranging from pouring all of the scotch in his house down the sink to taking up tai chi. The fact that Stark is aware of the options and their repercussions is enough to assign him responsibility for his alcoholism. But consider these possibilities: Tony may have inherited a gene that makes him particularly susceptible to addictive behavior, or he may have unresolved childhood issues with a domineering parent, or he may simply be too busy to go jogging or have a good cry to relieve his stress. These certainly do affect the difficulty of selecting some options over others; nonetheless, the difficulty of choosing an option—such as turning away from the bottle—does not relieve him of responsibility for choosing it.

The contemporary philosopher Harry Frankfurt argued that "a person is not morally responsible for what he has done if he did it *only* because he could not have done otherwise."[5] If this is correct, deciding whether Tony is responsible for his alcoholic drinking becomes a matter of examining his reasons for his behavior. Suppose we see Stark at a black tie affair sipping yet another glass of a nice shiraz. Assuming Tony is aware of his problem with alcohol, there seem to be three general explanations as to why he would not abstain. First, he could have the same sort of reason for drinking that a nonaddict has (say, because he likes the taste). A second possibility is that Tony chooses to drink for some reason not shared by the nonaddict (he knows he won't be able to concentrate later if his mind is obsessing about getting to a bar, so he gets it over with, so to speak). In both cases, Tony is drinking for a reason other than "*only* because he could not have done otherwise," and so is as responsible for his decision as the nonaddict is.

It is also possible, however, that Tony is being forced to drink, even though he'd prefer to abstain. Imagine that unbeknownst to Tony, Dr. Doom has managed to install a tiny parasitic worm into the decision-making faculties of his brain that will make him drink even if he doesn't want to. Clearly, if Tony chooses to drink, the worm's existence would be irrelevant and we would hold Stark responsible for his choice. On the other hand, if Tony tries to abstain, the parasite would override that choice, and Tony would have the wine anyway. In this case, his drinking would result not from his own choice, but from compulsion on the part of Doom's little brain worm. Tony would thus not be responsible for the action. Because Dr. Doom never did implant such a worm in his brain, Tony's alcoholic drinking is completely his choice. Under the choice model of alcoholism, Tony is wholly responsible for his alcoholism.

Tony knows that he shouldn't drink, yet sometimes he drinks anyway. If there is no Dr. Doom–style choice-controlling parasite involved, how can we make sense of this? Presumably, Tony believes that not drinking is a better option than drinking, and he wants to pursue that better option, yet he chooses the worse one. In *Protagoras*, Socrates tells us that "No one willingly goes after evil or what he thinks to be evil and when compelled to choose one of two evils, nobody will choose the greater when he may the lesser."[6] If this is so, there are a number of explanations for why a person might still choose against his best interests. It's possible that the person might be reasoning perfectly well but is basing his decisions on ignorance or misinformation. "Garbage in, garbage out," as they say, even if your reasoning process is faultless. So, for example, we can imagine someone who desires a body mass index like Ms. Marvel's, yet consumes only ice cream and malt liquor because she badly misunderstood a health article. Or, as happens in "Demon in a Bottle," Tony stands up a lunch date because he transposed digits in the restaurant's address.

A second possibility is that the person is acting not on his best considered judgment but instead is motivated by some other, less clearly rational basis, such as honoring a past promise or acting on a strong emotion. This sort of acting contrary to one's best interests is what brings down many villains, and perhaps it's what brings down Tony. For instance, once Tony is made a prisoner on Justin Hammer's floating island, Hammer—in the tradition of the vain Bond villain—can't resist explaining both why and how he managed to override Stark's control of the Iron Man armor. Rather than simply tossing Tony into shark-infested waters and getting on with his master plan, Hammer gives Stark information and time to act on it. Almost as often, the superhero might use the bad guy's arrogance or rage to lead him into a trap (it turns out that supervillains are particularly susceptible to "yo mama" jokes). Likewise, perhaps Tony drinks simply to satisfy an overwhelming desire for the sense of euphoria he feels after a couple of drinks, failing to recognize that drinking often gets him into a shark tank full of trouble.

A final way of explaining why we might choose the worse option instead of the better is that we simply lack the resolve to stick with our best intentions. Philosophers call this weakness of will, or *akrasia*.[7] So, perhaps Tony realizes he should not drink and he plans not to drink, but he just can't muster the will to resist the bottle. What all three of these possibilities have in common is that they make us doubt whether the choice the person ultimately makes is really free—could he really have done otherwise? As Plato wrote, no one could willingly choose the worse option, so perhaps Stark was compelled somehow, not by one of Dr. Doom's worms, but by something inside his head. That leads us to the disease model of addiction, which does maintain that at least some choices made by the alcoholic are not *really* his choice and therefore not his responsibility.

"Cause"—That's Why!

If we understand alcoholism as a disease, rather than as a choice, we paint the addict as a victim of some long chain of events over which he has no control. Like the person afflicted with chorea or dementia, the person is not responsible for his alcoholism or for choices made while under its sway. So, for example, when a thoroughly pickled Iron Man flies through a closed window, raining glass onto the busy street below, we would not blame Tony Stark for the damage; it was all the result of a disease over which he has no control.

This interpretation fits with the theory of *causal determinism*, the commonsense idea that all events in the world are caused by previous events. Of course, causal determinism is essential to our day-to-day lives; we depend on our actions to have effects on the world we live in. If Jarvis were to wake up from a sound sleep to the smell of smoke, he wouldn't think that the smell *just happened*; he would attribute it to some cause and would go looking for whatever is responsible. Even if Jarvis didn't find a guttering candle, embers in the fireplace, or Tony trying to make a grilled cheese sandwich (again), he wouldn't conclude that the smell "magically" appeared, but that there was a cause that had simply eluded him. If we don't accept this basic picture of cause and effect, we can't even start to explain how things happen; the concept of "explanation" and the scientific enterprise itself become incoherent.

But although we readily accept causal determinism as it relates to billiard balls and frying eggs—examples of cause and effect in the physical world that we can easily observe—many of us are uncomfortable with the idea that the more intrinsic parts of who we are, such as our thoughts, judgments, and purposeful acts, are also causally determined. If they were, it would seem to put us in the position of so many marionettes: the way Tony Stark acts, the way Rumiko Fujikawa feels, and the way Pepper Potts treats Happy Hogan, all become matters of finding which string is being tugged harder.

Furthermore, if all of our thoughts and actions are causally determined, we could not act any differently than we do. Stark couldn't be other than an industrialist, Iron Man's alter ego, or an alcoholic; these roles are "chosen" for him, and he only feels as if he chose them himself. In a determined universe, the choices we make are both effects of prior causes and causes of future events. If determinism is true, blaming Tony Stark for his alcoholic drinking would be not only inappropriate but also a misunderstanding of what made him who he is.

Blaming the Disease

Yet, should we resist making value judgments on alcoholics' behavior, even if we accept the disease model of alcoholism? The American Psychiatric Association defines *substance dependence* as a "significant impairment in functioning" resulting from a "maladaptive pattern of substance use."[8] This pattern is demonstrated if any one of the following is exhibited in a year:

> (1) recurrent use resulting in a failure to fulfill major obligations at work, school, or home; (2) recurrent use in situations which are physically hazardous (e.g., driving while intoxicated); (3) legal problems resulting from recurrent use; or (4) continued use despite significant social or interpersonal problems caused by the substance use.[9]

By its very definition, alcoholism makes reference to the individual's loss of control and how this loss brings harm to the alcoholic and those around him. As the contemporary philosopher Mike Martin put it, "The sickness of alcoholism is the disordered agency itself as defined in terms of overt behavior and failed intentions."[10] In this way, to be an alcoholic is to be someone with an impaired free will: Tony's judgment and capacity for self-reflection are muted, if not completely taken away from him by the addiction.

All things being equal, we each have a responsibility not to harm others; as such, we have certain obligations toward ourselves and others that demand prudence in our decisions. In this way, the alcoholic should be accountable for at least some of the damage—physical, emotional, and psychological—caused by his behavior. It's difficult to imagine an understanding of disease without the use of evaluative terms such as "wellness" or "suffering," "helpful" or "harmful": terms that are directly linked to behavior. That an impaired Iron Man misjudged the aftermath of a train wreck and caused a massive chlorine tank to burst, risking the lives of those on the scene and causing an evacuation of the area, seems a model example of someone who ought to be blamed for his behavior. If alcoholism is a disease, then we can't blame Iron Man for his actions—yet we do, and therein lies the conflict.

Choice and Responsibility

Whether everything that happens, including our own choices and actions, is the effect of some previous cause is a metaphysical question with serious repercussions for ethics. Responsibility, praise, blame, and guilt make sense only if we assume that the person we apply them to *chose* to act the way he did, or that he could have chosen to act in some other way instead. But if his choices and actions were merely the product of a prior set of causes—if he had no *real* choice at all—concepts like blame and praise don't make any sense. We can't hold a person responsible for something he had no choice in doing, any more than we can blame a puppet for the actions of its master.

Despite the strength of the causal determinist position in theory, in practice we certainly *feel* as if we make choices and take actions, and that we should be held responsible for them. We wouldn't punish supervillains if we didn't think they were truly responsible for their choices and actions. Responsibility requires free will, a Pandora's box for philosophers if there ever was one. Note that this doesn't mean "free" in the political sense, such as enjoying freedom of speech, movement, or association; one isn't free simply by virtue of not being locked up by S.H.I.E.L.D. Instead, free will involves the idea that a person truly makes decisions without being mechanistically made to do so by other forces or causes.[11]

A person acting on free will deliberates among options and then makes a choice. Such a person "could have done otherwise," could have made a different choice, and could have taken a different action. So while Ant-Man did choose to help Stark by infiltrating Ryker's Island to interrogate Whiplash, he could have chosen to do many other things instead, from skipping out altogether and going bowling to visiting Whiplash in his cell to play a few hands of canasta.[12] If this is true, then Ant-Man did have a true choice, he did enjoy free will—and he would be responsible for the choices he made.

Is He or Isn't He?

According to Martin, our understanding of alcoholism is "hamstrung by a morality-therapy dichotomy, [and] we seem to lack a coherent conceptual framework for saying alcoholism is both immorality and sickness"—that is to say, both choice and disease.[13] The choice model of alcoholism "employs concepts such as integrity and dishonesty, right and wrong, guilt and blame," while the disease model "employs concepts such as disease and symptoms, wellness and suffering, treatment and therapy."[14] So yes, Tony Stark must take responsibility for his being an alcoholic, but no, he is not responsible for his actions while drunk because he suffers from a disease that robs him of control over his actions. Does this make sense?

Recognizing that some cases of being diseased can be traced to deliberate actions taken by the person—arguably putting alcoholism in the company of sexually transmitted diseases or emphysema among smokers—some advocates of the disease model view addiction as a disease of a special sort that incorporates a limited amount of responsibility. Under this view, Tony is responsible for having started drinking but not for the disease itself; that is, he is responsible for having opened the "alcoholic floodgates," though not for his inability to close them. He is also responsible for whether he takes the first drink on any given day. There are things he can do to avoid taking the first drink, such as working the twelve steps—but once he takes the first drink, all bets are off. As they say in recovery programs, "It's the first drink that gets an alcoholic drunk." This doesn't mean that the alcoholic is massively buzzed by the first drink, but rather that his willpower is massively compromised by it. Once an alcoholic takes the first drink, the compulsion to take another and another is nearly irresistible, despite the negative consequences foreseen. As Tony thought to himself during a recent bout of temptation, "But it's never just one magnum of champagne. After that it's long nights alone with Jack and Jim and Johnnie and eventually Ol' Grand-Dad and some Tussin."[15]

This idea that the alcoholic is both blameworthy and a victim is prominent in the current therapeutic approach to alcoholism, but Martin is skeptical. He characterizes this approach as trying to have it both ways by taking "the condition of alcoholism—that is, the drinking problem that includes heavy alcohol consumption, alcohol dependency, impaired agency, and the need for help" to be sharply distinguished from "the harm caused by alcoholism."[16] While the separation of the former as a disease from the latter as a choice may serve practical medical and public policy interests, we don't need to look too deeply to see that this dichotomy is untenable.

The conflict between the disease model and the choice model becomes most problematic when attempting to address the progressive nature of alcoholism. Once alcoholism has developed beyond the earliest stages, the individual's capacity for choice becomes steadily more compromised; his "free will" erodes as alcohol damages the brain. Roughly put, while in the early stages of alcoholism, Stark would have greater control over whether to take the first drink. But as Tony's alcoholism develops, the various areas of his brain that mediate impulse control, prioritize the importance of environmental stimuli, and govern decision making gradually become unable to compensate for one another. The sad consequence would be a progressive loss of the ability to make and act on his choices, including the choice of whether to take the first drink.[17]

The psychiatrist Jeffrey Smith suggested that we imagine that "free will" is an organ of the body that can be compromised like any other organ by disease, trauma, and drugs.[18] Once compromised, this organ is unable to do its job to its full capacity. Think of Tony's heart; Iron Man's initial armor came into being not merely to facilitate escape from his captors, but also to keep Stark alive after his heart was damaged in Vietnam. Without the chest plate, Tony's failing heart was having a negative impact on the body's functioning in a number of ways, including making it progressively more difficult to breathe. Similarly, a compromised free will is unable to do its job of recognizing and choosing one's best interest as well as it would otherwise. As the damage to Tony's brain and body due to drinking increases, there is a corresponding negative effect on the functioning of the free will. Neither the choice nor the disease model alone seems capable of addressing the clinical situation of the progressive nature of alcoholism through time.

Drying Out

In our daily lives, we take free will as obvious; we could not act in the world otherwise. Although we recognize that our choices are restricted by the circumstances of our lives, we behave as if we are responsible for them. These circumstances may greatly affect how—and how well—one addresses alcoholism. At the end of "Demon in a Bottle," Stark "got the monkey off of his back" in only a few pages, but the images are revealing. We see Tony in the company of a selfless loved one as he faces the DTs; he has the luxury and the resources to put aside his job (as both Stark and Iron Man) and other personal responsibilities in order to have the time to dry out; and he has something very appealing waiting for him on recovery—satisfying, meaningful, and appreciated work.[19] The narrator reminds us of what is at stake: on the one hand, Tony "knows that merciful escape is but a shot glass away," but on the other hand, Stark's "life's dream has been to help others. . . . The drink or the dream? Each heads a path that he knows will take him through the rest of his life."[20]

In the epilogue to "Demon in a Bottle," Tony Stark reminds us that getting sober and staying sober is a struggle: "I am tired—but it's a good tired. I feel like I've just taken life's best shot, and I'm still standing. And somehow, my other problems don't seem so tough anymore."[21] As difficult as he may have found—and continues to find—his battle with alcoholism, his vast resources would seem to put him in an ideal situation for the fight. But as a quick glance at the supermarket tabloids will tell us, those with wealth and power like Stark have a particularly difficult time getting sober. As *Iron Man* star Robert Downey Jr. has demonstrated, celebrities can indeed end up looking at the world from the bottom of a bottle. According to Alcoholics Anonymous, an alcoholic is still an alcoholic even when he no longer chooses to drink. Such a person is considered to be a "recovering" alcoholic; it's not "recovered" but "recovering" because, as the claim goes, alcoholism cannot be cured, only treated. Regardless of whether alcoholism is in the end a choice, a disease, or some combination of the two, the key to sobriety for most recovering alcoholics and addicts is participation in a long-term recovery process taken "one day at a time."[22]

NOTES

1. All of these events happened in *Iron Man*, vol. 1, #120–128 (1979), since collected as *Demon in a Bottle* (2007).

2. Ibid. A few years later, a much more in-depth tale of Tony's struggle with alcoholism was told over three years of comics, starting with his temptation at the end of *Iron Man*, vol. 1, #166 (January 1983), his succumbing to the bottle at the end of #167 (February 1983), and his gradual descent into homelessness thereafter. In #182 (May 1984), sitting against the outside of a building in a raging blizzard, clutching a bottle purchased with his last few bucks, he says to himself, "I guess I'm dying. I guess it doesn't matter. I guess I don't care." Only when he delivers the child of his friend, a homeless woman who dies immediately afterward, does Tony realize the value of life and swear off alcohol. But the story doesn't end there, as he must fight to regain everything he lost during his relapse (including his company and his identity as Iron Man), a fight that does not end until #200 (November 1985). His fight with alcohol, however, never ends and is still a central aspect of his character to this day.

3. *Iron Man*, vol. 1, #128 (November 1979).

4. From "The Twelve Steps" (steps one and eight, respectively), in *Alcoholics Anonymous*, 4th ed., 2001, p. 58.

5. Harry G. Frankfurt, "Alternate Possibilities and Moral Responsibility," in his *The Importance of What We Care About* (Cambridge, UK: Cambridge University Press, 1988), pp. 1–10, at p. 10 (emphasis mine).

6. Plato, *Protagoras* (pp. 358c–358d), in *Plato in Twelve Volumes*, vol. 3, trans. W. R. M. Lamb (Cambridge, MA: Harvard University Press, 1967).

7. See the chapter by Mark D. White titled "Does Tony Stark Have an Iron Will?" in this volume for more on weakness and will and choice.

8. American Psychiatric Association, *Diagnostic and Statistical Manual of Mental Disorders*, 4th ed. (Washington, DC: American Psychiatric Association, 2000), p. 197.

9. Ibid., p. 199.

10. Mike W. Martin, *From Morality to Mental Health: Virtue and Vice in a Therapeutic Culture* (Oxford, UK: Oxford University Press, 2006), p. 90.

11. For more on free will and determinism, see Timothy O'Connor's "Free Will" in the *Stanford Encyclopedia of Philosophy*, http://plato.stanford.edu/entries/freewill/.

12. *Iron Man*, vol. 1, #125 (August 1979).

13. Martin, *From Morality to Mental Health*, p. 87.

14. Ibid., p. 88.

15. *Iron Man*, vol. 5, #1 (July 2008).

16. Martin, *From Morality to Mental Health*, p. 95.

17. For an accessible rundown on the physiology of this process, see Mark Moran's "Drug Addiction Erodes 'Free Will' Over Time," describing National Institute on Drug Abuse director Nora Volkow's study of the neurobiology of free will, in *Psychiatric News* 42 (2007), http://pn.psychiatryonline.org/cgi/content/full/42/13/16.

18. Jeffrey Smith, "Alcoholism and Free Will," *Psychiatric Times* 16 (1999), www.psychiatrictimes.com/display/article/10168/49816.

19. *Delirium tremens* (Latin for "trembling madness") is the name for the collection of physical symptoms (including fever, trembling, disorientation, and agitation) that accompanies withdrawal from long-term use of alcohol and other depressants.

20. *Iron Man*, vol. 1, #128 (November 1979).

21. Ibid.

22. Thanks to Dawn Jakubowski and Mark White for wading through some truly beastly drafts of this chapter.

PART THREE

THE IRON AGE: TONY STARK'S ROLE IN SOCIETY

TONY STARK AND "THE GOSPEL OF WEALTH"

Andrew Terjesen

Tony Stark is a billionaire playboy who does a lot of good, in addition to a lot of carousing. So, if he is committed to helping people, why doesn't he simply put his money into a number of worthy charities? And why is Tony Stark the only one who gets to wear the armor? Unlike his bat-fetish counterpart, the Iron Man armor is the source of all of Tony's crime-fighting abilities, and it could be worn by anyone. Of course, over the years, Tony has handpicked select individuals to wear one of his Iron Man armors (most notably, James "Rhodey" Rhodes and Pepper Potts). But the fact that they needed Stark's blessing means that he still completely controls access to the Iron Man technology and the good it can do. So, why doesn't he just mass-manufacture the Iron Man armor to create a battalion of superheroes? Let's see.

The Gospel of Andrew Carnegie:
Why Tony Stark Knows Best

Admittedly, Tony Stark does not put *all* of his money into his superhero activities; after all, he created the Maria Stark Foundation to finance charities and renovation projects. But even the Maria Stark Foundation has been used over the years to fund his "pet" superteam, the Avengers, and it's unlikely that the foundation's charitable activities go through as much money as do Tony's constant upgrades of his armor. Not only does he use expensive, cutting-edge technology, but he also does not intend to put the armor on the market to recoup the costs of the upgrades.

Although some people might find the way he uses his money to be wasteful, an argument in favor of it can be found in the work of the Gilded Age industrialist Andrew Carnegie (1835–1919). Carnegie is not often thought of as a philosopher, but philosophy is really just about offering and scrutinizing arguments for believing one thing over another. Thus, anyone can potentially be a philosopher. In Carnegie's case, he wrote a short essay titled "The Gospel of Wealth" that was intended to advocate for greater philanthropic activities among the rich.

Carnegie's reasoning clearly applies to Tony Stark. According to Carnegie, the wealthy have distinguished themselves because they have a particularly rare talent for organization and administration. Carnegie was not saying that every rich person is particularly intelligent or talented, because he knew that some people inherit a great deal of wealth and are simply competent enough to hang on to it and others squander it. A classic example of this would be Tony's only living relative, his ne'er-do-well cousin Morgan Stark, who has frittered away his fortune and ended up helping Stark's enemies, including Count Nefaria and his daughter Madame Masque, to work off his debts.[1] Carnegie did not think much of people like Morgan and argued that one should leave only moderate sums to one's family in order to prevent wealth from being wasted in the hands of the less skilled.

Carnegie didn't merely argue that we shouldn't leave our money to our families when we die; he also stated that we shouldn't leave it for public use after our deaths. Carnegie's point is that the unique abilities of those who are self-made billionaires—like Tony Stark—make them the only people who are qualified to determine what to do with that wealth. Consider the following passage from his essay:

> We shall have an ideal state, in which the surplus wealth of the few will become, in the best sense, the property of the many, because administered for the common good, and this wealth, passing through the hands of the few, can be made a much more potent force for the elevation of our race than if it had been distributed in small sums to the people themselves.[2]

According to Carnegie, if Tony Stark gave a hundred dollars to every person in America, it would not do much for society as a whole. If Mrs. Arbogast, Pepper Potts, and Happy Hogan knew how to make the most out of the money they had, then they would already be wealthy. With a hundred dollars, they would all buy something that they think they need, but they would probably not consider pooling their money with that of other recipients to fund large-scale projects that could benefit society overall. On the other hand, if Tony kept that money, he could use it to fund a project that he determines is best for society, thereby making everyone better off.[3]

Are the Rich Really Different from Us?

If you're skeptical of Carnegie's claim that Tony Stark is much better at money management than is the rest of the Marvel Universe, you're not alone. Carnegie's claim rests on the assumption that in the competitive world of business, only the truly skillful come out on top. This may sound suspiciously like the notion of "survival of the fittest," and that's because Carnegie was directly influenced by the philosopher who coined that term, Herbert Spencer (1820–1903). Spencer's philosophy is often called "social Darwinism," but that's misleading, because Spencer was promoting the idea that the human mind and human society evolved even before Darwin published *On the Origin of Species* in 1859. Spencer's theory of human evolution was not based on the biological arguments of Darwin; instead, he argued that everything naturally becomes more complex over time, whether it be federal government or the long-running plot line of *Iron Man* (teenage Tony Stark—really?). Those who can handle the increased complexity will thrive, and the rest will fall by the wayside.

Perhaps it is too much to argue that every self-made billionaire is the next step on the evolutionary ladder, but it makes sense to think that someone who is able to maintain a fortune over the long haul has more skill than luck. Look at Tony: he was born into wealth and was able to build much greater wealth on top of that. In fact, he's lost and regained his wealth a number of times. He turned Stark Industries into Stark International and helped found Circuits Maximus, Stark Solutions, and two separate companies named Stark Enterprises. Other superheroes (I'm looking at you, wall-crawler) have not demonstrated the same business acumen. Tony Stark does seem particularly well equipped to determine how his wealth ought to be redistributed. As Abby St. Clair, who ran the Haven (one of Tony's projects for helping kids on the streets), observes, "He's been on the top and he's been on the bottom and he's done all 12 steps and more . . . he knows there's no easy answer, but every solution to every problem has to start somewhere."[4]

Arguments against the idea that Tony Stark knows best usually begin by denying that he is any different from the rest of us. In other words, there is no reason why Tony

Stark morally deserves the amount of wealth that he has. Consequently, there is no reason why he should have the right to determine what to do with it. The problem with such an argument, at least when it is applied to Tony Stark, is that there *is* something really different about him. He is Iron Man. Or, more to the point, he created the Iron Man armor, one of the most technologically sophisticated pieces of equipment in the Marvel Universe. Tony stands apart from most billionaires; I don't think Donald Trump could build even an outhouse without hiring someone.[5]

The Gospel of Intellect

To ignore Stark's intellect is to ignore what makes him so wealthy. So, even if we don't accept the idea that the rich are different from the rest of us, we must accept that Tony Stark is unlike most other people. His ideas and opinions demand a much greater degree of respect from us than do those of some random person on the street.

At the very least, Stark thinks his intellect gives him the right to determine how his creations are used.[6] In effect, he applies Carnegie's argument to the technological realm. Rather than arguing that Tony has a right to determine how his wealth is used because he is obviously skilled at managing wealth, one could argue that Tony has a right to determine how the Iron Man technology is used because he is obviously skilled at understanding how it works. So, if Tony decides that only he should be allowed to have Iron Man armor, we need to respect this distribution of the technology as being for the best. If he gives it to someone else whom he deems capable of using it, as he does with Rhodey and the War Machine armor, we need to regard that as being the best choice as well.

We see Stark's attempts to control access to the Iron Man technology most dramatically in the "Armor Wars" story line.[7] On discovering that the criminal Clay Wilson's

"Force" armor incorporates a design of Stark's that Wilson got from arms dealer Justin Hammer, Iron Man embarks on a crusade against everyone who has gotten technology from Hammer. Tony is clearly upset that villains such as the Crimson Dynamo, Titanium Man, the Raiders, and Mauler have, in Tony's words, "drawn blood with my sword."[8] It might seem that Tony is simply upset that Spymaster stole his technology and that he feels responsible for all of the harm it caused, but Stark's actions during "Armor Wars" suggest a different underlying motive.

In order to keep Hammer from getting his hands on Stark technology again, Iron Man also neutralizes the armor of S.H.I.E.L.D.'s Mandroids and Project Pegasus's Guardsmen. These are armors he built for those organizations to help them capture superpowered criminals and keep them in prison. It might seem that this is only an extension of his mission to keep his technology from causing more harm, but Stark is also taking control of the technology. His actions as Iron Man show that he does not trust even the good guys to use his technology wisely and keep it from falling into the wrong hands. The only person who should be able to determine who gets Iron Man technology is Stark himself.

This point is driven home when Stark has a "tapeworm" computer virus created that erases his designs whenever someone enters them into a computer.[9] Presumably, the program will keep people from using a design like Stark's, regardless of whether they came up with it on their own or stole it from him. Stark thus makes himself the judge of who can use that technology, even planning to forgo use of the technology himself, fearing that others might get their hands on it. He builds another suit of armor, however, to stop an out-of-control Firepower, who is using the last bit of working Iron Man technology, but Stark equips this armor with a self-destruct chip that he will activate when he's done with it.

Tony's reason for building the armor to stop Firepower, rather than letting another superhero do it, is that there are "very few people powerful enough to stand against them, to offer protection for the blameless and innocent. And with this armor I'm one of those few."[10] At the end of the issue, Tony decides not to destroy the new armor because, he says, "I do have a responsibility to keep my inventions from evil hands—but I have a greater responsibility to oppose evil any way I can." Tony clearly believes that he—and no one else—has the intellect and moral judgment necessary to use the Iron Man armor wisely. But if protecting the innocent was so important, couldn't he at least have left some armor in the hands of Nick Fury and Project Pegasus? There does not seem to be any reason that he should be allowed to take risks that they can't, unless one accepts the idea that Tony Stark has intellectual capabilities that those individuals lack, which give him better judgment.

Better Judgment? Have You *Met* Tony Stark?

If the argument for allowing Tony Stark to monopolize the Iron Man technology is based on the idea that he clearly has better judgment than everyone else, then that argument is on some pretty shaky legs. When Tony found out that there was a name missing from Hammer's list, he reasoned that it was the superhero Stingray. Instead of calling him up and finding out whether it was true, Iron Man went after Stingray and defeated him in combat. When he tried to neutralize Stingray's powersuit, he discovered that he had been mistaken: it did not contain any Stark technology.[11] Tony's reckless behavior during "Armor Wars" continued as his actions led the Titanium Man armor to malfunction and kill its occupant.[12]

Aside from his questionable behavior in those situations, his entire life casts doubt on the claim that he knows best, especially the sordid details of his private life as Tony Stark. Unlike some other billionaire superheroes, he didn't have to *pretend* to be a playboy as part of some plan to scare the crap out of street criminals. Throughout his life, he has behaved in a reckless manner and has not treated those who cared about him very well. His lowest point came when his alcoholism began to interfere with his role as Iron Man and forced him to relinquish that responsibility to Rhodey.[13] But even after he started on the road to recovery, he did not show good judgment with his friends. One notable instance is when he faked his death and left Rhodey in charge of Stark Enterprises.[14] Tony did not seem to realize that when he revealed that he had faked his death, this would cause a huge rift between himself and Rhodey (a man who had always stood by him, even during some of his more questionable actions during "Armor Wars").

In the story line "The Best Defense," the perception that Stark is still very much an egotistical and childish individual is reflected in the attitude of Department of Defense official Sonny Burch. He uses Stark's exposure of his secret identity to nullify the government's agreement not to make use of any of the patented technology Stark had created for them. Burch states that he doesn't "think it's very patriotic for the country's greatest munitions developer to sit on the sidelines, playing with his toys all by himself!"[15] In other words, using all of his best technology to play superhero and refusing to let anybody else "play" do not reflect the most mature judgment. ("These are *my* repulsors—get your own!")

The Best Defense against the Misuse of Technology

When Sonny Burch begins to distribute Stark technology to select government contractors, Stark objects. This time, however, he doesn't go all "Armor Wars" on the problem. Stark's objection is that the government is "risking lives with equipment that only I understand!"[16] The various accidents that occur while the government contractors try to make Stark's patents work highlight his point.

So maybe Carnegie's point was too strong. He seemed to believe that massive wealth accumulation showed that someone was very smart *in general*. But, as some of the mistakes that Stark has made illustrate, one can be very smart about managing a tech company or very knowledgeable about robotics, while being no smarter than anyone else in every other area of life. Stark's knowledge about how his technology works simply means that he can see the dangers of implementing it and can provide guidance on how to avoid those problems.[17]

Perhaps recognizing that he is not uniquely qualified to determine who gets to use certain technology, he does not try to stop government production. Instead, he proclaims, "I need to be where I can see everything!"[18] Tony thus decides that he must try to become secretary of defense so that he can oversee the production of his technology. Once he gets the post, he is still not the ultimate decision maker, because he reports to the president; nor is he the only one initiating decisions, as projects can start at lower levels and work their way up to him. Instead of exercising sole control, he rides herd on the institutional structure.

During his time as secretary of defense and later director of S.H.I.E.L.D. (following the "Civil War" event), Stark begins to make his technology much more readily available. He even equips S.H.I.E.L.D. teams with armor based on his design. By that point, he has abandoned Carnegie's idea that he is uniquely qualified to make decisions about how to use his technology, in favor of the more moderate idea that he has certain knowledge that no one else has (because much of his technology is leaps and bounds ahead of the state of the art) that must be incorporated into the decision-making process.

Civil Wars, Secret Invasions, and the Fall of Iron Man

It's not too long, though, before Tony once again falls into the trap of thinking that he is the only person who really knows how to use government resources and technology. Claiming that he is a futurist, Tony determines that the future holds only devastation. A war between superheroes is inevitable because "we're warriors with weapons and ideals and things to fight for—things worth dying for. . . . It's our defining characteristic. We fight . . . I knew there'd be a war of heroes."[19] Thus, Tony endorses the Superhuman Registration Act (SHRA) as a way to prevent the inevitable conflict and sets into motion the events that lead to the *Civil War* mini-series (2006–2007).

Tony claims that he could largely predict what side most heroes would fall on and makes plans to win without casualties or the large-scale damage that the SHRA was intended to prevent. In his pursuit of victory, Stark embraces a number of questionable projects, including a detention center in the Negative Zone (which lacks due process), cloning Thor, creating a team of mostly psychotic supervillains to hunt superheroes who refuse to register, and trying to get Spider-Man on his side by bribing him with the Iron Spider armor (armor that Tony designed to let him control Spider-Man if he switches sides). He may even have staged an attack by Norman Osborn using the nanites that were supposed to keep his team of psychotic superhero hunters under control.[20]

In the end, Tony "wins" the Civil War and is even able to reconcile with many of those who opposed the SHRA. His idea of government superteams in every state (the "Fifty-State Initiative"), using registered heroes, begins to bear fruit.

But it all falls apart when the "Secret Invasion" (2008–2009) by the imperialistic Skrull race is revealed. In fact, by the end of the (not-so) Secret Invasion, the prevailing attitude is that Tony Stark's actions before, during, and after the Civil War made the world vulnerable to a Skrull takeover. After the Skrull invasion has been thwarted—conveniently, by the end of the *Secret Invasion* series—Tony Stark is ruined and Norman Osborn (yes, the former Green Goblin!) now holds Tony's old position of power and prominence in the U.S. government. Only drastic action by Tony denies Norman access to the Iron Man technology and the database of heroes' secret identities that Tony had compiled as part of the SHRA.[21]

Despite the unfortunate consequences of his actions, Tony does follow Carnegie, almost to the letter. Carnegie said that the duty of the man of wealth is "to consider all surplus revenues which come to him simply as trust funds, which he is called upon to administer in the manner which, in his judgment, is best calculated to produce the most beneficial results for the community."[22] Of course, Carnegie also said that the wealthy man has a duty to be a model of thrifty and moderate living, but we've already established that Tony isn't perfect. Ironically, it's Tony's taking control of everything and trying to run it for the common good that makes the country vulnerable to the Skrull invasion.

Another Scotsman famous for writing about wealth would have pointed out that Carnegie's idea of charging the wealthy man with the stewardship of society has a fatal flaw. In the words of philosopher and economist Adam Smith (1723–1790), "I have never known much good done by those who affected to trade for the public good."[23] Smith expressed a great deal of skepticism concerning the ability of a single individual (or even a small body of individuals) to determine what is best for everyone. Indeed, Tony's failure during the Civil War seems to illustrate the dangers of putting one's fate into the hands of a single person, no matter how intelligent he or she might be.

Despite what some on the "right" might say, Smith's skepticism does not commit us to believing that government causes more problems than it solves. Instead, the point of Smith's skepticism is that if Tony decides what is best for everyone without asking any of them, there's a good chance he is going to get it wrong. Democratic institutions do a good job of channeling people's ideas of what is best, but Tony ignores (and maybe even subverts) them when they disagree with what he and Reed Richards and Hank Pym think is best.[24]

The Invisible Power Gauntlet of Adam Smith

We shouldn't, however, decide how to administer wealth and technology in society simply on Adam Smith's say-so. That would be trading the presumptuousness of Tony Stark for the presumptuousness of Adam Smith. Rather, we need reasons for following Adam Smith's lead on this issue. The common perception is that Smith would not think that Tony should be put in charge of America's technology and superhumans because "the invisible hand of the market will regulate society more effectively." As I will argue, this perception is not actually very fair to Smith.

Smith's famous metaphor of the invisible hand appears only once in *The Wealth of Nations*, in the following passage: "By preferring the support of domestic to that of foreign industry, he intends only his own security; and by directing that industry in such a manner as its produce may be of the greatest value, he intends only his own gain, and he is in this, as in many other cases, led by an invisible hand to promote an end which was no part of his intention."[25] The metaphor appears in the context of a very specific issue (domestic versus foreign investment) and only once, so we should be careful before attributing the unrelenting faith in free markets of many modern-day economists to Smith. Plus, he did say "as in many other cases," not "in all cases," suggesting that he did not believe in an underlying principle that always produces the best results. Rather than thinking of Smith as someone who believed "the free market knows best," it would be better to think of Smith as someone who believed that "attempts to regulate people's individual judgments on a grand scale rarely work out well."

Adam Smith would not have been committed to the idea that the citizens of Earth, if left to their own devices, would have developed a better defense against the Skrull invasion than Tony did. Heck, there were powerful arguments during the Civil War against the idea of unlicensed heroes running around doing whatever they think is best. It's not that Smith had unwavering faith in the "market"—it's that he would have had even less faith in Tony Stark. Having examined some of Tony's foibles, we can understand Smith's point. The real danger is when you combine unreliable judgment with the amount of power that is centralized into Stark's hands. When you or I make a mistake, we need a cleanup in aisle seven. When the director of S.H.I.E.L.D. goofs, the Skrulls invade, and the Wasp (among others) dies.

Carnegie's unwavering faith in people like Tony Stark is grounded in his commitment to Spencer's social Darwinism. One of the problems with social Darwinism is that it is based on the idea that Tony's natural talents must be much greater than everyone else's. If they weren't, then Tony would not be an improvement on humanity, he'd merely be lucky. Also, without going into technical detail, it really wouldn't be evolution if there was no significant advantage that could be passed on to one's offspring. Smith flatly disagreed with this premise; in *The Wealth of Nations*, he stated that "The difference of natural talents in different men is, in reality, much less than we are aware of."[26] He even later attributed the belief that people are naturally gifted—as opposed to talents being largely developed by practice and experience—to the "vanity of the philosopher."[27] Smith's egalitarian beliefs are one of the main reasons for his skepticism toward someone like Tony trying to decide, all by himself, what is best for society. Putting too much unchecked power in one person's hands treats the rest of us as ill-equipped to deal with the situation. Smith thought this went against common sense, and maybe we should too. Otherwise, we need to start treating Bill Gates and Warren Buffett as the first examples of *homo superior economicus*.

Another Reason to Give Back

Tony's role in making Osborn's "Dark Reign" possible seems pretty good evidence against Carnegie's ideas about how the rich should conduct themselves. This, however, does not mean we should disregard everything that Carnegie had to say. The reason that Carnegie wanted to put a moral burden on the wealthy to care for the whole of society was that he believed it was inevitable that an unequal distribution of wealth would occur in a free capitalist society.

Carnegie emphasized the problems of unequal distribution in his sequel to "The Gospel of Wealth," titled—what else?—"The Gospel of Wealth II." In that essay, he talked about how, no matter how equal the playing field, chance events can lead one person to accumulate vast amounts of wealth while someone else goes broke. Tony had a lot of success as an arms manufacturer before he developed the Iron Man armor, but had there been a downturn in demand for weapons, his company might have folded before he had a chance to move into other sectors of the market. Tony's skills had enabled him to parlay his government contract work into a fortune, but no one has the skill to control every chance event that affects the world of business. One particular "chance" event that Carnegie really thought mattered was the community one lived in. Almost as if he were describing

Tony Stark, Carnegie wrote, "The inventor's wealth is in great part dependent upon the community which uses his productions."[28]

Tony Stark benefits from his intellect, but mostly because the community values it. Certainly, not every era has welcomed technology with open arms. Recognizing that one's wealth is a product of chance should encourage one to give back to those who have not been as fortunate. Even if we are not convinced by Carnegie's "gospel," we should not forget that basic point. As it happens, Adam Smith also encouraged the rich to be magnanimous. In his discussion of a tax on luxury carriages (presumably, that would be an SUV tax today), Smith did not argue that the wealthy should pay the tax because they are causing more wear and tear on the road. Instead, Smith said that "the indolence and vanity of the rich is made to contribute in a very easy manner to the relief of the poor, by rendering cheaper the transportation of heavy goods to all the different parts of the country."[29] Tony has no reason to complain if the taxes on his luxury cars are higher than everyone else's, because he can afford it. Smith is encouraging him to be magnanimous about his wealth.

Tony Learns His Lesson?

As mentioned earlier, Smith is skeptical of the idea that a powerful individual really knows what is best for society. But the thing about skepticism is that it can be counterbalanced by other concerns. In *The Wealth of Nations*, Smith makes it clear that there are public works projects and public institutions that must be put in the hands of government because "though they may be in the highest degree advantageous to a great society [they are] of such a nature that the profit could never repay the expense to any individual or small number of individuals."[30] So perhaps someone needs to oversee the activities of superhumans who take the law into their own hands.

That someone might as well have been Tony. The problem is, Tony did not keep in mind the need to be magnanimous (because, after all, his ability to oversee that activity is a chance event). In the case of intellect, magnanimity would mean listening to and considering what people have to say, even if they are not as brilliant as you—but he did neither.

Post–Secret Invasion, Tony seems to realize that he needs to change his approach to problems. While trying to stop a volcano from destroying one of his plants, Iron Man digs a trench with his repulsor beams. One of his employees points out that it isn't working. Stark's initial response is to say, "I know what I'm—" but before he finishes his sentence, he says, "No. You're right," and changes tactics.[31] In that moment, Tony begins to practice the magnanimity that Smith advocated. Tony's intellect and familiarity with the Iron Man armor make him the best choice to pilot it.[32] In that sense, Carnegie was right. But the important thing Tony needs to remember is Smith's skepticism toward anyone who tries to decide what is best for everyone else. Even if he is a hundred times smarter than everyone else or a million times more wealthy, Tony has to recognize that he will make mistakes and will not always know what is best for everyone. That magnanimous attitude leads him to listen to his employees and take what they say seriously.

Undoubtedly, there will be times when he needs to trust his judgment and act—as, later in the issue, when he dramatically airlifts the lab out of the volcano's way. But such "only seconds before the lava kills us" scenarios are pretty rare. We should never forget Smith's skepticism and his reluctance to trust our fates to people simply because they are richer, smarter, or generally more successful than us. On the other hand, we should not dismiss Carnegie's ideas completely. There may be reasons why Tony's judgment should carry more weight than someone else's when we deliberate. Of course, the rich and successful should meet us halfway and heed Carnegie's call for philanthropic action—not because they are best suited to do it, but rather because they owe it to the society that made their success possible.

NOTES

1. *Tales of Suspense* #67–68 (1965); for more on Madame Masque, see the chapter "Engendering Justice in Iron Man" by Rebecca and Gary Housel in this volume.

2. Andrew Carnegie, "The Gospel of Wealth," in *The "Gospel of Wealth" Essays and Other Writings* (New York: Penguin, 2006), p. 8.

3. In *Iron Man: The End* (2008), a possible future Tony Stark puts his entire fortune into a space elevator, because he believes that humanity's future is in space travel. No one else (private individual or government) is willing to make that financial commitment.

4. *Iron Man*, vol. 3, #51 (April 2002).

5. Editor's note: The opinions in this chapter are solely those of the chapter's author and do not reflect the opinion of the editor (who *will be* the first "Philosopher Apprentice").

6. One might argue that Tony has a right to control the technology he develops because it is his intellectual property, but I will not rest my argument on that issue. For an exploration of the nature of intellectual property and what technology Stark actually "owns," please see Daniel Malloy's chapter in this volume ("™ and © Stark Industries: Iron Man and Property Rights").

7. *Iron Man*, vol. 1, #225–232 (1987–1988).

8. Ibid., vol. 1, #225 (December 1987).

9. Ibid., vol. 1, #230 (May 1988).

10. Ibid., vol. 1, #231 (June 1988).

11. Ibid., vol. 1, #226 (January 1988).

12. Ibid., vol. 1, #229 (April 1988).

13. Stark's refusal to acknowledge his problem during the "Demon in a Bottle" period (*Iron Man*, vol. 1, #120–128, 1979), despite Bethany McCabe's repeated interventions, is also a sign that he does not always demonstrate the clearest judgment. For more on this topic, see the chapter by Ron Novy, titled "Fate at the Bottom of a Bottle: Alcohol and Tony Stark," in this volume.

14. *Iron Man*, vol. 1, #284 (September 1992), reprinted in *Iron Man: War Machine* (2008), which includes *Iron Man*, vol. 1, #280–291 (1992–1993).

15. Ibid., vol. 3, #73 (December 2003); the "The Best Defense" story line appeared in *Iron Man*, vol. 3, #73–78 (2003–2004).

16. Ibid., vol. 3, #74 (January 2004).

17. Which is not to suggest that his judgment along these lines is perfect either. Several of his creations show poor judgment regarding the consequences of creating

that technology, such as the supercomputer Cerebus that conquered one alternate future (*Iron Man*, vol. 1, #5, September 1968), the Life Model Decoy of Tony Stark that tried to replace him permanently (*Iron Man*, vol. 1, #17, September 1969), and the sentient, homicidal armor ("The Mask in the Iron Man,"*Iron Man*, vol. 3, #26–30, 2000). For more on the moral responsibility Tony bears for his creations, see the chapter by Christopher Robichaud ("Can Iron Man Atone for Tony Stark's Wrongs?"), and for more on the sentient armor, see the chapter by Stephanie and Brett Patterson ("'I Have a Good Life': Iron Man and the Avenger School of Virtue"), both in this volume.

18. *Iron Man*, vol. 3, #74 (January 2004).

19. *Civil War: The Confession* (May 2007). Is perceiving the future a "superpower" of Tony's? If so, it would be the kind of thing that sets him apart and once again gives force to Carnegie's argument (transformed into a "Gospel of the Futurist"). But honestly, other than as a metaphor for his genius compared to the rest of us, calling Stark a futurist seems to take away from what makes him an interesting hero: that he's just a normal person using technology to become more.

20. *Civil War: Front Line* #11 (April 2007). For more on Tony's actions, motivation, and rationale during the Civil War, see the chapter by Mark D. White, titled "Did Iron Man Kill Captain America?" in this volume.

21. See the "World's Most Wanted" story line in *Iron Man*, vol. 5, #8–19 (2009).

22. Carnegie, "The Gospel of Wealth," p. 10.

23. Adam Smith, *The Wealth of Nations* (Indianapolis: Liberty Fund, [1776] 1984), IV.2.9.

24. Actually, it turned out to be a Skrull impersonating Pym (see *Secret Invasion* #1, June 2008)—Tony and Reed have no such excuse.

25. Smith, *The Wealth of Nations*, IV.2.9.

26. Ibid., I.2.4.

27. Ibid.

28. Carnegie, "The Gospel of Wealth II," in The *"Gospel of Wealth,"* p. 63.

29. Smith, *Wealth of Nations*, V.1.75.

30. Ibid., V.1.69.

31. *Mighty Avengers* #21 (March 2009).

32. And the dangers of mass-producing the armor so that every person could have his or her own WMD show why Tony (and those he trusts) is the only one who should be allowed to pilot it.

™ AND © STARK INDUSTRIES: IRON MAN AND PROPERTY RIGHTS

Daniel P. Malloy

> Do you really think that just because you have an idea, it belongs to you?
>
> —Obadiah Stane, *Iron Man* (2008)

Officially, Iron Man is an employee of Stark Industries. The armor he wears is property of the corporation, the technology that powers it is owned by the company, and even the Iron Man identity belongs to Stark Industries, in the same way that Tony the Tiger belongs to the Kellogg Company, and Bugs Bunny belongs to Time Warner. Iron Man, unlike any of his colleagues in the spandex business, is a corporate mascot.

This makes Iron Man nearly unique among superheroes. Certainly, others have backers of various sorts, and those relationships are often complex. The X-Men could not exist without Charles Xavier's fortune, Captain America owes his membership in the superhero club to the U.S. government, and Nick Fury is inseparable in our minds from S.H.I.E.L.D. But Iron Man's relationship to Stark Industries (or whatever company Tony Stark is running at the moment) is unusual because it is one of ownership. Iron Man is not a soldier like Captain America or Nick Fury; nor is he a spy or a vigilante, a covert operative with no open connection to his backers. Iron Man is more like Mickey Mouse—just as Mickey belongs to the Walt Disney Company, Iron Man belongs to Stark Industries. One cannot look at Mickey Mouse without thinking of Disney, and because of this, Disney strictly controls the use of his ratlike image. In the same way, wherever Iron Man is, there Stark Industries is as well. As we'll see, this situation raises some complex philosophical questions about property and responsibility.

Tony's Best Toy

In the broadest terms, a piece of property is a thing owned by some person. When we speak of owning a "thing," we are not speaking strictly of a physical object. Rather, "thing" can refer to an object, an idea, or an image, any one of which may be owned. Now, what do we mean by "own"? To own a thing is to have the right to decide how it may be used and by whom. For instance, if I own a bicycle, it is my right to ride it or not, and to decide whether anyone else may ride it, and if so, when and to where. When someone steals my bicycle, this person has done no harm to the bicycle itself, nor has he or she actually wounded me, but the thief has violated my rights of ownership. He or she has robbed me of my ability to decide what may be done with the bicycle.

The ownership of the Iron Man armor is similar, in many ways, to the ownership of the bicycle. The armor is a material thing, and owning it means that Stark Industries can decide how it is used and by whom. There is, however, a key difference between the armor and the bicycle when it comes to responsibility. The armor, unlike the bicycle, has enormous destructive potential. If I lend my bicycle to someone who I have every reason to believe knows how to ride it, and she gets into an accident with it, I am not responsible for the accident. In fact, I may actually expect that person to pay for repairs to the bicycle. If, however, Stark Industries were to allow someone to use the Iron Man armor, and that person caused an enormous amount of damage with it, then those injured by the armor could rightly present the bill to Stark Industries. Ownership of the armor brings responsibility for how it is used and by whom, and added responsibility flows from the added destructive power of the Iron Man armor. When I lend my bike, there is no reasonable expectation that the person I lend it to will destroy a building with it. On the other hand, the Iron Man armor is easily capable of destroying a building—or several. So, in allowing someone to use the armor, Stark Industries has the responsibility of gauging what type of person this is. Is she likely to use the armor correctly? If there is a reasonable expectation that the person will use the armor for the wrong reasons, then Stark Industries is responsible for the consequences.[1]

This is linked to similar aspects in the ownership of an idea or an image. With a material object such as the Iron Man armor, ownership is fairly cut and dried. If I own it, I can decide what to do with it. If I want to use it, I can. On the other hand, if I feel it is too dangerous to be used by anyone, I can destroy it. Stark believes that the Iron Man armor can be used for the good of the world—provided that it is used by him (or by a trusted ally, such as James "Rhodey" Rhodes). He thus refuses to allow anyone else to use the armor, and he refuses to produce suits for anyone else (although he does often design and build technology for his fellow superheroes). But think about it: however much good Stark can do with his suit, wouldn't he be able to do more for the world if he built more suits? Say, a small army of dedicated and completely trustworthy individuals, all armed with Iron Man technology?[2]

Owning Ideas and IDs

Here we move beyond the question of the ownership of the armor itself and into the ownership of the technology behind it. We thus enter a more nebulous arena, the ownership of an idea. This involves both the ownership of an idea with practical application and also the ownership of an image. To put it in concrete terms: Apple, Inc., owns the technology behind the iPhone, but the company also owns its image. The mucky-mucks at Apple would be very concerned if someone started to degrade the image of the iPhone, but they would be far more concerned if someone were to copy the technology of the iPhone. Similar though they are, ownership of an idea and ownership of an image each carry with them different rights and responsibilities.

Tony Stark owns not only the Iron Man armor but also the ideas—the designs and the technologies—that go into the armor. His rights in this domain are similar to his rights over the armor itself. As long as he has exclusive ownership of the technology, he can decide how it may be employed and by whom. So, for example, regardless of how much good an army of Iron Men might do, Stark cannot justifiably be forced to build such an army. The technology belongs to him, so it is his decision whether to use it to build more than one suit of Iron Man armor, just as it is his decision whether to let anyone else use the armor itself. If someone else attempts to use the Iron Man technology without Stark's permission (as has happened on numerous occasions), Stark can demand that this person stop.

The logic is similar with respect to Iron Man's image or identity, perhaps the strangest aspect of Iron Man as a superhero.

It's one thing to have armor or a technology that is the property of a company, but it's another thing altogether to have that company own one's identity. This ownership of an identity should not be confused with slavery; it is rather more like that warning of mothers everywhere that everything a child does reflects well or poorly on her. Good children are believed, rightly or wrongly, to be the product of good mothers, where a bad child "clearly" has a bad mother. I bring this up not to comment on the wisdom or lack thereof of this reasoning, but to draw a parallel with the ownership of an identity: we can say the mother is claiming ownership over the child's identity.

In a parallel way, corporations own the identities of their mascots (although this time as a legally recognized right). When you see someone dressed as Ronald McDonald, it is natural to link that image to the McDonald's corporation. As such, McDonald's has a vested interest in what a person dressed as Ronald does. Someone dressed as Ronald visiting children in a hospital looks good for the company, whereas that same person robbing a bank would reflect poorly. The same is true of Stark Industries and Iron Man. In truth, it is impossible at any given moment to tell who is wearing the Iron Man armor—Rhodey has filled in for Tony many times over the years, and no one has been the wiser. Once a person dons the armor, he is, for all intents and purposes, Iron Man. And whatever he does with the armor will reflect on Stark Industries. Thus, the company retains the right to dictate how the armor is used, both on the basis of its ownership of the armor itself and on the basis of its ownership of the Iron Man persona.

At its most basic level, the ownership of a thing can be summed up as the right to decide how it is used and the responsibility to ensure that it is used sensibly. But what is the basis of this right? What grants Tony Stark or Stark Industries any right to declare that the Iron Man armor shall be used in this or that way, or that the Iron Man technology may or may not be used by this or that person or group? In sum, what is the moral basis of this idea of ownership? And what does that basis tell us about the more difficult-to-define types of property, such as intellectual property?

Stealing Tony's Stuff

Control of the Iron Man technology and various attempts to wrest control away from Stark by various means and by different villains have formed the basis of any number of Iron Man story lines, as well as the 2008 *Iron Man* film (in which the dramatic tension is caused almost entirely by Obadiah Stane's desire to control Stark Industries). To discover the basis of Stark's property rights, let's look at one example where Stark's rights were clearly violated: the Armor Wars.

Called "Stark Wars" when it was first published and subsequently renamed "Armor Wars" when Marvel reprinted the story line in a trade paperback, the events are triggered when Stark defeats the villain Force in battle.[3] Examining Force's new armor, Tony finds that it is powered by his own designs. Spymaster, as it turns out, had stolen the designs, which then made their way onto the black market. So Tony engages armored heroes and villains alike to disable any and all systems based on his designs, a rampage that ultimately results in the death of Gremlin. Tony's actions may be morally questionable in general, but the issue is what gives Stark the right to decide who gets to use his designs and for what purposes. The easy answer is, as we saw earlier, his ownership of those designs; however, when we examine that answer, it turns out to be circular. So we must go deeper and look into the moral basis of property.

There are two basic theories about the moral basis of property, if we exclude those that reject the existence of private property altogether (such as Pierre-Joseph Proudhon's claim that "property is theft").[4] These theories are the natural law and social contract theories. According to the *natural law theory*, property is a natural right, which is to say that it exists "in the world," apart from human society and its conventions. That is not to say that we are all entitled to property, but that we are all entitled to the opportunity to earn property and to be secure in that property. According to natural law theory, the moral ground of property is, essentially, our existence in this universe. A human being, simply by virtue of his or her existence, can claim a right over some property, given that he or she has done something to earn that right (more on this in a moment).

On the other hand, we have the *social contract theory* of property. According to this theory, property is not a natural thing—rather, it is the creation of society. Social contract theory relies on an individualistic view of humanity: a human being outside of society, having no dealings with other humans, would have no call to claim or press a right to something she considered "hers" and therefore off limits to others. It is only once this individual enters into society with others that it becomes necessary to negotiate what will constitute the difference between "mine" and "yours." As the social contract theorist Jean-Jacques Rousseau (1712–1778) put it, "The first man who, having enclosed a piece of ground, bethought himself of saying 'This is mine,' and found people simple enough to believe him, was the real founder of civil society."[5] The moral basis of property is thus the agreement at the heart of society.

Putting a Locke on the Armor

Starting from these broad sketches of the competing theories, we can now look at them in detail and see how they relate to Iron Man and the Armor Wars. In dealing with natural law theory, our main source is John Locke (1632–1704) and his theory of *original appropriation*. According to Locke, every human being is born with one piece of property that can never be taken by or sold to another under any circumstances: namely, one's own body. The way something becomes one's property is when one puts the labor of one's body into it.[6] Take the example of picking apples. Suppose there is an apple tree in a field that no one owns. Anyone who wishes to may pick some apples from the tree—within reason. (The apple picker has a duty to take only as much as she needs and to leave "as much and as good" for others. There is no sense in her picking all of the apples out of the tree; they would rot long before she had the chance to eat them.) Once she has picked the apples, even though the tree does not belong to her, the apples are hers. She has invested her labor in them: changed them and improved them in some way (no matter how minimal). Her natural right to her own body can therefore be extended to the things she applies her body to improving.

How does this apply to Stark's stolen Iron Man designs? Clearly, the designs represent a substantial investment of Stark's labor, though not his physical labor. The designs are the product of his mind. This distinction does not affect the case. If Stark's body is his own property, then his mind most certainly is as well. Therefore, when Spymaster took those designs, he robbed Stark of an extension of himself. According to natural law theory, Spymaster's actions are comparable to taking Stark's arm or leg. His property, intellectual or otherwise, is in a sense a part of himself; his mind is in his designs. What Spymaster stole was not merely something of Stark's, but a part of Stark. By this logic, many other crimes can be seen as a violation of property rights. Indeed, when Locke laid out his list of inalienable rights—life, liberty, and property—he claimed that in truth, the first two are based on the third.[7] Someone who takes my life has taken my first piece of property, my body, away from me. In the same way, anyone who limits my liberty—say, by tying me up—robs me of the right to choose how I am going to use my property. So long as I am tied up (provided, of course, that I am tied up against my will, which raises entirely different questions), I cannot use my property, my body, as I would. In the same way, by stealing Stark's designs, Spymaster impinges on Tony's ability to use them as he desires.

The natural law theory of property seems convincing, but it has some drawbacks. Most especially, natural law theory seems to be utterly inflexible. Our competing theory, the social contract theory of property, does not suffer from this flaw. Here we call on one of Locke's successors, the Scottish philosopher David Hume (1711–1776), whose theory of property proves an interesting and valuable counterpoint to Locke's. According to Hume, private property and property rights are based on an *original agreement*. Historically, this agreement never took place, but that is not the point; the agreement is implied. The idea of the agreement underlies all of our dealings with one another. What makes a thing mine or yours is that we act as if we had agreed to the idea that one can have exclusive rights over a thing because we can all benefit from it. Private property is a fiction but a socially necessary fiction. This justification of private property is *consequentialist* in nature, meaning that the reason we agree to it is that it gives rise to common advantage.[8] Thus, social contract theory allows for greater flexibility in our observance of property rights than does the natural law theory, which is rigidly absolute.

Even with the flexibility of the social contract theory, however, it still provides no justification for Spymaster's actions in the Armor Wars. Taking Stark's designs is still a morally wrong act, only for a different reason: Spymaster's theft violated the social contract. This may not sound as bad as it does under the Lockean theory, where the theft is a violation of Stark's own body, but bear in mind that this contract is the basis of society. Under the Lockean theory, Spymaster violated Stark's rights; under the Humean theory, he has broken his own link with society. Far from making himself simply Stark's enemy, Spymaster's actions make him the enemy of society itself. And this is true of any theft; the person who steals my bicycle is just as much the enemy of society as is the person who steals another's life or liberty. Breaking the contract is a costly prospect (and helps explain why we consider such acts to be crimes against society, rather than merely personal injuries).

To get at the heart of the differences between these two theories of property, however, we must examine a different kind of case: one in which they will disagree as to who is in the right. Only by examining such a case can we determine where our sympathies lie. In doing this, we will also deal with the complex and controversial issue of intellectual property.

I Am/Own Iron Man

In the final scene of the first *Iron Man* film, Tony Stark announces to the world, "I am Iron Man." In the film, the announcement results in a confrontational visit from Nick Fury, the director of S.H.I.E.L.D., but it seems to have no other repercussions (at least, in the first movie!). In the Marvel Comics Universe, however, the same announcement got Stark into serious trouble with the U.S. government.[9] Stark Industries had contracts to supply the U.S. military with technology, including weapons, but Stark naturally wanted to keep the Iron Man technology for himself. So the contracts all stipulated that the government would have no rights to Iron Man technology; it would be used only by a Stark employee (namely, Tony's fictitious bodyguard). The instant Stark revealed his identity, that clause in his military contracts was voided. The U.S. military immediately began to develop weapons based on the Iron Man technology, and Stark, whatever his objections, had no legal recourse. In order to monitor the use of his armor, he sought and accepted the post of secretary of defense.[10] This was short-lived; ultimately, he had to convince the public that someone else was in the Iron Man armor in order to regain control of his designs.

This case is not as clear cut as Spymaster's theft. Here, no one has broken the law, except perhaps Stark himself, who could, potentially, be charged with identity fraud. He was masquerading as someone else—a fictitious bodyguard—in order to gain something: exclusive rights to his Iron Man technology. The government was acting within its legal rights in duplicating Stark's technology, because Stark nullified the contract. In appropriating his technology, the government had the law on its side. So, there is no question of the legality of its actions, unlike the Spymaster case.

But were these actions *moral*? The distinction between legal and moral justifications is an important one, because an action can be both legal and moral, or it can be one but not the other, or neither. For example, when I'm asked by my friends, "Have you been drinking?" and I say that I haven't, even though I have, I have done something immoral but not illegal. There's no law against lying to your friends. If, however, a police officer asks me that question when I'm behind the wheel of a car, and I lie again, I have done something illegal as well as immoral. In the case we're dealing with, the appropriation of Stark's technology is perfectly legal, but the question of its morality has yet to be determined.

On the one hand, the government does have moral justifications for its actions. Here we fall back to Hume's social contract theory and its consequentialist basis. The government is justified in appropriating Stark's technology because this will allow it to better defend citizens from superpowered threats. It is, after all, part of any government's job to protect its citizens. By appropriating Stark's technology, some of the most advanced weaponry ever designed, the government is able to perform this function all the more effectively.

On the other hand, however, there is something disturbing about the government's actions, despite this consequentialist justification. Part of it may simply be a natural distrust of government agencies—yes, there are good moral reasons for the appropriation, but there seems to be no way of guaranteeing that Stark's technologies will be used solely for protection and defense. In fact, there is a more basic intuition that the appropriation is simply wrong. Our sympathies are with Stark. He has poured his labor and money into these technologies. He has a huge personal stake in how they are used, both as their originator and as Iron Man. And it is difficult to see how the government's use of his designs against his will is not simply another case of theft. Certainly, the law is on its side, but our moral intuition tells us that the Iron Man technology is Stark's, regardless of contracts. It is his time, money, and labor that developed the designs and the armor itself, and it is his reputation on the line whenever and wherever the technology is used. That is what is at stake in the Armor Wars, and it crops up again here. It would seem that while the legal interpretation is based on a social contract theory of property, the moral intuition about the case is more akin to natural law (placing restrictions on the consequentialist nature of the social contract).

Selling Ol' Shellhead

Before we're done, let's look at one more aspect of Iron Man as property. So far, we've dealt strictly with cases in which the Iron Man technology was appropriated against Tony Stark's will. However legal the government's appropriation was, Stark did not want it to happen. This has shown us some of the downfalls of the social contract theory when applied to intellectual property. As a result, we seem to be forced to rely on natural law theory to understand intellectual property.

Now, let's take a hypothetical example to see a problem that faces the natural law theory. Suppose that Stark were to decide to sell Iron Man, lock, stock, and barrel—or, in this case, armor, designs, and identity. As the owner, it is his right to sell his property. So that's it: Tony Stark is no longer Iron Man. There's another person who now owns and uses the armor, the technology, and the name of Iron Man. Although others have worn the armor in the past, it has always been temporary; this is permanent. In exchange for a certain amount of money, Stark has relinquished all rights to Iron Man. Here's our question: would the man (or the woman) behind the mask be Iron Man? I can't help but think that he or she would not. Ownership of something like Iron Man is not that easy to pass on.

And I believe that this intuition applies to all intellectual property. To remain within the comic book realm, take the example of Jerry Siegel and Joe Schuster, the men behind Superman. Siegel and Schuster sold the rights to their character to DC Comics very early on and famously believed that they had been swindled. Swindle or no, the sale was legal. Nevertheless, when the controversy came to broad public view on the 1978 release of the *Superman* movie, the public's sympathies were on the side of the creators. So much so, in fact, that Time Warner, which by then owned DC Comics and Superman, gave Siegel and Schuster lifetime pensions and health-care benefits, in spite of being under no legal obligation to them whatsoever.[11]

The point is that despite the legal sale of a piece of intellectual property, our moral intuition still tells us that it belongs to the person who created it. The identity of Iron Man, the responsibility for what someone in the armor does, will always fall to Tony Stark. So it seems that even the natural law theory of property falls short when dealing with intellectual property. There is something unique about intellectual property. When I buy a chair from someone, there is no question that the chair is now mine. But when an idea is bought and sold, be it for a piece of technology or a song or a movie or a character, in some sense that idea still belongs to its creator. The buyer has really only bought the right to use it. That is why, whatever else Tony Stark does in his continuing adventures in the Marvel Universe, he will always be Iron Man. Whatever his rights over the property, he can never get rid of it. And we should all feel a bit comforted by that.

NOTES

1. See the chapter "Can Iron Man Atone for Tony Stark's Wrongs?" by Christopher Robichaud in this volume for more on the responsibility involved with using the Iron Man armor and technology.

2. For more on this theme, see "The Five Nightmares" (*Iron Man*, vol. 5, #1–6, 2008; 2009 trade paperback), particularly the conversation between Tony Stark and Maria Hill, deputy director of S.H.I.E.L.D., in #4 (October 2008).

3. *Iron Man*, vol. 1, #225–231 (1987–1988).

4. Pierre-Joseph Proudhon, *What Is Property?* trans. and eds. Donald R. Kelley and Bonnie G. Smith (New York: Cambridge University Press, 2002).

5. Jean-Jacques Rousseau, *The Social Contract and Discourses*, trans. G. D. H. Cole (Rutland, VT: Charles E. Tuttle, 1996), p. 84.

6. See John Locke, *Two Treatises of Government*, ed. Peter Laslett (New York: Cambridge University Press, 1993), pp. 289–291.

7. Ibid., pp. 323–324.

8. David Hume, *A Treatise of Human Nature*, eds. L. A. Selby-Bigge and P. H. Nidditch (New York: Oxford University Press, 1978), pp. 484–501.

9. *Iron Man*, vol. 3, #55 (July 2002).

10. "The Best Defense," *Iron Man*, vol. 3, #73–78 (2003–2004).

11. For more on this, see Gerard Jones, *Men of Tomorrow* (New York: Basic Books, 2004), pp. 316–322.

TONY STARK, PHILOSOPHER KING OF THE FUTURE?

Tony Spanakos

In a recent series of stories in Marvel comic books, Tony Stark has been portrayed as a genius whose ability to read future situations allows him to serve as a sort of puppet master. His skill provides strategies that eventually play out in the "Civil War" between heroes and aid him as director of S.H.I.E.L.D., the international security organization. Stark disassembles the Avengers, sanctions the assembling of the New Avengers, assigns the new Omega Flight to Canada, and sends newly registered heroes to provide defense of the United States and the world, including the former villains who form the new Thunderbolts.

The idea of the brilliant and virtuous decision maker calls to mind the famous discussion of the philosopher guardian (also called a philosopher king) in the political utopia presented by Socrates in Plato's *Republic*.[1] In particular, the Avengers (old, New, and Mighty) and other registered heroes resemble the

Republic's "guardian class." But would Socrates consider Tony Stark/Iron Man an example of the type of philosopher guardian that he would want to govern his ideal city? The answer is no, but to understand why, we need to think about the ideal city, Iron Man, and the Avengers.

Is All That Glitters Gold?

Socrates proposed a "noble lie" in order to help us think about what an ideal society, a *kallipolis*, would be like. If people believed this lie, they would live in the sort of harmony necessary for his utopian project. He said that all people have elements of gold, silver, and iron in them, placed by God, but they have them in different proportions. The difference in the makeup of the souls of the people within society corresponds to three basic functions or classes: guardian rulers, auxiliary guardians, and farmers or craftsmen. The guardian rulers are primarily gold, the auxiliary guardians more silver, and the workers have iron or bronze.[2] The guardians should both live and be trained differently from workers, so as not to be tempted with material wealth and possessions.[3] In superhero language, we the people are pretty much farmers and craftsmen, the utterly ordinary people about whom there is little interest on the part of Socrates (and most comic book writers until recently). Our activities and lives are dependent on the protection and governance that come from others. But what about superheroes? Are they guardians, and is Tony Stark a philosopher king? If philosopher guardians have lots of gold in them, then billionaire industrialist Tony Stark is as good a place as any to look, or is he?

Tony Stark seems to be very much in the mold of a philosopher king. Socrates told us that philosopher kings should be separated from others who are less capable of performing the same tasks and that they should be taught mathematics, astronomy, music, and dialectics, in addition to engaging in physical exercise.[4] Similarly, Tony Stark is a child prodigy, whose wealthy pedigree puts him in boarding schools that effectively isolate him from both his family and from people of lower levels of intelligence and wealth. He graduates from MIT at the young age of fifteen, and his field of study, engineering, would have pleased Socrates, who was rather obsessed with mathematics and logic.[5]

So, Stark's background makes him a good candidate for philosopher king. Indeed, superheroes in general form a kind of protector class above ordinary citizens. When superheroes act as individuals, they potentially subvert the order established by us mere mortals (clearly, Bruce Wayne does this as the Batman, as does Frank Castle as the Punisher).[6] And when they act together, they place limitations on the current order or impose their own. The Avengers, for example, were created to deal with challenges that were beyond what individual heroes and governments could handle, particularly reining in a renegade hero, the Hulk. Over time, as Marvel writers became more ambitious, the Avengers expanded their concerns to intergalactic invasions and genocidal wars involving mutants.

Typically, superheroes such as the Avengers form a separate class in society, using their powers and abilities to protect the citizenry. But superheroes are also expected to be moral. For instance, superheroes typically do not kill, even when we the readers are über-convinced of the justifiability of killing a Magneto, Red Skull, or Super Skrull. (There are superheroes who kill, of course—Wolverine and the Punisher are two who come to mind—but this clearly sets them apart from Captain America, Iron Man, and the rest.) The Avengers, and superheroes more generally (though not supervillains), are like Socrates' guardian class, both physically capable and morally fit to serve and protect.

Superheroes Rule—but Should They?

If the superheroes are a sort of guardian class with more power than Socrates could imagine (and with remarkably high moral standards), we might ask, "Why is the world so stinky?" Or, more specifically, why does the existence of morally good superheroes not bring about a better form of order?

One answer Socrates would probably have given is that the world of superheroes is most certainly not his ideal city (*kallipolis*). The problem is that while superheroes may be very good guardians, they are guardians of someone else's order, the institutions and the governments of normal men: people without powers, who are also often without scruples. These days, superheroes are increasingly venting along similar lines. After the United Nations disavows its relationship with the Avengers, a number of Avengers feel "sideswiped" and Hawkeye says, "All we've done for them and at our worst moment—boom! Sold us out. . . . We aren't politicians, we're superheroes. We're the guys people can count on because they know they can't really count on anyone else. And if I'm mad about anything, it's that I knew this was coming one day."[7]

Yes, Hawkeye, the problem is that although superheroes have superpowers, save the world, and show mercy to their enemies, politicians and capitalists (such as Roxxon Oil and Obadiah Stane in the *Iron Man* stories) are often entirely unheroic. They use their less-than-super powers in ways our superheroes cannot counter. But this is really nothing new. We've known this for years. For instance, Bruce Wayne was hunted by the law in his early days as Batman, although he was arguably the most virtuous man in Gotham. What matters for us is that after considerable years of frustration, Tony Stark is willing to do something about it.

Remarkably, Socrates foresaw this. He knew that his philosopher guardians, those who truly sought understanding of the ideal forms that comprise the "actual" reality (as opposed to the one that we perceive—more on this later), might not be inclined toward rule. The problem is quite simply that no one despises political life more than philosophers do, and, unfortunately, people who want to rule are people who seek private gain and are therefore least prepared to rule justly.[8] The ideal society would be governed by those who have the least "interest" in governing and, for that reason, Socrates suggested that the philosopher guardians be "compelled" to govern the city.[9]

"Tony Stark makes you feel, he's a cool exec with a heart of steel"[10]

So, where does Tony Stark fit into this equation? And why is he different from other Marvel superheroes? Stark's "power" derives not so much from his intelligence but from his understanding of future realities. After all, Reed Richards (Mr. Fantastic), Hank Pym (Ant-Man/Giant-Man), and Doctor Octopus are all brilliant scientists, but none of them is quite like Stark, who says, "This is what I do. I'm an inventor. I can envision the future . . . I see what we will need and I invent the thing that will help us get there. That's how I invented my armor. That's how the Avengers were born."[11] This side of Tony Stark received little attention in early *Iron Man* stories, but it has nevertheless been an important part of the overall plot.

For example, Stark has been central to the changes within the Avengers and the various rules that govern the Marvel universe. Not only does he uniquely realize the need for the Avengers, but he puts his money where his mouth is by bankrolling them, too. Given his importance in terms of vision and finances, it is not surprising that Tony is the one who finally breaks up the team in 2004's *Avengers Disassembled*, and it is Tony whom Captain America tries to convince about the need to reassemble the Avengers soon thereafter.[12] But it is important to note that Tony had already considered the idea ("Guess we shouldn't have broken up the Avengers").[13]

He is also the one who tells Maria Hill, director of S.H.I.E.L.D., that they are re-forming the Avengers.[14] When Tony Stark assembles, disassembles, and reassembles the Avengers, he is something like the Socratic philosopher guardian, because the Avengers do not serve his private interests but serve what he perceives to be a collective good. And like the philosopher guardian, *he* defines the role of the Avengers.

In the *Civil War* story line, he goes even further and redefines the role of superheroes altogether. Here, we see Stark's role grow considerably in shaping the reality that he and others inhabit. Here, Stark's concern is not limited to the Avengers, but to the continued viability of superheroes as a whole. This is where the link between his envisioning the future and crafting methods to accommodate it today are most visible. The ability to link perception of the true reality with the institutions and practices necessary to foster good behavior, appreciation of the beautiful, and justice in society was critical to the Socratic philosopher guardians. After all, what would be the sense of emerging out of the cave of shadows, if the newfound wisdom of the philosophers were not used to bring about justice?[15] In fact, Plato said that "There can be no happiness, either public or private . . . until political power and philosophy entirely coincide."[16]

This is what Stark does when he calls together Mr. Fantastic, Black Bolt, Prince Namor, Doctor Strange, and Professor Xavier, to address a problem they share.[17] Normal people are tired of superheroes, no longer trust them, and want to place clear limitations on them. Stark tries to convince the "leaders" of the superhero community that they need to support superhero registration with the government. Initially, he fails to win over some of his colleagues. But after a reality TV stunt involving some young heroes goes wrong and kills hundreds in Stamford, Connecticut, Stark receives more support from Mr. Fantastic and others.[18] Eventually, the superhero world is split in half between pro- and anti-registration groups, with Stark leading the pro side.[19]

At the end of the *Civil War* arc, Stark says to the mother of one of the victims of the Stamford disaster, "A hundred ideas for a better world and we aren't even at number fifty yet. Doesn't that sound exciting to you? Believe me, ma'am, the superhero community just found the greatest friend they'll ever have. . . . The best is yet to come."[20] At this point we realize that Stark was not merely a participant in the Civil War but was the unseen hand, anticipating and manipulating the actions of superheroes and government officials. He was able to craft the world in which he lived through predictions of probabilities using the deliberative and rational part of his soul, ignoring the challenges posed by the appetitive and honor-seeking parts.

Stark emerges from the Civil War victorious, even if he appears somewhat unscrupulous. He then commissions the Mighty Avengers, assembles Omega Flight to replace the deceased Alpha Flight as Canada's new superhero team, and oversees the creation of the new Thunderbolts, a group of former villains who have registered with the government. In addition, he serves as the director of S.H.I.E.L.D. Holy conflict of interests, Batman! Certainly, Tony Stark is busy, especially if we throw in all of the womanizing. But is there really a conflict of interest? Are Tony Stark's private interests, behavior, and tactics in winning the Civil War consistent with those of a Socratic philosopher guardian?

Philosopher King or Puppet Master?

Socrates wanted his philosopher guardians to be virtuous, unconcerned with private and material gain, and technically skilled in the art of governing. Beyond that, they also needed an understanding of justice, beauty, and the good in their purest forms. So, is Tony Stark really a philosopher guardian?

Let's start with whether he is virtuous. Although Stark's private life is exciting, it's not exactly moral. Stark's conception of the beautiful and the good are too superficial

and material and he is too much a slave to his passions. By
contrast, the philosopher guardian must be temperate and
detached. The *Republic* opens with Cephalus and Socrates
agreeing that "old age brings peace and freedom from all such
things [sexual desire]. When the appetites relax and cease
to importune us . . . we escape from many mad masters."[21]
Similarly, the appetitive aspects of the souls of Socrates' philosophers are controlled by the rational parts of the soul.
Otherwise, they would be enslaved by their desires and be
neither free nor capable of making wise decisions.[22]

Socrates made clear that the rationality and virtue necessary for philosophers makes no space for philandering.[23] This
is a far cry from Tony Stark's dalliances in *Ultimates*, which
put his teammates and the world at risk.[24] Notoriously, Stark
is also an alcoholic. In the 1980s, "Demon in a Bottle" highlighted Stark's struggle with alcohol, which cost him friends,
loved ones, and the reputation of Iron Man. In the end, it
nearly destroyed him, but he did manage to recover.[25] For
the most part, though, the shortcomings of Stark's personal
life do not affect his judgment as a hero. For nearly half a
century, he showed consistently good judgment and has saved
the world too many times to count, both on his own and
with the Avengers and other heroes.

More to the point of morality, Socrates went to great
lengths to make it difficult for philosopher kings and auxiliary
guardians to have money and property.[26] The idea is that
attachment, especially to material things, can create private
interests, which will prevent the auxiliary guardian and the
philosopher king from defending the interests of the city.
Instead, they would use their power to defend their own private
interests. Here, Tony Stark scores highly, because his interest in
money seems minimal. He bankrolls the Avengers, a group that
he considers necessary to the well-being of the planet, although
it provides no personal benefit to him. It certainly is a financial
drain, and it draws considerable time away from his womanizing

activities, which even the least qualified philosopher would consider a "private interest." So, while Tony is certainly rich, this does not represent the type of distraction or conflict of interest that Plato was concerned about.

Tony Knows Armor, Tony Knows Women, Tony Doesn't Know Diddley

Okay, so he is not so bad a guy, but is he really a philosopher king or merely a puppet master? Is he, as he says, someone who sees the future and responds, or is he, as Socrates would want, someone who pierces through perception to see the underlying forms that sustain reality and then crafts a world that is best for the soul? This is where Tony Stark scores worse—a *lot* worse . . .

Socrates was insistent on the need for philosopher guardians to rule because they alone have the knowledge necessary to rule justly. One limitation of the craftsmen and the workers is that their knowledge is partial, particular to their profession and their personal needs. The knowledge of the craft corresponds to what Socrates called *technê*, and the lower crafts are distinct in that they are essentially material. In other words, the ordinary craftsman's knowledge produces something tangible, such as a basket or a ship. The *technê* employed by philosopher guardians does not produce anything tangible, but, then again, neither does that of teachers (and no one is claiming that teachers should rule). "True philosophers" are different, in that they do not only learn the "petty crafts," but they also "love the sight of truth."[27] Here Socrates argued that while philosopher guardians must know the *technê* of ruling, this type of knowledge is insufficient to make laws and govern the city in a way that is best for the soul.

Understanding (*epistêmê*), as opposed to craft, requires knowing the world as it is, the "real" reality, a world that is knowable only through contemplation. The famous allegory of the cave describes the intense philosophical journey from a cave of shadows toward a light that reveals the true forms underlying reality.[28] A true philosopher is committed to a lifestyle consistent with that allegorical journey: "the one who readily and willingly tries all kinds of learning, who turns gladly to learning and is insatiable for it, is rightly called a philosopher."[29] Philosophers are literally "lovers of wisdom," whose love is so great that they cut away all the material obstacles and items that mask the truth, which is to be found in permanent forms. It is only from these forms that justice, beauty, and the good life can be understood. Without understanding these forms, even the person best trained in the craft of ruling would not rule in the way that is best for the souls of the people. Therefore, the philosopher guardian must know the craft of governing and understand the forms, must have *technê* and *epistêmê*.

Socrates asked, rhetorically, "Since those who are able to grasp what is always the same in all respects are philosophers, while those who are not able to do so and who wander among the many things that vary in every sort of way are not philosophers, which of the two should be the leaders in a city?"[30] He considered those who have "no clear model in their souls and so . . . cannot . . . look to what is most true, make constant reference to it, and study it as exactly as possible" to be blind and incapable of acting to "establish here on earth conventions about what is fine or just or good, when they need to be established, or guard and preserve them, once they have been established."[31] Socrates wanted knowledge deduced from abstract principles that are ultimately true. This is consistent with his obsession with mathematics and his argument that *epistêmê* is logical and deductive.

So far, so good, for Tony Stark, MIT-trained engineer, right? But deduction is based on starting from first premises to make sense of the many phenomena that exist and take place within the world. Stark takes the world for what it is.

He is more ambitious than some superheroes in the methods he employs in order to try to change the world. But he does not try to know the world as a Socratic philosopher would. He does not struggle to cut away behind the shadows of shadows to uncover ultimate forms that define justice, goodness, or beauty. He does not make his decisions on how to arrange the chessboard of superheroes based on this ultimate understanding of knowledge. His thought process is occasional, rather than continuous, and his understanding of the world is partial and contextual. He responds to problems, predicts future crises, and imagines solutions to each. In each case, he considers what is just and good to do in each situation, but his ethics are based on the situation, not on any commitment to permanent forms of justice and goodness. Unfortunately, his knowledge is primarily *technê* (craft) and not at all *epistêmê* (understanding).

Although Stark takes the initiative to put the Avengers together, to disassemble and reassemble them, and to push for the Superhuman Registration Act, he is still very much *re*acting to circumstances. What differentiates him from other comic book heroes is that these are future circumstances, whereas other heroes react to the present. After the Civil War is over, Tony has a very "stark" monologue in which he reveals a tremendous amount about himself, telling the corpse of Captain America he saw that "a war was coming . . . I saw us fighting each other," and that he set in motion the circumstances that would allow for the best possible outcome. This is who he is as a superhero. He predicted the change in popular sentiment toward superheroes and that it would divide the superhero world. More damning, he says, "I knew that you would force me—no, that's wrong. You didn't force me. But I knew that I would be put in the position of taking charge of this side of things. Because, if not me, who?" But, as he confesses with respect to Cap's death, "The thing I can't live with . . . has happened. . . . It wasn't worth it."[32]

What Stark's confession reveals is that he crafted the Civil War based on his perception of the future, not due to any true understanding of justice, beauty, or the good life. His admission that "it wasn't worth it" suggests that either he has an understanding of "justice" but employed *technê*, which ended with an unjust result, or that his methods and/or goals during the conflict were guided by a lower and therefore not ultimate form of justice.

Tony Stark's puppet mastery, then, is not nearly as Socratic as it first appears. In truth, rather than understanding the world in its depth, Stark simply reacts to the world he observes, and he anticipates the reactions of others to that world better than most. He is quite skilled at understanding situations and creating conditions in which people will act as he expects or wants. But he is *only* a problem solver: a technically trained genius who has mastered the craft of maximizing outcomes in many circumstances. Stark is not a philosopher. He does not pursue knowledge for its own sake but as a way to react to a current or future "problem."

Over Four Thousand Words to Say No

So, what's the point? If Tony Stark is not a philosopher guardian, why wasn't the "no" in the second paragraph sufficient? Why did we need another few thousand words just to return to the same answer? Tony Stark seems so much like a philosopher king to us because we've read neither Plato's *The Republic* nor *Iron Man* carefully enough. A philosopher king in daily life seems to mean a very intelligent ruler who moves people around like pieces on a chessboard, and a quick reading of Stark's involvement in recent arcs of *Avengers* and *Civil War* shows him doing just that. Tony Stark becomes a "philosopher king" to us precisely because we have lost the ability to understand what it means to be a philosopher. And, in so doing, we cut away the power of the Socratic *kallipolis* from its roots in *The Republic* and instead made it a banal sticker that we apply to a country's president or the intentions of a revolutionary movement. To that end, the problem is less with Tony Stark than with us.

The Spanish philosopher José Ortega y Gasset (1883–1955) was convinced that the "backwardness" of Spain in the twentieth century was not due to structural economic problems or poor political organization. Instead the backwardness was caused by Spaniards not thinking deeply. His solution to the crisis in Spanish thinking, proposed in his *Meditations on Quixote*, was to demonstrate that by reading Cervantes' *Don Quixote* "meditatively," Spaniards would not only understand the text better but would learn how to think more deeply and, in the process, would develop the skills necessary to get beyond their "backwardness."[33] This meant approaching the text closely, then pulling back to gain distance, and then going back onto a specific point, before beginning the process again. In other words, we should read deeply, interrogate texts by looking at them in detail, and analyze them using wisdom gained from other texts.

By considering superheroes as guardians and Tony Stark as a philosopher guardian, only to demonstrate the limitations of those ideas, we are able to understand both Socrates and Iron Man better. Tony Stark's concept of the beautiful is Natasha Romanova in black spandex because she fits with our understanding of the beautiful, not Socrates'. Although comics are slow to challenge our notions of the beautiful, there is no question that recent Marvel story lines have deliberately raised the question of the appeals and the dangers of a Socratic-style philosopher king, albeit incompletely. Nevertheless, the creators of these story lines are not responsible for their failure to challenge Socrates. If we want them to write high-quality, sophisticated, *serious* work—without giving up the pulp—we need to read them seriously.

We've done that in this chapter, and this entire book is an effort to improve our reading. The more meditative readers we are, the more we insert Socrates, Ortega, Saint Augustine, Kant, and others into our experiences reading comic books, the more it will encourage the type of *Iron Man* comic books and movies that inspires deep thinking and makes us better readers. Could reading *Iron Man* save the world in the twenty-first century? It's up to us, true believers.[34]

NOTES

1. Although Plato is the author of *The Republic*, the main character, Socrates, espouses his views through dialogue with others. Scholars have debated to what extent the views expressed by Socrates in the *Republic* represent Plato's thoughts or a specific phase of development of his thought. For the sake of simplicity, this chapter will use "Socrates" to represent the character Socrates in Plato's *Republic*, not the thought of Plato per se or even the views of Plato's Socrates that appear in other dialogues in which Socrates is a character.

2. Plato, *The Republic*, trans. G. M. A. Grube and C. D. C. Reeve (Indianapolis: Hackett Publishers, 1992), p. 415.

3. Ibid., pp. 416^d4–417^b6.

4. Ibid., pp. 535–540.

5. *The Official Handbook of the Marvel Universe Update '89 #4* (October 1989).

6. For more on how Batman in particular does this, see Tony Spanakos, "Governing Gotham," in Robert Arp and Mark D. White, eds., *Batman and Philosophy: The Dark Knight of the Soul* (Hoboken, NJ: John Wiley & Sons, 2008), pp. 55–69.

7. *Avengers #502* (November 2004), reprinted in *Avengers Disassembled* (2005).

8. Plato, *Republic*, pp. 520e, 521b, 521a.

9. Ibid., p. 521b.

10. These are the opening lines to the jingle for the *Iron Man* animated television series; see http://homepage.mac.com/jjbeach/einheri/music/ironman.html.

11. *Civil War: The Confession* (May 2007).

12. *New Avengers #3* (March 2005).

13. Ibid., #2 (February 2005).

14. Ibid., #4 (April 2005); these issues of *New Avengers* are available in the trade paperback *New Avengers: Breakout* (2005).

15. Plato, *Republic*, pp. 513–516.

16. Ibid., pp. 473c–473e.

17. *New Avengers: Illuminati* (one-shot, May 2006).

18. *Civil War* #1 (July 2006).

19. For more on the Civil War, superhero registration, and Tony's role in it, see the chapter by Mark D. White, "Did Iron Man Kill Captain America?" in this volume.

20. *Civil War* #7 (January 2007).

21. Plato, *Republic*, pp. 329^{c}4– 329^{d}1.

22. Ibid., pp. 442^{a}6–442^{b}2.

23. Ibid., pp. 442^c–443^{b}1.

24. *Ultimates 2* #9 (January 2006).

25. For more on Tony's battles with alcohol, see the chapter by Ron Novy titled "Fate at the Bottom of a Bottle: Alcohol and Tony Stark" in this volume.

26. Plato, *Republic*, pp. 416d–417b.

27. Ibid., pp. 475^{e}1–475^{e}4.

28. Ibid., pp. 514–521a.

29. Ibid., pp. 475^{c}5–475^{c}7.

30. Ibid., pp. 484^{b}4–484^{b}7.

31. Ibid., pp. 484^{c}7–484^{d}3.

32. *Civil War: The Confession* (May 2007).

33. José Ortega y Gasset, *Meditations on Quixote*, trans. Evelyn Rugg and Diego Marín (Chicago: University of Illinois Press, [1914] 2000).

34 The author would like to thank Rob Delfino, Michel Spanakos, Photini Spanakos, and Mark White for their comments.

PART FOUR

THE MIND INSIDE THE IRON MAN

IRON MAN IN A CHINESE ROOM: DOES LIVING ARMOR THINK?

Ron Novy

And yet what do I see from my window but hats and coats which may cover automata? Yet I judge these to be men.

—René Descartes

Imagine that you have been given an afternoon to examine Iron Man. As you work your way up from the jet thrusters in his boots, Iron Man peppers his small talk with descriptions of each bit of equipment, its composition, function, and so forth. As you linger on the strange combination of fly-wheels and silicon chips within the knee joint, you're told that this particular configuration was developed after a devastating tackle by Crimson Dynamo left both the armor and its wearer nearly crippled. Reaching Iron Man's helmet, you lift the visor to see not Tony Stark's mustachioed smirk, but simply more circuit boards and shiny brass cogs. The voice modulator continues its running description: something about an early encounter with Mister Doll that led to a redesign of the louvers in the helmet's cooling system. You miss nearly all of the details, focused as you are on the empty space within the suit, the hollow where you had expected to see the thinking, breathing human with whom you thought you'd been speaking. Seeing your confusion, Iron Man says, "What is—so—hard to believe? . . . You knew that I was always a possibility."[1]

In 2000's "The Mask in the Iron Man" story arc, Iron Man's armor—like Victor Frankenstein's monster—is imbued with consciousness by a great bolt of lightning.[2] The most advanced cybernetic equipment of the Marvel Universe became sentient: a "Living Armor" that feels pain, learns new things, and acts on abstract principle. Could something like the Living Armor—a thinking, autonomous machine—exist in our world? And if so, how would we know? At various times, Stark has programmed the suit so that he and his armored bodyguard could appear together in public. Without opening the crunchy metal shell and finding Tony in the soft chewy center, how could we tell a preprogrammed but empty Iron Man suit from Stark in armor or either of these from the Living Armor? In this chapter, we'll look for the answer in, of all places, a Chinese Room!

Of Blenders, Toasters, and Living Armor

The plot of "The Mask in the Iron Man" is straightforward: While fighting villain-for-hire Whiplash, Iron Man is led into a trap in which his bondage-enthused adversary calls lightning down upon him. This literal and figurative shock is a pain-filled spark of life, which creates the Living Armor. Stark initially welcomes the enhanced abilities that come with the use of a sentient tool, but as the Living Armor becomes more violent and independent (eventually killing Whiplash in a vengeful rage), Stark realizes that this autonomous and deadly superweapon must be stopped. When Stark refuses the Living Armor's demand that they merge into "a perfect union of man and machine," he is taken to a remote island of the Bikini Atoll to be tortured into meeting the demand that they become "a perfect Iron Man." In the ensuing struggle, Stark suffers a heart attack. And in what seems to be a moment of remorse or possibly love, the Living Armor tears out its own mechanical heart and places it in the chest of his creator, saving Tony Stark and ending its own brief existence.[3]

As it happens, the philosopher and mathematician Gottfried Leibniz (1646–1716) imagined himself confronted by an apparently intelligent machine. Leibniz asked that we visualize this machine scaled up in size "until one was able to enter into its interior, as he would into a mill." As we tour every nook and explore every cranny of this mill-size mechanical mind, we "would find only pieces working upon one another, but never would [we] find anything to explain perception. It is accordingly . . . [not] in a machine, that the perception is to be sought."[4] Following Leibniz, the fact that we would find no element in this great clockwork that could not be fully explained by the same mechanical rules that govern the movements of washing machines and locomotives demonstrates that despite the outward *appearance* of having thoughts, perceptions, and such, there is nothing that gives us reason to believe that the machine *actually* has any of these things. Contrary to appearances, Leibniz would find that the Stark-free armor lacks the capacity to think; a mind's thinking—unlike a blender's blending or a toaster's toasting—is simply not the sort of thing that is subject to the rules of physics.

Functionalism, or If It Walks Like a Robot...

"Can a machine think?" is the sort of question you cannot answer in a particularly satisfying manner without having already worked out some other pretty big philosophical questions. What do you mean by "thinking"? How do you define "machine"? Where do you stand on the question of the relationship of mind to body? These all seem to need some answers prior to wading into a discussion about artificial intelligence. So, in an effort to sidestep some of the larger items on this carousel of metaphysical baggage, the mathematician Alan Turing developed a test to determine whether a machine can function *as if* it were thinking: that is, does the machine function as well as a human in the relevant ways? Basically, the question "Can a machine think?" is put aside in favor of "Can a machine pass the Turing Test?"[5]

The Turing Test itself consists of a number of sessions in which a person—say, personal assistant extraordinaire Pepper Potts—is seated at a computer terminal having a text-based conversation with an unknown partner. Pepper is told that her conversation partner is either a human or a computer programmed to hold a conversation. After having some time to interact with her conversation partner, Pepper is asked with whom she was interacting. If she is unable to correctly identify her partner as either human or computer at a rate better than chance (i.e., more than half of the time), we say that the computer has passed the test. That is, if Pepper can't tell the difference between the two, there is good reason for her to doubt that there is a difference.

The Turing Test assumes that *functionalism* is correct in accounting for minds and their thoughts. Functionalism defines a thing in terms of what it does, rather than what it is made of. So, for example, anything that tells time is a clock, whether it's made of metal, plastic, wood, or stone.

Imagine that Stark's mentor Ho Yinsen had been kidnapped by the communist warlord Wong-Chu.[6] Were a rescue to be mounted, it would look quite different depending on just who was making the attempt: S.H.I.E.L.D. might send a stealthy raiding party led by the Black Widow; the Scarlet Witch might bend reality with a hex to teleport Yinsen out of danger; while Thor might simply march verily through the front door swinging his hammer. With respect to Ho Yinsen's rescue, any successful strategy would do—that is, would be *functionally equivalent* to any other. Put another way, the escape could be realized in multiple ways, but if they all get the same results, then the rescuer fulfills the same role or function in each case.

This idea, that the role something plays is given priority over its appearance or physical makeup, has its place not only in comparing daring rescues but in the philosophy of mind as well. So when a functionalist is discussing "thinking" or "minds," what matters is that the function or the role is *instantiated* somehow—that it exists in some form, not whether it occurs within a cranium among the organic goo, a shiny metal box packed with wires and transistors, or a Rube Goldberg construction of bowling balls, piano wire, and wedges of cheese.

Look Out, Tony—Intelligent Earthworms!

This idea of functional equivalence has underwritten much of the discussion of artificial intelligence since Turing, but functionalism has had a much longer history in our effort to understand intelligence. Seventy-seven years after Mary Shelley's story of a sentient golem awakened with a bolt of lightning, Charles Darwin published his last and probably least-read major work, *The Formation of Vegetable Mould, through the Action of Worms with Observations on Their Habits*, a study of the creation of topsoil (which he calls "vegetable mould") through the digestive action of earthworms.[7] His extended study led him to conclude that "castings" (Victorian decorum prevented his identifying the material as "worm poo") added one to three inches of topsoil per decade. More interesting, though, is Darwin's claim "that worms, although standing low on the scale of organization, possess some degree of intelligence."[8]

Darwin had observed that at night, earthworms plugged their burrows with leaves, and that these plugs were consistently put into place by being pulled into the burrow by the narrow ends. Darwin considered four different explanations for the phenomenon: (1) chance; (2) a process of trial and error; (3) a specialized earthworm instinct; and (4) intelligent problem solving by the earthworm. The experiments themselves consisted of observing the earthworms' behavior when presented with both familiar leaves and with a variety of materials previously unknown to the worms (exotic leaves and triangles of stiffened paper).

Darwin dismissed the first two options, given the consistency of the results and the lack of supporting observations, respectively. From this, Darwin inferred that the earthworm behavior is a response to sensory input regarding the shapes of the objects—either option 3 or option 4. Darwin found the claim that the earthworm has a specialized "leaf-grasping" instinct to be insufficient to explain the ability to make burrow plugs of previously unfamiliar materials. Having eliminated the competing hypotheses, Darwin concluded that

> If worms have the power of acquiring some notion, however rude, of the shape of an object and of their burrows, as seems to be the case, they deserve to be called intelligent; for they then act in nearly the same manner as would a man under similar circumstances.[9]

The claim that earthworms solve the puzzle in more or less the same way that you or I would may strike even Count

Nefaria and the Ani-Men as strange, for it implies that the same measuring stick for intelligence can be applied to all comers—human, schnauzer, computer, or Martian—with the difference between them being one of degree, rather than of kind. Functionalism, and the Turing Test specifically, is concerned with countering our presuppositions underlying this "strangeness."

As If!

Darwin's experiment takes the earthworm to be what the contemporary philosopher Daniel Dennett called an *intentional system*, "a system whose behavior can be (at least sometimes) explained and predicted by relying on ascriptions to the system of beliefs and desires."[10] In other words, we can often explain a thing's behavior only by interpreting its actions *as if* it were motivated by and for something.[11] When your dog scratches at the door, we expect it means she wants to go outside. As often as not, we even assign reasons as to why the dog wants to go out: to relieve herself, to investigate a strange smell, or to play in the sun with the neighborhood children (who may very well be the source of the smell). Although this system for predicting and explaining behavior isn't foolproof—your dog might be stalking a bug or just be plain nuts—without taking an "intentional stance" toward the behavior, you get no explanation at all (and risk a soiled rug).

In his article "Intentional Systems," Dennett sketched a way to evaluate the "mental capacity" of evermore "intelligent" computers, such as IBM's chess-playing Deep Blue or David Cope's music-composing Experiments in Musical Intelligence.[12] Dennett asked that instead of trying "to decide whether a machine can *really* think, or be conscious, or morally responsible," we should consider "viewing the computer as an intentional system. One predicts behavior in such a case by ascribing to the system *the possession of certain information* and by supposing it to be *directed by certain goals*, and then by working out the most reasonable or appropriate action on the basis of these ascriptions and suppositions."[13] It seems unavoidable that we adopt this intentional stance whenever we sit across the chessboard from any opponent. Whether playing against fellow Avenger Steve Rogers or Jocasta, the computer that runs Stark House, it is necessary for Stark to credit his opponent with possession of certain background knowledge regarding the rules of chess, with having the goal of winning the match, and with having a strategy for reaching that goal.[14] Stark would neither be able to predict an opponent's next move nor be able to interpret past behaviors if he didn't assume he (or "she") was trying to win the game. Similarly, the earthworm's burrow-plugging behavior can be explained and predicted by ascribing to it beliefs about the prevailing conditions and a desire to shut off its burrow. And, in their final confrontation, both Tony Stark and the Living Armor could not avoid taking each other as intentional—or thinking—beings.

Crediting others, be they animals or artifacts, with intentionality is not to say that they in fact have intentions, but rather that they behave *as if* they have them. Ascribing intention to an earthworm, another human, Deep Blue, or the Living Armor allows us to predict future actions and interpret those in the past. Just as important, because we don't have direct access to the mental states of earthworms, robots, or members of our own family, behavior is—in a sense—all we have to go on.[15]

The Attack of the Chinese Room

Let's suppose that the contemporary philosopher John Searle is secretly one of the Mandarin's many sleeper agents, and he has captured Tony Stark's chauffeur Happy Hogan. Furthermore, as dastardly henchmen are prone to do, Searle has placed Happy in his latest diabolical device, the "Chinese Room."[16]

Happy—who speaks only English and a few cheesy French pick-up lines he picked up from Stark—has been confined to a small room and provided with a thick book of tables with which to look up Chinese symbols. From one slot in the door he receives cards containing Chinese symbols that represent questions, and through another slot he returns other cards that contain different symbols as indicated in his large book. To an outside observer who understands Chinese (such as the Mandarin), the interaction appears to be a conversation—a question goes in and an answer comes out—and he may conclude that Happy knows Chinese. Nonetheless— and here's the diabolical part of Searle's device—Happy will not be released from the room until he *really* understands Chinese. If Searle is right, this means that Happy will never get out, for although he may be a terrific manipulator of symbols, he doesn't understand what any of those symbols really mean.

This device itself is modeled on an advanced computer that behaves *as if* it understands Chinese—that is, Chinese symbols are fed into the computer as input, a program "looks up" the symbols, and other Chinese symbols are produced as output. For every question in Chinese that is fed into the computer, an appropriate answer in Chinese is spat out. The computer is so finely tuned at this process that the Mandarin himself would be convinced that he was interacting with a native speaker of Chinese. But does the computer really *understand* the Chinese language? No more than Happy Hogan does, according to Searle.

The Chinese Room thought experiment is intended to show that even when something can pass the Turing Test, this does not mean that it understands. Merely tricking an observer into believing that Happy or the computer has true understanding is quite a different matter from actual understanding.[17] As with Leibniz's mill-size mechanical mind, proponents of the Chinese Room argument appear to base their claims on the intuition that a mechanical device is simply not the sort of thing that can think, despite strong appearances to the contrary.

But perhaps we should not be so quick to accept Searle's hard and fast distinction between *merely* appearing to understand Chinese and *really* being able to understand Chinese. How do we judge understanding except by the appearance of understanding? If we ask how we know that the Mandarin is *really* able to understand Chinese, we presumably would cite his behaviors such as negotiating with Yellow Claw in Cantonese or ordering food at a Szechuan restaurant without resorting to pointing to the "number four" on the menu. If we doubt that the computer or that Happy understands Chinese, despite behavior indicating otherwise, it seems we should also doubt whether the Mandarin *really* understands Chinese, despite his behavior indicating otherwise.

Although the Mandarin's behavior seems to demonstrate that he understands Chinese, if we look into the brain processes connecting his input to his output, we would find only physical stuff: gray goop and firing neurons. As with Leibniz's tour of the "mental mill," we shouldn't expect to find a few sacks of "understanding" tucked away behind some random dendrites. Because a computer in principle can pass a behavioral test as well as a native speaker can, it would seem that we lack good reason to say that one understands Chinese while the other doesn't. If it is unreasonable to attribute understanding on the basis of the behavior exhibited by a computer, then it seems equally unreasonable to attribute understanding to humans on the same basis.

Simulating Stark

Opponents of the notion that machines can have minds might claim that understanding is merely "simulated" by the Living Armor; it's simply a "neat parlor trick." These folks are right to point out that we don't confuse a computer simulation of an asteroid strike with an actual asteroid strike or consider people mass murderers for shooting characters in a video game. Sometimes, though, it isn't quite so easy to lay out the distinction between a thing and its simulation: Does one walk or merely simulate walking with a prosthetic leg? Are manufactured objects such as titanium hips or acrylic dentures simulations or duplications of their user's original parts? The functionalists avoid these questions, because they evaluate a thing's performance or role, not its origin or physical composition, as important.

Against the functionalists, Searle apparently believes that minds can exist only in a limited number of biological systems, which are the product of a long evolutionary process, while a computer is "just" an artifact that simulates the thinking properties of its biological creators. So, for Searle, a mechanical system can simulate intelligence and appear indistinguishable from human behavior, all without understanding a single thing.

This, of course, is a problem. Biological evolution relies on selective forces that operate wholly on the basis of behavior. If there is no recognizable difference in the behavior of a system that understands (such as Tony Stark) and one that does not (such as the Living Armor), these selective forces cannot select for "real," rather than "merely simulated," understanding. If this is so, then regardless of whether they truly understand or merely appear to understand, minds are no more or less well adapted than they would be otherwise. And so we are left with the possibility that evolution could as easily have selected for the simulation—which would place us all in the Chinese Room.

My Aching Shellhead

Leibniz and Searle share an intuition about the systems they consider in their respective thought experiments. In both cases, they consider a complex physical system composed of relatively simple operations—such as the Living Armor in "The Mask in the Iron Man"—and note that it is impossible to see how understanding or consciousness could result. This simple observation does us the service of highlighting the serious problems we face in understanding meaning and minds. Nonetheless, it is difficult to imagine how you or I—or Tony Stark—could meet the same criteria demanded of Leibniz's mental mill, hapless Happy in the Chinese Room, or the Living Armor. For as much as we might wish to deny it, we, too, are each a sort of machine. And if you don't think so, try to prove it. (Good luck!)[18]

NOTES

The chapter epigraph is from René Descartes, Second Meditation, in *The Philosophical Writings of Descartes*, vol. II, trans. John Cottingham et al. (New York: Cambridge University Press, 1984), p. 21.

1. *Iron Man*, vol. 3, #28 (May 2000).

2. Ibid., vol. 3, #26–30 (2000).

3. See the chapter in this volume by Stephanie and Brett Patterson ("'I Have a Good Life': Iron Man and the Avenger School of Virtue") for more on "The Mask in the Iron Man."

4. Gottfried Leibniz, *Monadology*, in *The Rationalists*, trans. George Montgomery (Garden City, NY: Doubleday, 1974), p. 457.

5. Alan Turing, "Computing Machinery and Intelligence," *Mind* 49 (1950): 433–460.

6. Or, if you prefer to follow the version given in the *Iron Man* film (2008), imagine that Yinsen is captured by the Ten Rings, a Talibanesque organization in Afghanistan.

7. Well, I'm sure *you've* read it, but do you know anyone else who has?

8. Charles Darwin, *The Formation of Vegetable Mould, through the Action of Worms with Observations on Their Habits* (New York: Appleton & Co., 1907), p. 98.

9. Ibid.

10. Daniel C. Dennett, "Intentional Systems," *Journal of Philosophy* 68 (1971): 87.

11. You've probably noticed that Dennett is using the word "intention" in a specialized sense, rather than in the ordinary meaning of a "plan," but his exact meaning isn't important for our purposes. For the brave among you, see Pierre Jacob's "Intentionality" in the *Stanford Encyclopedia of Philosophy*, http://plato.stanford.edu/entries/intentionality.

12. While the story of Deep Blue's development and eventual victory over world chess champion Garry Kasparov is well known, the Experiments in Musical Intelligence (EMI) project is less familiar to most of us. Cope, a professor of music theory and composition at the University of California at Santa Cruz, has produced several albums of EMI compositions, as well as a number of books on artificial intelligence and musical creativity.

13. Dennett, "Intentional Systems," p. 90.

14. In the 2008 film *Iron Man*, the sarcastic mainframe computer is called Jarvis, after Tony Stark's Alfred Pennyworth–like comic book butler Edwin Jarvis.

15. Since its introduction in 1971, Dennett has tweaked and expanded the idea of "intentional systems"; for instance, see his 1989 book *The Intentional Stance* (Cambridge, MA: MIT Press).

16. The "Chinese Room" argument is regularly included in readers for introductory philosophy courses. It first appears in John Searle's article "Minds, Brains and Programs,"*Behavioral and Brain Sciences* 3 (1980): 417–457.

17. Searle has since put forward a positive case for the claim that programs are not the same as minds. Roughly put, (1) computer programs are *syntactic*, i.e., they "merely" manipulate symbols; (2) mental content is *semantic*, i.e., our thoughts represent things and we know what it is that they represent; (3) mere manipulation of symbols is not sufficient for semantic meaning; and therefore (4) minds are not programs. (See his 1990 article "Is the Brain's Mind a Computer Program?" *Scientific American* 262, pp. 26–31.)

18. I thanks to Jake Held and Dawn Jakubowski for talking me through earlier drafts of this essay.

FLEXING HIS INTELLIGENCE: TONY STARK'S BRAINY BRAWN

Phillip S. Seng

Unlike in movies centered on a flashy suit of armor, technological gadgetry, and lots of big explosions, the most important attribute on display in the *Iron Man* films is not brute force—it's intelligence. Robert Downey Jr.'s performance deserves much of the credit for causing us to overlook this point. His flippant style of delivering lines and ability to ooze into the role of the wealthy playboy divert our attention from Stark's smarts. Aside from the brief biography we hear at the awards ceremony that Stark skipped in Las Vegas early in the first film, little is made of his intelligence.

Intelligence can be defined as the mind at work within and through the body. And while this definition may sound strange, it helps to resolve long-standing philosophical debates, such as the relationship between the mind and the body. Stark's armor is basically a mechanized version of his usual bodily functions: sensor arrays, an alloyed layer of dermal protection, and means for propulsion, among other functions.

Although it certainly increases Stark's powers of sensation, protection, and motion, the philosophically important effect of Iron Man's suit of armor is that it heightens the distinction between the mind of Tony Stark and the body of Iron Man. In other words, the classic philosophical problem of the separation of mind and body is reinforced by the very nature of Iron Man.

Never Mind the Armor

The philosopher René Descartes (1596–1650) claimed that the essence of a person—the one undeniable, persistent, and immutable thing about a human being—is that she is, at rock bottom, a sort of mental substance, a thinking thing. The rest of a person—her body, experiences, and relationships with people and the world—is secondary to her mental essence. Thus, Descartes viewed humans as a combination of two substances: one mental and one physical. The mind is housed within a physical body and controls the body as though the body were a suit of armor built for the protection and mobility of the mind. It's pretty clear how Iron Man seems to support this old philosophical argument: Stark is the consciousness controlling the "body" of the Iron Man suit. The virtual butler in the movie, Jarvis, even fits into this scheme as the immaterial mind within the physical armor.

One of Descartes' biggest problems was working out how the nonphysical mind and the physical body communicate. Descartes claimed that the two substances actually join in the brain's pineal gland. Stark, on the other hand, solves the problem of bridging mind and body by making his armor, the "body," capable of communicating with him verbally. In other words, Stark built a body that could meet the mind a bit more than halfway. But then again, Stark and the armor are both physical objects, so he hasn't really solved the mind-body problem Descartes was considering. (Nice try, though, Tony.)

At first glance, Iron Man seems to support Descartes' description of how human beings exist in the world: we are basically physical shells of flesh directed and controlled by minds. Some bodies are stronger than others, just as some minds are, well, stronger than others. Iron Man is the suit of armor Tony Stark puts on when he wants to go out and do some good in the world (or break flight altitude records on a whim). But Tony Stark *is* Iron Man—he said so at the news conference at the end of the first movie. And just like that, we have to rethink our philosophical analysis. If a person *is* anything at all, it's the mental part he or she should identify with, not the physical. So, Stark should just be Stark, but he says he is not only Stark, but also Iron Man. What on earth can philosophers do to make this problem go away?

Many, *many* philosophers have tried to find their way out of Descartes' mind-body problem. Most of them just end up getting lost in re-creating another type of dualistic worldview. Descartes' view of the world is *dualistic* because he suggests that reality is composed of two separate things or substances, one mental and the other physical. Other philosophers prefer to think of minds and bodies not as separate entities but rather as united in form and function.

By now, you may be wondering what Iron Man has to do with any of this. Iron Man draws our attention to the physical body of the "superhero," but as I said earlier, the real power behind Iron Man is Tony Stark's intelligence. Now, I know what you're thinking: isn't "intelligence" simply another way of saying what Descartes meant by "mind"? Well, to put it simply, no, but more on that in a few pages. The mind and the body are not two separate and distinct substances. In fact, many philosophers in the twentieth century tried to put the mind back in the body, so to speak, and their efforts are important for our understanding of what intelligence really is. But first, let's take a moment to laugh at Tony Stark.

Separation Anxieties

I think the funniest scenes in *Iron Man* are those in which Stark is learning how to fly. He first has the propulsion too strong, and he flips head over heels into the concrete ceiling. He then reduces the power, manages to stay aloft, and flies over his very expensive cars. In the interim, he develops stabilizers to put on his palms so that he can adjust his pitch and orientation while in the air. He figures out what power level is necessary for carrying the weight of his body and the suit. And he learns to tell his robot not to douse him with the fire extinguisher unless he actually is on fire. We laugh at these mishaps because they make Tony more human to us; he's not merely the eccentric but suave billionaire we see in other scenes (such as when he decides to buy a painting by Jackson Pollock and has it sent straight to storage). These scenes also show us something very important about the process of learning and how the mind and the body interact in everyday activities.

Stark begins with 10 percent thrust capacity when he first tests the propulsion of the boots. The quick editing of this scene—cutting it quickly after Stark slams into the concrete ceiling joist and falls to the ground—makes the process of creating, testing, renovating, and building his armored suit seem like a lot of fun and games. In reality, the quick snippets the audience sees are just a snapshot of what was surely a long, tedious, painstaking process. It is as though Stark has to relearn walking. His body is trying to learn a whole new system of motion, and his mind has yet to incorporate all of the new parameters for responses and actions to bring about the desired movements. In effect, Stark's mind and body are trying to get back into sync.

In these scenes we see what philosophers call the *embodied mind*. According to the philosophers John Dewey (1859–1952) and Maurice Merleau-Ponty (1908–1961), the mind is naturally inseparable from and continuous with the body. Dewey defines mind in this way:

> Mind denotes the whole system of meanings as they are embodied in the workings of organic life. . . . Mind is contextual and persistent; consciousness is focal and transitive. Mind is, so to speak, structural, substantial; a constant background and foreground; perceptive consciousness is process, a series of heres and nows. Mind is a constant luminosity; consciousness intermittent, a series of flashes of varying intensities.[1]

For Dewey, the complement of mind is not the body, as Descartes believed, but consciousness. Mind is the whole system of habits and expectations that a person has and depends on for moving about in the world. The simple act of walking presupposes that the ground will continue in front of our feet where we will step. We take the next step presuming that it can resemble the last step, unless we've noticed something different about the ground in front of us. When we walk and talk with a friend, we don't always have to concentrate on where we walk, but our minds are always taking in the perceptions of the ground and the people and the buildings around us. Whatever we happen to be focused on at any given moment is what we are actually conscious of, but our minds are processing all of the other sights and sounds and smells and other sensations that simply do not gain our conscious attention.

Stark has obvious difficulties balancing while he is learning to fly—in fact, his learning to fly can also be seen as learning to balance while not on the ground. His habits of walking and standing will not help him while he's in the air because his habits are based on the support of a firm ground beneath his feet. He needs to pay very close attention to all of his movements while flying because he has not learned which actions will result in which effects. Balancing while airborne is not the same sort of skill as balancing while standing on solid ground, so he needs to relearn how to maintain his balance in a new situation. Basically, his mind needs to change to accommodate his new abilities.

The next time we see him in his lab, Stark is testing the full armor. Jarvis is installed in the suit as well, and Stark has a running dialogue with his virtual butler. Stark asks Jarvis to "import all preferences from home interface" so that he can "start the virtual walk-around." Jarvis proceeds with "importing preferences and calculating virtual environment," believing that Stark simply wants to see how the suit manages the storage and display of the information. But Stark has Jarvis perform a "check on control surfaces" so that he can put the suit to an actual flight test. And then he's off, out of the garage and into the open night sky. This scene is a sort of preamble to the real excitement, which is watching Stark fly and seeing the suit as it darts over the city skyline at night. But the testing and loading of all the things Jarvis talks about are necessary for the flying to be possible at all.

Merleau-Ponty argued that "spatial existence is the primary condition of all living perception."[2] He meant that all of our perceptions—our very sense of the world about us and all the knowledge we have of it—are rooted in our relationships with other things in space. When we move about in the world, we engage the world in more ways than we could possibly count or keep track of with our conscious awareness. That's why Dewey claimed that a person's mind is not the same thing as a person's consciousness.

Merleau-Ponty said that we make sense of the world from our own perspective or point of view first, and then learn how to generalize and take on other points of view. So, when Stark asks Jarvis to import his preferences from his home computer system, he's telling Jarvis that he wants the suit to configure the environment for him—Tony Stark. In other words, when Stark is in the suit, he wants the suit to interact with Stark and the world—to move and react, expect and anticipate—just the way the house computer interacts with Stark while he's at home. How warm or cold should the suit be? The same temperature as Stark likes his house. Humidity levels? Keep them at the same level as the house. And on and on with all of the other preferences Stark has programmed into his home computer: phone numbers, e-mail addresses, and so on. We can imagine that the list of information stored in Stark's home system is very large indeed (especially if we include his little black book!).

All of this information is stored by the computer (by Jarvis) and is ready when needed. Jarvis, in a sense, is the mind of the suit, and Stark is the consciousness of the suit. When Jarvis states that he (or it?) is "calculating virtual environment," we are looking through Stark's eyes at his helmet's visual display. Images are calculated into their 3D forms from sensors of the suit. If it were merely Stark's eyes looking at the cars in the garage, he could never see the far sides of the cars. He would be able to see only the surfaces. Yet we see the computer calculating, into its virtual environment, the full dimensions of the cars and other objects in the garage. Stark knows these only from personal experience with his cars, but Jarvis programs the data into the suit so that when Stark walks near a car, he will not walk into it. In short, Stark's armor must make it seem that Stark's body ends not with his skin but with the exterior of the armor. The armor is therefore his body. And Jarvis becomes the system of electronic habits and the systems processing the multitude of calculations that are needed every second to exist in the world.

Merleau-Ponty wrote that "Our own body is in the world as the heart is in the organism: it keeps the visible spectacle constantly alive, it breathes life into it and sustains it inwardly, and with it forms a system."[3] In other words, a human being's center is his or her body—we are oriented around our bodies and we come to know the rest of our experience through our bodies. The centrality of the body in Merleau-Ponty's philosophy is a reversal of the philosophy of Descartes, who believed not only that the mind was something separate and distinct from the body, but that it was of primary importance. Merleau-Ponty and Dewey sought to change the course of philosophy by focusing on how a person finds meaning in the world of everyday life, and this new kind of philosophy began by reorienting our understanding of how we exist in the world in terms of mind and body. When Stark creates the suit and imports Jarvis into it, he is not assuming some all-knowing or all-powerful computer mind. Instead, he imports Jarvis into the suit so that the suit will act according to his own preferences and habits and will act just like his own flesh, moving when he moves and ducking when he ducks.

Things Left Unsaid

When Stark wants to do something in the armor, he often commands Jarvis to make it happen. When he wants to test the armor's altitude limits, he tells Jarvis, "C'mon!" and flies as high as possible. Before his initial flight out of the garage, he counts down so that Jarvis knows when to engage the thrusters, and later, when Stark tries to outrun a missile, he commands his flares to fire.

Why would Stark have to give all of these commands if the armor were really another skin? Wouldn't it simply respond to his thoughts and impulses? After all, the armor does seem to be a part of Stark at other times in the movie. Just think of when Stark flies into Golmera and lands in a perfect three-point stance. As Stark is about to shoot the men ravaging Golmera, he pauses because they have leveled their guns at women and children. Then we see the armor target six gunmen, and before anyone can think about dodging or reacting, his shoulder-mounted guns pop out and all six are dead. We didn't hear Stark utter a single command.

Of course, we as audience members are subject to the choices of the sound editors; sometimes we hear Stark's voice inside his suit, and other times we hear the environment from outside the suit. So it would make sense that we don't always hear Stark's commands. But it does seem that the armor can react to Stark's thoughts. Consider those nifty little palm-based repulsors Stark created, which double as weapons and flight stabilizers. When Stark stands down in the face of the threatened villagers, he lowers his hands and the repulsors give a mechanical "whirring" sound as they spiral closed. This sound effect mimics Stark's feelings, and the closure of the weapons coincides with his demeanor. In a sense, the armor behaves precisely as if it were Stark's body: when Stark stands down, his armor does likewise. When Stark watches the reports of the attacks on Golmera while at home, he's testing out the palm stabilizers/weapons. When he gets angry, the shutterlike closures on his palms flare open; when he calms down, they close up. What can explain this kind of responsiveness except that the suit *is* Stark's body and is thereby connected (somehow) to his mind?

(Artificial) Intelligence

This chapter began with the strange claim that Stark's distinguishing quality as a superhero isn't his high-tech armor at all, but rather his intelligence. Recognizing that the mind and the body are intimately related, and that our entire understanding of our world depends on our embodied existence, helps us see what Dewey meant by "intelligence."

According to Dewey, a "man is intelligent . . . in virtue of his capacity to estimate the possibilities of a situation and to act in accordance with his estimate."[4] In other words, intelligence implies action, not merely the ability to think about possible actions. To be intelligent means to act for those things that one can reasonably conceive of gaining.

Daydreaming is not intelligence—it is a flight of fancy. Stark's vaunted brainpower would not be intelligence if it did not actually produce results. But sometimes results are denied or frustrated, so, of course, intelligence does not imply successes. Dewey wrote that one must be able to act "in accordance with his estimate," not that his estimate must always be 100 percent correct. So Stark might be wrong in some instances. Consider the end of the first movie when he thinks Stane will be killed or otherwise disabled after falling out of the sky. When Stark acts on his incorrect estimates and begins to remove his helmet, he soon realizes his mistake.

In most movies, the good guy wins and the bad guy loses. But why does it always seem that the good guy is the more intelligent one? Couldn't the villain be more intelligent and yet the hero wins out of luck or by accident? There seems to be a correlation between being good and being intelligent in Dewey's understanding of the meaning of "intelligence." Intelligence is actually a sign of the kinds of judgments a person makes: "Intelligence . . . is associated with *judgment*; that is, with selection and arrangement of means to effect consequences and with choice of what we take as our ends."[5] And furthermore:

> Because intelligence is [a] critical method applied to goods of belief, appreciation and conduct, so as to construct freer and more secure goods, turning assent and assertion into free communication of shareable meanings, turning feeling into ordered and liberal sense, turning reaction into response, it is the reasonable object of our deepest faith and loyalty, the stay and support of all reasonable hopes.[6]

Intelligence is the activity of selecting goals that help us live in the world. And it's not concerned with our living only as individuals, but as a community. The first quotation above conveys Dewey's opinion that intelligence involves overt action and the ability to distinguish between various goals. Stane's goals are power and money, both of which used to be Stark's goals as well, but we witness his shift in values as the movie develops. It is in that process, before our very eyes, that we see the growth of Stark's intelligence. Yes, he was always the smartest person in the movie, but he met his match with Christine Everhart, the *Vanity Fair* reporter who sees him on both sides of his "mid-life crisis."

Earlier in the movie, when Stark "loses some sleep with" Everhart, he's unaware of Stane's underhanded dealings on behalf of Stark Industries. Not only is he ignorant, but his demeanor suggests that he could not be bothered to care about the less fortunate people of the world. After his experience in captivity and his friendship with Yinsen while building the first suit of armor, Stark changes the direction of his life and adopts goals that will help others make their lives more fruitful and meaningful as well. This aspect of Stark's conversion illustrates what Dewey meant when he wrote that intelligence is concerned with goods and meanings that are sharable. Stark comes to care about more people than merely himself, and thus he is more intelligent than Stane, who cares only for his own selfish goals.

Putting One's Mind into a Body

Iron Man makes us reconsider the mind-body problem because it seems as if the suit is the technological body and Stark is simply the brainpower behind the suit. Using the philosophies of Dewey and Merleau-Ponty, we are able to understand how Descartes' conception of the mind-body problem may have been mistaken. The mind and the body are not two separate and radically different kinds of things. Instead, the mind and the body are intimately connected, even necessarily connected, allowing them to function intelligently in the world.

So, what about Jarvis? Jarvis is the artificial intelligence of Stark's mansion and also of Iron Man. Stark is inside the Iron Man suit, of course, but the mind that is actually making sure that the suit functions correctly with all of the "terabytes of calculations" is Jarvis. Stark can't possibly keep track of every possible function of the suit's components all of the time. I've suggested that Jarvis is the mind of the Iron Man suit. This claim makes sense if we understand that Jarvis is a representation or manifestation of Stark's mind. If Stark were able to take a physical snapshot of his mind—simply create a complete duplicate at any one instant and move it to another place or container—that may explain how he created Jarvis.[7] After all, Jarvis has all of Stark's personal preferences, all of Stark's data, everything that is necessary to make Stark feel as if he's in his own skin. If we understand Jarvis in this way, then "he" is similar to what Dewey meant by the term "mind." Jarvis is Stark's mind, made manifest in the virtual world. Thus, it's no wonder that Iron Man defeats Stane's overpowered behemoth; two minds are better than one!

NOTES

1. John Dewey, *Experience and Nature* (Carbondale: Southern Illinois University Press, [1925] 1981), p. 230.

2. Maurice Merleau-Ponty, *Phenomenology of Perception*, trans. Colin Smith (London: Routledge & Kegan Paul, 1962), p. 109.

3. Ibid., p. 203.

4. John Dewey, *The Quest for Certainty* (Carbondale: Southern Illinois University Press, [1929] 1988), p. 170.

5. Ibid., p. 170.

6. Dewey, *Experience and Nature*, p. 325.

7. That, in fact, is what he did in the *Hypervelocity* miniseries (2007), as a backup measure in case of his early demise.

DOES TONY STARK HAVE AN IRON WILL?

Mark D. White

Tony Stark is a fantastic hero but a very imperfect man, justly infamous for his numerous dalliances with women—and especially for his recurring problems with alcohol. As with most Marvel superheroes, Tony's imperfections are very normal: Spider-Man lacks self-confidence, Mr. Fantastic lives inside his mind most of the time, and the Hulk has "anger issues" (to put it mildly). Only Daredevil approaches the deep psychological turmoil that characterizes Batman; the rest of the Marvel heroes are very recognizable and down to earth in their flaws. But one thing that sets Tony apart in this regard is that his particular flaws reflect problems with self-control, or "weakness of will," especially with regard to the bottle (and the demon within it).

The Akratic Avenger

Philosophers also struggle with weakness of will (sometimes called *akrasia*)—academically speaking, of course.[1] (We are a very moderate people and never take things to excess, I assure you.) Among the many curious aspects of self-control is why we even need it, because the term itself implies that we are *not* always in control of ourselves. But if we do not control ourselves, who does?

This paradox has led some philosophers to suggest that weakness of will simply does not exist; something else must explain apparent cases of it. The philosopher Donald Davidson (1917–2003) asked, in the title of one of his most famous papers, "How Is Weakness of Will Possible?"[2] His answer was that it is impossible for a person to judge that one thing should be done, and know that it can be done, but then do something else. So, in a case of what appears to be weakness, the person must not have *really* judged the original action to be best; perhaps it was a preliminary judgment, contingent on some circumstance that didn't come about, or simply hasty. Whatever the case, the person *must* have changed her mind—revised her judgment—before acting on it, and that explains her mysterious "akratic" action. As Davidson asked near the end of the paper, "Why would anyone ever perform an action when he thought that, *everything considered*, another action would be better?"[3]

Imagine that Natasha Romanova, the Black Widow, receives an order from Nick Fury, director of S.H.I.E.L.D., to spy on a suspected arms smuggler. As a loyal S.H.I.E.L.D. agent, she knows she should follow Fury's orders, and there is no reason why she can't. She judges that the best thing for her to do would be to spy for Fury, but she doesn't—she chooses to stop by Tony Stark's place to catch up on Avengers business instead. Davidson would explain this by saying that before she chose to visit Stark, she must have changed her mind about the best action—she simply could not have visited Tony if she truly believed that spying for Fury was the best action. Maybe she suspected that the order came from a villain impersonating Fury, and she went to Stark instead to ask for his help investigating the matter. Or maybe she was starting to question her S.H.I.E.L.D. loyalties. But according to Davidson, she must have revised her judgment so that seeing Stark was judged the best thing to do (which, of course, is what she did).

In the same spirit, some philosophers question whether akratic action is a result of free choice—how could a person freely act against her best judgment? They claim instead that such action is compelled: the person is being manipulated by external forces (such as mind control) or internal drives (such as addiction), either of which the person finds irresistible.[4] Tony Stark definitely knows about both of these: for example, during the "Avengers Disassembled" story line, Tony's mind is mysteriously taken over, causing him to feel, act, and appear as if he were drunk. Of course, this being Tony, it all happens in front of the UN General Assembly, causing an international incident, forcing him to resign as U.S. secretary of defense and ultimately leading to the breakup of the Avengers.[5] Later, in "Execute Program," the son of Ho Yinsen (the man who helped Tony build the first Iron Man armor) takes control of Tony's mind and forces him to kill the men responsible for Yinsen's death (and hundreds of innocent bystanders in the process).[6] In both cases, Tony's choice was co-opted; these actions certainly were not the result of his judgment at all, though it was his body "executing the program." He was certainly not free, but no one would call these examples weakness of will anyway—Tony's will was not weakened but rather was taken out of the picture completely.

Addiction may seem like a different matter, because it is often seen as the result of previous choices freely made by the addict (although this is subject to debate). Nonetheless, once a person is addicted and under the thrall of his drug of choice—or simply the desire for it—his judgment may not have the same influence on his choices that we may otherwise assume. (His judgment may be impaired as well, of course, but that's another matter.) After Tony loses his cool with the Avengers' butler Jarvis near the end of "Demon in a Bottle" (prompting the good man's resignation), he immediately says to himself, "I didn't mean to snap at Jarvis like that. I don't even know why I did it."[7] But was he truly coerced into acting like he did, as with the incident at the UN? Did he really have no control at all? Obviously, Tony didn't feel that way, based on his apology to Jarvis in the next issue, in which he denies any excuse for his behavior and instead takes responsibility for it—which he would not have had to do if his actions had been compelled.[8]

Is it possible that all of this discussion about weakness of will misses the point? Maybe a person's best judgment doesn't have to determine her choice, and that choice can still be considered free, not coerced, controlled, or impaired. As we'll see next, one philosopher not only claims that this is possible, but that it is common and indeed provides strong evidence *for*, rather than against, rationality.

Enter the Searle

In his book *Rationality in Action*, the contemporary philosopher John Searle questioned the traditional position in philosophy, normally traced back to David Hume (1711–1776), that a person's judgment, based on her beliefs and desires, completely determines her actions.[9] He claimed that such a model represents "human rationality as a more complex version of ape rationality," characterized by mindless pursuit of desires to seek out food, shelter, and a mate.[10] Such behavior is not really rational, Searle claimed, because there is no rational deliberation involved. The animal doesn't have to think about its goals or its needs; it simply reacts to urges and drives.

Ironically, Searle also offered the heroin addict as a poster child for the traditional model.[11] In the worst case, the heroin addict has lost all ability to reflect and deliberate on his situation. He does not think about why he needs the drug; he just does what he has to do to get it. Another contemporary philosopher, Harry Frankfurt, would call such an addict a *wanton* (as opposed to a *person*, as he uses the term), because he does not—indeed, *can* not—reflect on his own wants and desires.[12] To Frankfurt, a person has both first-order and second-order desires. *First-order* desires are normal wants: desires for cake, jet boots, love, or world domination. (Hey, different strokes.) Wantons certainly have those; our heroin addict obviously has a strong desire to obtain heroin. But a person (in Frankfurt's sense) also has *second-order* desires, which are desires about his first-order desires. I may want a Boston creme doughnut, but I don't *want* to want the doughnut—I know it isn't good for me, although I have a strong desire for it. Tony has always wanted to be with Pepper Potts, but he doesn't *want* to want to be with her, because he feels that his heroic lifestyle would put her in danger. And although he often craves a drink, he doesn't want this craving; he reflects on his alcoholism and takes steps to maintain resolve in the face of temptation. (More on this later.)

In the ideal case, a person orients his choices with his second-order desires, thereby deciding what to choose, or which desires he will indulge and which he won't. Of course, nobody does this perfectly, and when a person succumbs to his rejected first-order desires—which are often very strong, especially for addicts—that is a case of weakness of will. But our heroin addict, who is unreflective, doesn't have second-order desires; he simply satisfies his first-order desires, like an animal—or a wanton, to use Frankfurt's term.

What Searle and Frankfurt have in common is that they both sever—or at least loosen—the tight link between desire and choice. While Searle doesn't explicitly endorse second-order preferences, he does support *desire-independent reasons*, factors other than desires that can influence our choices. Commitments, such as promises, are the simplest example: suppose Captain America wants to have lunch with longtime love Sharon Carter but remembers that he promised Iron Man that he'd help him design some Avengers training exercises. His only desire at the time may be to meet Sharon (who's much better company than Tony Stark), but he recognizes the commitment he made to Tony. Captain America, of course, would not break a promise, but even if he did—in some alternate universe where up is down and Doctor Doom is a preschool teacher—the promise would still be a reason guiding his action, even if it was not the decisive reason in the end. In Frankfurt's language, Cap would have a second-order desire to keep his promise, which he would stick to if—well, *because*—his will is strong. But whichever way you look at it, Cap would honor his commitment, even though it means not following his desires.

What Happens in the Gap
Stays in the Gap

So, if we recognize desire-independent reasons, we can include them with normal desires and beliefs in the traditional model of rational decision making, and it's basically the same: all of these factors influence a person's best judgment, which then determines her choice and action.

Not so fast, said Searle. Even after a person reaches her best judgment, perhaps after much deliberation, soul-searching, and pro-and-con lists, there is still no guarantee that she will follow it. Animals would, and so would heroin addicts, but not a truly rational person. Why not? Searle argued that rationality has "gaps," holes in the road, so to speak, in which true choice occurs:

> We presuppose that there is a gap between the "causes" of the action in the form of beliefs and desires and the "effect" in the form of an action. This gap has a traditional name. It is called "the freedom of the will."[13]

In other words, after arriving at a judgment, the person must *do* something—she must *make* a choice: "making up your mind is not enough; you still have to do it."[14] It isn't made for her from some complicated formula or algorithm combining her desires and beliefs; if there were such a mechanism, this would result only in her judgment. But choosing is itself an action, and so the person must act, she must choose—*she* must decide. If the traditional model is to be believed, then "we would not have to *act on* our intentions; we could, so to speak, wait for them to act by themselves. We could sit back and see how things turned out. But we can't do that, we always have to act."[15]

Remember Black Widow's situation from earlier: she knew she should follow an order from Nick Fury but chose to hang out with Tony Stark instead. Under the traditional model of choice, we would have to assume that she revised her judgment so that seeing Tony was now the "best" action. But Searle considers that a very limited idea of choice, arguing instead that there is no contradiction between judging that obeying Fury is the best thing to do, all things considered, but choosing to do something else. Somewhere in the gap between judgment and choice, she decided to see Tony, simple as that.

But why? What explains her decision? Searle has a very simple answer: *nothing*. "What fills the gap? Nothing. Nothing fills the gap: you make up your mind to do something, or you just haul off and do what you are going to do."[16] Nothing can explain or model what happens in the gap because that is where true choice occurs. This choice is not determined by other factors (desires, beliefs, or reasons in general), which are limited to influencing a person's judgment. These things can help determine the best thing to do, but they can't make you do it. Her choice is her own—it is her will—and she can choose to follow her judgment (and do Fury's bidding), or she can choose to go against her judgment (and see Tony).

Mind you, we're not saying that it's not a good idea for Natasha to follow her best judgment; after all, that's what judgment is for! But a person is free to choose to go against her judgment, too, and it is this ability that makes her truly rational, simply because she is actually making choices rather than following her desires and beliefs like an animal.

Saving Weakness of Will

Searle's idea of gaps gives us a neat and tidy solution to the paradox of weakness of will. The reason weakness of will is so difficult for the traditional model of choice to deal with is that there is no will in that model to be weak. Desires and beliefs determine choices, just as a computer's program determines its operation. (No one ever called a robot weak-willed, right?) There is no room in this model for a will—and therefore no room for it to fail or be weak either. As Searle explained, many philosophers think "that in the case of rationally motivated actions, there is some sort of causally necessary connection between the psychological antecedents of an action and the intentional performance of the action." This denies a person any true choice or role in the matter, and therefore "you get into the problem that weakness of will, strictly speaking, becomes impossible."[17]

But in Searle's theory, the gap is the seat of true choice or of the will itself, and therefore makes room for it to be weak (or strong). As we mentioned, it is usually a good idea for a person to make choices in line with her judgment (such as following second-order desires in Frankfurt's framework). But it takes will, or willpower, to do this, especially when following your best judgment involves sacrificing your desires, perhaps to satisfy a commitment. So the more reliably a person follows her judgment (or second-order desires), the stronger her will is—and the less she does this, the weaker her will is. Thus, weakness of will simply means failing to make choices in line with your best judgment. Although the traditional model of choice puzzles over weakness of will, it makes perfect sense in Searle's concept of rationality, because Searle makes room for true choice—good or bad.

So, let's consider Tony's drinking again. As we said, Tony is definitely self-aware and reflective, as least when he's sober. Even though he often—perhaps always—wants to have a drink, his judgment is that he shouldn't have one, and to his credit most of the time he doesn't, even during stressful events like the Civil War.[18] Most of the time, he makes choices that correspond with his judgment, so he exhibits strength of will. But in those cases in which he succumbs to his desire for a drink, it would be absurd to say that he revised his judgment and decided that having a drink—"just this one time"—would be a great idea. (Certainly, people rationalize in this way, but they wouldn't have to rationalize if their judgment had truly changed.) For instance, we see Tony struggle with—and ultimately succumb to—the temptation to drink at the beginning of the three-year conflict with Obadiah Stane. Tony continually maintains that the costs of indulging his desire for alcohol are too high, but in the end, Stane's manipulations (one of which, naturally, involves tempting Stark with a woman who then betrays him) loosen his resolve, and Tony drinks.[19] It makes much more sense to follow Searle and simply say that he still judged sobriety to be the best path, but in a moment of weakness chose a more immediately attractive one.

And Searle emphasized that this choice is free, not coerced: akrasia "is but a symptom of a certain kind of freedom," namely, freedom of the will.[20] Searle even gave the example of drinking: "I had another glass of wine in the teeth of my judgment that I should not have another glass of wine. But my taking the glass of wine was no more compelled or forced or determined than was my strong-willed action when I acted according to my best judgment."[21] Searle said the choice to take the additional glass of wine is irrational, because it goes against his better judgment. But the fact that he has the chance to make that bad choice shows he is a rational person in general who truly makes choices, even if some of those choices end up being irrational.

Super-strength . . . of Will

Scholars—not only philosophers, but psychologists and economists, too—spend a lot of time explaining why and when people succumb to weakness of will, but they spend very little time trying to understand how people *resist* such urges. Although they make some room in their models for weakness of will—for example, by introducing short-term preferences that tend to dominate long-term ones—those models are still essentially deterministic, representing akratic action as a result of desires and beliefs, only more broadly understood. If a temptation is too strong, then the person *will* succumb to it, and if it's not, then the person *won't*, end of story. The person still has no choice and no true sense of will to be weak—it's simply a weak model.

Can we recharge this model, just as Tony recharged his early chest plate? Like Searle and his gaps, some contemporary philosophers take the idea of a will seriously and maintain that there is a faculty of choice, above and beyond desires and beliefs. This idea is called *volitionism*, because it maintains that an act of volition or choice is necessary to put desires and beliefs into action—or not. The philosopher R. Jay Wallace referred to the traditional model of choice as the "hydraulic conception," because it "pictures desires as vectors of force to which persons are subject, where the force of such desires in turn determines causally the actions the persons perform."[22] As a result, "action is traced to the operation of forces within us, with respect to which we as agents are ultimately passive, and in a picture of this kind real agency seems to drop out of view."[23] Like Searle, Wallace maintained that choice is something we actually do; as Wallace said, "When we exercise our power of self-determination by actually making a decision, the result is something we have done, not something that merely happens to us."[24]

It is very easy for the traditional model to explain Tony succumbing to alcohol: his immediate desire for a drink was stronger than his more considered desire to stay sober. Yet sometimes Tony resists the bottle *even when* his desire for it is very strong—and we admire him for his restraint. The traditional model cannot explain his restraint, however, because desires determine choice, yada yada. It's as if by letting weakness of will into their models, philosophers ruled out the possibility of strength of will! On the other hand, if we follow the volitionists and recognize the existence of a will, not only can we more easily explain when it is weak in the face of temptation, but also when it is strong and resists temptation. Tony judges sobriety to be his best option overall but nonetheless desires a drink now—when his will is weak, he succumbs, and when it is strong, he perseveres.

The natural next question is: what explains whether a person's will is weak or strong? One contemporary philosopher, Richard Holton, modeled strength and weakness of will by analogy to a muscle.[25] Just as a muscle gains strength through repeated use and withers away with neglect, the will grows stronger the more we use it and weaker the more we ignore it. Dieters often find that passing up a dessert one night often makes it easier to pass it up again the next; alcoholics try to avoid taking even one drink, for fear that it will lead to more lapses in the future. Furthermore, the will, like a muscle, can be weakened through overuse or even by general exhaustion; this is how Obadiah Stane is able to engineer Tony's relapse by putting him through a series of orchestrated disasters, frustrations, and betrayals—including keeping him awake and busy for far too long![26]

This approach suggests that the way to defeat weakness of will is not exclusive reliance on elaborate support mechanisms (such as Weight Watchers or automatic savings plans) but also continual exertion of mental effort to strengthen our wills.[27] Like many recovering alcoholics, Tony attends Alcoholics Anonymous meetings, but in between the meetings, if his sponsor isn't available, it's all him. As he thinks to himself during one of many moments of temptation, "I need to be strong."[28] He must have continual resolve—because if his resolve isn't there when he needs it, the bottle surely will be.

Amazing and Inspiring

Iron Man is perhaps the most human of the Marvel superheroes, not only for lacking superpowers or mutant genes but also for lacking perfect willpower. If John Searle is right, Tony's weaknesses, particularly with regard to alcohol—even if he never succumbs to it—show that he is truly a rational person and also very human. His constant struggle with his demons actually helps us identify with the rich, handsome, brilliant Tony Stark. For all the worldly goods he has and all the attention he enjoys, he wages a daily battle between his will and his desires. At the end of the day, the strength of Iron Man's armor may amaze us, but the strength of Tony Stark's will inspires us.

NOTES

1. For an introduction to the topic, see Sarah Stroud and Christine Tappolet, eds., *Weakness of Will and Practical Irrationality* (Oxford, UK: Oxford University Press, 2003), especially the introduction by the editors.

2. Donald Davidson, "How Is Weakness of Will Possible?" in his *Essays on Actions and Events* (Oxford, UK: Oxford University Press, 1980), pp. 21–42.

3. Ibid., p. 42 (emphasis mine).

4. For an excellent treatment of this issue, see Gary Watson, "Skepticism about Weakness of Will," in his *Agency and Answerability: Selected Essays* (Oxford, UK: Oxford University Press, 2004), pp. 33–58.

5. *Avengers* #500 (September 2004), reprinted in *Avengers Disassembled* (2005); and "The Singularity," in *Iron Man*, vol. 3, #86–89 (2004), collected as *Avengers Disassembled: Iron Man* (2007).

6. *Iron Man*, vol. 4, #7–12 (2006), collected in trade paperback in 2007.

7. Ibid., vol. 1, #127 (October 1979), reprinted in *Demon in a Bottle* (2007), which collects #120–128 (1979).

8. Ibid., vol. 1, #128 (November 1979). Interestingly, Jarvis offers Tony's illness as an excuse; see Ron Novy's chapter titled "Fate at the Bottom of a Bottle: Alcohol and Tony Stark" in this volume for more on the choice and disease interpretations of alcoholism. For a survey of perspectives on addiction from philosophers, psychologists, and economists, see Jon Elster, ed., *Addiction: Entries and Exits* (New York: Russell Sage Foundation, 1999).

9. John Searle, *Rationality in Action* (Cambridge, MA: MIT Press, 2001). The traditional model of choice is defended by philosophers such as Donald Davidson; see his "Actions, Reasons, and Causes," in *Essays on Actions and Events*, pp. 3–19.

10. Searle, *Rationality in Action*, p. 5.

11. Ibid., p. 13.

12. Harry G. Frankfurt, "Freedom of the Will and the Concept of a Person," in his *The Importance of What We Care About* (Cambridge, UK: Cambridge University Press, 1988), pp. 11–25. For an application of this idea to a man and his dog, see my "Is Brian More of a 'Person' Than Peter? Of Wills, Wantons, and Wives," in J. Jeremy Wisnewski, ed., *Family Guy and Philosophy: A Cure for the Petarded* (Malden, MA: Blackwell, 2007), pp. 163–174.

13. Searle, *Rationality in Action*, p. 13.

14. Ibid., p. 232.

15. Ibid., pp. 232–233.

16. Ibid., p. 17.

17. Ibid., p. 229.

18. See *Civil War: The Confession* (May 2007), reprinted in *Civil War: Iron Man* (2007).

19. See *Iron Man*, vol. 1, #166–167 (January–February 1983) for the beginning of Tony's descent. He doesn't give up drinking this time until the end of #182 (May 1984), during which time Stane takes over Stark's company and James "Rhodey" Rhodes takes over as Iron Man. The Stane saga ends in #200 (November 1985), which is also when Tony again assumes the Iron Man identity full-time.

20. Searle, *Rationality in Action*, p. 233.

21. Ibid., p. 236.

22. R. Jay Wallace, *Normativity and the Will: Selected Essays on Moral Psychology and Practical Reason* (Oxford, UK: Oxford University Press, 2006), p. 172.

23. Ibid., p. 174. Another contemporary philosopher, J. David Vellman, offered a similar criticism of the traditional model, in which "reasons cause an intention, and an intention causes bodily movements, but nobody—that is, no person—*does* anything. Psychological and physiological events take place inside a person, but the person serves merely as an arena for these events: he takes no active part" ("What Happens

When Someone Acts?" in his *The Possibility of Practical Reason* [Oxford, UK: Oxford University Press, 2000], pp. 123–143, at p. 123).

24. Wallace, *Normativity and the Will*, p. 58.

25. Richard Holton, "How Is Strength of Will Possible?" in Stroud and Tappolet, *Weakness of Will and Practical Irrationality*, pp. 39–67.

26. For empirical evidence, Holton relied upon the groundbreaking work of psychologist Roy Baumeister and his colleagues; see, for instance, Mark Muraven and Roy F. Baumeister, "Self-Regulation and Depletion of Limited Resources: Does Self-Control Resemble a Muscle?" *Psychological Bulletin* 126 (2000): 247–259. (I discuss this concept more in a chapter on willpower in Jane Dryden and Mark D. White, eds., *Green Lantern and Philosophy* [Hoboken, NJ: John Wiley & Sons, 2011].)

27. For this approach applied to procrastination (commonly held to be a specific type of weakness of will), see my "Resisting Procrastination: Kantian Autonomy and the Role of the Will," in Chrisoula Andreou and Mark D. White, eds., *The Thief of Time: Philosophical Essays on Procrastination* (Oxford, UK: Oxford University Press, 2010), pp. 216–232.

28. *Iron Man*, vol. 3, #18 (July 1999).

PART FIVE

THE VIRTUE OF AN AVENGER

DOES TONY STARK
USE A MORAL
COMPASS?

Sarah K. Donovan and Nicholas P. Richardson

Tony Stark's life is riddled with moral contradictions. Consequently, it's difficult to draw any tidy moral lessons about him. What moral compass, if any, does he follow? To address this question, we'll focus on the "Armor Wars" and "Extremis" story lines, and along the way we'll introduce the three major schools of moral philosophy: utilitarianism, deontology, and virtue ethics.[1]

Does Tony's Moral Compass Point to
the Greater Good?

In "Armor Wars," Tony examines the confiscated equipment of the villain Force (Clay Wilson) and discovers that it contains technology stolen from his own lab. Tony realizes, of course, that if Force had access to his technology, then so did other criminals. His suspicions are confirmed when he breaks into Justin Hammer's computer and obtains a list of criminals to whom this technology was sold. As we might expect, Tony feels personally responsible for the chaos and destruction created by those who used the technology he created, and he sets out to recover his technology from villains who would use it to harm innocent people. Similarly, in "Extremis," Tony Stark remains remorseful of his weapons-designing past and continues to struggle to be a "good" person. Even though the technology has evolved over time, the moral issues facing Tony Stark are unchanged.

Clearly, Tony has a moral compass. But what kind? Perhaps he is a utilitarian. *Utilitarianism* is concerned with the outcomes of actions, rather than with the actions themselves or the people taking the actions. More specifically, the classical utilitarians, such as Jeremy Bentham (1748–1832) and John Stuart Mill (1806–1873), believed that all people naturally seek happiness and that happiness is gained by maximizing pleasure and minimizing pain. So, the principle of utility is to seek the greatest amount of happiness for the greatest number of people.[2]

At its core, utilitarianism is really about equality, or the idea that no one person is more important than any other. In other words, if the greater good is achieved by sacrificing the happiness of your child, this is understandably tragic, but you cannot protest that it is unfair on the grounds that your child is more important than other people (he or she would simply be more important to *you*). Furthermore, you have to calculate the happiness of all of the individuals affected by an action and determine how happy or unhappy it will make each person and how long that happiness or unhappiness will last. You also have to be realistic about whether the planned action will successfully achieve the projected ends. It might seem that many questionable actions, such as those that sacrifice the (legitimate) happiness of the few to increase the happiness of the many, could be justified according to this theory, and in its simple form this is true. But if you account for all of the complexities involved in utilitarian decision making, it ends up being a more cautious and judicious system than it first seems.[3]

Tony exhibits some elements of utilitarian thinking—certainly, he is concerned about the greater good—but ultimately this is not the best theory to describe who he is as a moral agent. In "Armor Wars," he finds the utilitarian mantra of the "greatest amount of happiness for the greatest number of people," and the sacrifice of innocent people that this may allow, morally unacceptable. (Of course, he has less of a problem sacrificing criminals, so this is a bit murky.) In this story, Tony is intent on recapturing his stolen technology and is in turmoil about the possibility of even one innocent person dying in that process—a process that could potentially save many lives, and one that a true (but simplistic) utilitarian would approve of.

Consider that when he confronts the Controller at his base of operations, Tony discovers that the villain has cultivated a group of human zombies, one of whom is killed when he gets in between Iron Man and the Controller. Tony is outraged and says, "My whole reason for coming here was to keep anyone else from being harmed by my technology! And now, because of that technology, someone has . . . died!"[4] Also, recall the series of events in which Iron Man is trying to save a military plane and its pilots from an attack by the Raiders. After Iron Man uses a negator pack on one Raider, another one threatens to shoot one of the pilots. Tony thinks, "My whole reason for being here is to save lives! I can't be responsible for the loss of one, even if it means failure!"[5] He changes tactics in order to save the pilot's life, even at the possible cost of not saving many lives in the future.

In the end, Tony accepts some aspects of the utilitarian perspective, but it is not the best theory to describe his approach to morality. Besides Tony's unwillingness to sacrifice even one person for the "greater good," utilitarianism poses a second major problem for him. When we say that traditional utilitarians focus on outcomes, this also means that the primary focus of the theory is not the motives of the individual agent. For example, when Tony saves the pilot's life, the utilitarian concern would simply be whether the outcome is successful. If the life is saved, then it is irrelevant whether Tony did it because he wants to be a good person or because he wants to appear to be a good person or for some other reason. As we will see, however, Tony is obsessed both with doing good deeds and with being a good person, so we need another ethical theory to determine his moral compass.

Does Tony's Moral Compass Point to Duty?

Whereas utilitarianism focuses on the consequences of actions, deontology focuses on the actions themselves and the motives behind them. The word *deontology* comes from the Greek and refers to binding obligations and duties. The leading deontologist, the philosopher Immanuel Kant (1724–1804), argued that if we used our reason correctly, we would all come up with the same basic moral rule, what Kant called the *categorical imperative*. In essence, this moral rule instructs us that it is our duty to perform actions that we could rationally will that everyone else could perform, and also that it is our duty never to treat people merely as means to our ends but always as ends in themselves.[6]

Kant's theory is appealing insofar as it provides us with firm duties and obligations, but it also becomes indeterminate when confronted with two competing moral obligations or duties. A famous (some would say infamous) example concerns what you ought to do in a situation in which you must lie in order to save a life. Imagine the following situation: Iron Man is visiting you and the Crimson Dynamo comes to your door and asks whether Iron Man is there, in hopes of killing him.

Is it ethical to lie in order to save Iron Man's life? Kant says no—the moral imperative is not to lie, even though a life is at stake.[7] But more reasonable examples can certainly be imagined. What if Tony promises to help Happy Hogan move into a new apartment, but then he receives an emergency call for Iron Man to help the Avengers? Tony may certainly feel a duty to both, but he can help only one—what to do? A choice has to be made, but Kant provided little guidance in such situations.

In the end, Kant's theory is too idealistic and rigid for Tony Stark. While Tony exhibits idealistic thinking at times, he is ultimately too pragmatic to subscribe to a moral theory that is so strictly rule driven. Tony, after all, is sometimes willing to bend rules to get the outcome he desires. For example, in "Armor Wars," after Tony has discovered that his technology has been stolen, he tries to use legal means to retrieve it. But when he realizes how slow the process will be, he says, "I believe in the law, and in the system. But the people I'm up against don't. Maybe it's time for lives to mean more than rules. It's a tough decision; perhaps the toughest of my life. But with the government's support, or its hindrance . . . by the law, or against it . . . I'm going to get back what's mine."[8] Although at times Tony subscribes to black-and-white moral thinking about right and wrong, and in this sense has some affinity for Kant's ethics, he is no absolutist.

Tony's decision is fueled by emotion, but Kant did not place much value on emotion. Rather, he believed that reason is what makes us most human; we are most truly engaged in moral reasoning when we are guided solely by reason and not by emotion. Tony Stark, of course, is not a man driven by reason alone. His emotional life is part and parcel of his vision of who he ought to be. "Armor Wars" and "Extremis" are replete with examples of Tony struggling with and being guided by his emotions. Indeed, Tony's emotional turmoil is a common theme in the *Iron Man* series as a whole.

Finding Tony's Moral Compass
in Emotion

With Aristotle (384–322 B.C.E.) as our guide, we shift our focus from how we judge whether a person is moral to how a person *becomes* moral. Rather than discard emotions from the moral equation, Aristotle suggested training them and using them to form a virtuous character; hence, his moral system is known as a type of *virtue ethics*. In short, Aristotelian virtue ethics holds that a person of moral virtue is also a person of character; such a person exhibits moderation. She is able to hit the mean, the moderate balance point, between excess and deficiency. For example, in a situation in which a dear, trusted friend needs to borrow money for food, it would be moderate and generous to lend money. In a situation with a friend who has a known gambling problem, however, lending money would be foolish. A person of moral virtue knows the difference between the two situations.[9]

According to Aristotle, we learn moral virtue through habituation and practice. To *do* good, moral training must become so much a part of who we are that we barely have to think about it as we do it. In the first stages of becoming a good person, we observe and imitate those around us. In this sense, learning moral virtue is a little like learning a sport. If Happy and Pepper want to learn to play soccer, they have to study the rules of the game, train for endurance in running, and practice exercises that will teach them skills such as kicking and dribbling the ball. Only when they have mastered these skills will they be able to seamlessly employ them in a real-time game. In the same way that Happy and Pepper cannot play soccer well (or *be* good soccer players) unless they have so thoroughly absorbed the microlevel skills (so that they can focus on the game as a whole and not on how to properly kick the ball), so a person of character cannot act appropriately in different situations without the automatic skills that habituation has provided. Tony Stark, as Iron Man, has achieved this at a certain level, using his formidable intellect, together with his accumulated experience in many morally problematic situations, to develop habits that lead to sound moral character.[10]

The "Armor Wars" and "Extremis" story lines both demonstrate the degree to which Tony is preoccupied with the question of how to *be* a good person in the Aristotelian sense. For example, although his pragmatic side recognizes that the world is not a neat and tidy moral universe, he worries almost obsessively about being good. Tony wants to *do* good, but that is not enough for him—he also strives to *be* good. Aristotle's views on moral virtue and habituation can help us to think through why this approach to ethics best suits Tony Stark.

Tony's Moral Compass Found!

"Extremis" presents us with four interrelated examples of Tony's Aristotelian desire to be good and not merely to do good, all of them linked with Tony's past as a weapons designer and his uncertainty about the moral good done by Iron Man. Succinctly put, his concern is this: is Iron Man only another weapon, or does he represent the promise of a world without war? In "Extremis," Tony decides in favor of the latter.

In the first example, when Tony's personal secretary Mrs. Rennie calls him in his garage, where he has been a recluse for six weeks, Tony looks at himself in the mirror and says, "What are you looking at?" He examines his face and continues to say to the mirror, "I hate it when you look at me like that."[11] This response to his own reflection is a clear indicator of an inner conflict, related to his history as a weapons designer.

The second example is found in the same issue when Tony is interviewed by the documentary filmmaker John Pillinger.

Pillinger steers the interview in a negative direction that would indict Tony as a warlord who creates weapons that kill children, but Tony defends himself at every turn. At the end of the interview, Pillinger asks Tony why he would take an interview with him when he knows what his work is like (think of Pillinger as a kind of Michael Moore). Tony counters with a thought-provoking question that shows us once again the turmoil beneath the surface: "I wanted to meet you. You've been making your investigative films for what, twenty years now? I wanted to ask: Have you changed anything? You've been uncovering disturbing things all over the world for twenty years now. Have you changed anything? You've worked very hard. Most people have no idea of the kind of work you've done. Intellectuals, critics and activists follow your films closely, but culturally you're almost invisible, Mr. Pillinger. Have you changed anything?" Pillinger responds honestly that he doesn't know. Tony says back, "Me neither." The interview and Tony's question to Pillinger cut to the heart of Tony's inner turmoil. Pillinger may appear to be a good person, but has he done any good? Tony appears to have done some good, but is he a good person? Tony would like to both be a good person and do good—but is this possible? Becoming Iron Man is his solution.

The third example is found after Maya Hansen, an old friend and colleague, has called Tony in distress. The Extremis virus that she helped create, which was funded by the army to produce superhuman warriors, has been stolen. Tony brings Maya to see their old friend and mentor Sal Kennedy. Before Sal becomes aware of the full import of the danger Extremis poses, he offers an unsolicited diagnosis of both Tony's and Maya's lives that once again underscores Tony's inner turmoil. He says to Tony, "You can barely look at yourself in the mirror, can you, Tony? You're rich now. Independent. I have a feeling you do good works, when you can. But it's not enough. You have intellect and power, but it's not enough. It's like there's a dam across your life."[12] Sal, in effect, says that even if Tony *does* good, Tony does not feel that he *is* good. Tony's response is that Iron Man is somehow the solution to this dilemma.

The final example takes place after Maya has told Tony about the destruction that Extremis can cause. Tony springs into action and starts to don the Iron Man armor. As he makes his final preparations, he sees his reflection in a computer monitor and says, "Oh, *now* you can look at me?"[13] Iron Man is clearly the key to solving Tony's inner turmoil. Tony is torn about whether the good he does with Iron Man is good enough. Tony wants to be a good person, but it is Iron Man who does good deeds. The Extremis virus presents the solution, a way for Tony to *be* Iron Man in the truest sense. As Tony says to Maya, "Make me the Iron Man inside and out."[14] If Tony can be Iron Man, then he thinks that he can both be a good person and do good deeds. He won't have to instruct the Iron Man armor to do what he thinks is best; he will be the Iron Man inside and out.[15]

Tony's approach is Aristotelian because it joins the person with the deeds. In contrast to utilitarianism, Tony's Aristotelian approach focuses on a moral agent, rather than on the deeds or the outcomes, and it does not necessarily condone the sacrifice of some for the many. In contrast to Kantian moral theory, Tony's approach takes emotions into consideration and is not based in firm rules. Aristotle's concern with both doing good and being a good person allows for making decisions tailored to the situation. This explains why Tony will not simply walk away from the weapons industry and feels compelled to retrieve his stolen technology. There is no hard and fast universal rule to guide him in this regard—it simply comes down to his own judgment, based on his character.

Can You Find Your Moral Compass?

As readers, we are led to ask reflective questions of ourselves by the dilemmas that Tony faces. For example, are you concerned about being a good person and doing good deeds, or is simply doing good deeds enough? Or, perhaps, would you be satisfied with merely appearing to be good?

"Armor Wars" and "Extremis" demonstrate that Tony is not concerned with whether he appears good, but rather with being good. He would never have risked his company and alienated his friends, including Captain America and the Avengers, if this weren't the case. Aristotle said that in contrast to the person of character, anyone "can experience fear, confidence, desire, anger, pity, and generally any kind of pleasure and pain either too much or too little, and in either case not properly." But the person of character, because he has aligned who he is with what he does, has a different experience. As Aristotle continued, "But to experience all this at the right time, toward the right objects, toward the right people, for the right reason, and in the right manner—that is the median and the best course, the course that is a mark of virtue."[16] Only the actions of a person of character or virtue seamlessly display who that person truly is, regardless of the situation.

Tony would add that the mark of virtue also involves not being overly influenced by the opinions of others with respect to what he thinks is the right thing to do. This can be a lonely path. As Tony himself says in "Armor Wars" about his mission to destroy all of his stolen technology, "So far, the quest has been costly: I had to fire myself, as Iron Man from Stark Enterprises . . . my personal life is a shambles . . . and I've lost one of my oldest friends [Captain America]."[17] It can be alienating to align one's actions with one's beliefs, especially when one's concept of virtue conflicts with society's. Despite this challenge, Tony perseveres because he wants to be a good person and not merely appear to be so to those around him. Would you make a similar sacrifice for your moral beliefs? We can all hope we never have to face that question, but it's worth thinking about all the same.

NOTES

1. "Armor Wars" appeared in *Iron Man*, vol. 1, #225–232 (1987–1988), and "Extremis" in *Iron Man*, vol. 4, #1–6 (2005–2006); both have since been collected in trade paperback.

2. This is commonly referred to today as *hedonic utilitarianism*; some modern utilitarians deemphasize happiness and prefer to orient their ethical decision making around well-being or preference-satisfaction. For more on the varieties of utilitarianism (or consequentialism in general), see Walter Sinnott-Armstrong, "Consequentialism," *Stanford Encyclopedia of Philosophy*, http://plato.stanford.edu/entries/consequentialism, particularly section 3.

3. For more on the practical complexities of utilitarianism, see J. Robert Loftis, "Means, Ends, and the Critique of Pure Superheroes," in Mark D. White, ed., *Watchmen and Philosophy: A Rorschach Test* (Hoboken, NJ: John Wiley & Sons, 2008), pp. 47–60.

4. *Iron Man*, vol. 1, #225 (December 1987). Note that although Tony is concerned about the innocent man who died, he is not worried about whether the Controller survived the scuffle, which shows the ambiguity of his feelings toward utilitarianism and the meaning of the equality behind it.

5. Ibid., vol. 1, #226 (January 1988).

6. Ideally, these two formulations of the categorical imperative are equivalent, because they both rely on the equal dignity and worth of all rational beings (like us). For the basic treatment, see Kant's 1785 book *Grounding for the Metaphysics of Morals* (we recommend the translation by James W. Ellington, 3rd ed. [Indianapolis: Hackett Publishing, (1785) 1993]).

7. The original example from Kant, on which this example is based, comes from his "On a Supposed Right to Lie because of Philanthropic Concerns," which can be found in the edition of the *Grounding* cited in the previous note (pp. 63–67).

8. *Iron Man*, vol. 1, #225 (December 1987).

9. In this chapter we limit our discussion to Tony and moral virtue; for a discussion of Tony Stark and the other virtues, see the chapters in this volume by Carsten Fogh Nielsen ("Flawed Heroes and Courageous Villains: Plato, Aristotle, and Iron Man on the Unity of the Virtues") and by Stephanie and Brett Patterson ("'I Have a Good Life': Iron Man and the Avenger School of Virtue").

10. Again, see the chapters by Nielsen and the Pattersons for different perspectives on Tony's virtue.

11. *Iron Man*, vol. 4, #1 (January 2005).

12. Ibid., vol. 4, #2 (February 2005).

13. Ibid., vol. 4, #3 (March 2005).

14. Ibid., vol. 4, #4 (October 2005).

15. Of course, this view becomes problematic in the following story line, "Execute Program" (*Iron Man*, vol. 4, #7–12, 2006; 2007 trade paperback), when Iron Man's mind—and therefore Iron Man's system itself—is hacked and controlled by a killer.

16. Aristotle, *Nicomachean Ethics*, trans. Martin Ostwald (Englewood Cliffs, NJ: Prentice, 1962), p. 43 (1106b 18–24, by the marginal notation that is standard in any respectable edition of the text, including this one).

17. *Iron Man*, vol. 1, #229 (April 1988).

FLAWED HEROES AND COURAGEOUS VILLAINS: PLATO, ARISTOTLE, AND IRON MAN ON THE UNITY OF THE VIRTUES

Carsten Fogh Nielsen

Iron Man vs. Tony Stark

There can be little doubt that Iron Man is a hero. Selflessly putting his own life at risk, Iron Man employs the superhuman powers of his armor to conquer evil, fight crime, help the helpless, and generally make the world a better place. This, most people would probably agree, is what heroes do, and Iron Man should thus be ranked alongside other illustrious characters such as Superman, Wonder Woman, and Spider-Man as a true superhero.

What about Tony Stark, the man behind the iron mask? Here opinions are much more likely to differ. Even after donning the Iron Man armor and making serious attempts to undo the suffering caused by the high-tech weaponry produced by Stark Industries, Tony Stark remains a morally ambiguous character. As depicted in the comics for decades and as portrayed by Robert Downey Jr. in the films, Stark is not a flawless knight in shining armor. He is a charming and intelligent man, but he is also an arrogant, self-centered, and slightly immoral womanizer; he's a playboy incapable of committing to long-term relationships; and he's just a little too fond of heavy drinking and partying.

Some people might say Tony has minor character flaws but otherwise is quite an admirable person. Other people, however, might find his moral defects utterly reprehensible. Although people will disagree about the seriousness of Tony Stark's moral failings, they will likely all agree that he is not a fully virtuous human being.

Perhaps surprisingly, this agreement raises a host of problems. Because Tony Stark quite clearly is not a fully virtuous person, how can we then expect him to make the right decisions or to act in morally appropriate and admirable ways when he wears the Iron Man armor? And to what extent should Stark's moral flaws influence our moral evaluation of Iron Man? Should we continue to regard Iron Man as a (super)hero, even though we know that his alter ego Tony Stark is less than fully virtuous? Shouldn't superheroes be morally virtuous through and through? Stark and Iron Man, after all, are one and the same person. So how can our moral evaluation of one differ from that of the other? Or, to put the point more generally: Is it possible to be virtuous in some respects but not in others? Can you be a truly virtuous person if you are not completely virtuous in every respect?

Virtues Unite!

At the root of these questions is an ancient philosophical idea that can be traced all the way back to the very beginning of Western philosophy, which we will call the "unity of virtue thesis" (or UVT for short). According to the unity of virtue thesis, possession of one virtue necessarily entails possession of *all* the virtues. Or, put another way, being morally virtuous implies that you possess *all* of the virtues, not merely some of them. Moral virtue is to be construed as a unity; a person cannot be in possession of one moral virtue without being in possession of all of them, and if she lacks a single virtue, then she is not truly virtuous.

What does this have to do with Tony Stark and Iron Man? Well, if UVT is true, then it provides us with an answer to the problems we encountered when attempting to evaluate Tony Stark's (and Iron Man's) moral character. According to UVT, a virtuous person possesses every moral virtue. This, quite clearly, is not true of Tony Stark. He is arrogant and self-centered; his excessive consumption of alcohol indicates that he is not in possession of the virtue of moderation; and his social life seems to indicate that he has not (or at least not yet) acquired the virtues associated with maintaining meaningful and prolonged romantic relationships. Tony Stark is clearly lacking in the virtues department, which, according to UVT, means that he cannot be considered morally virtuous at all. And because Tony Stark and Iron Man are one and the same person, we cannot—and should not—regard Iron Man as a morally exemplary character, despite the fact that Iron Man appears to be doing good in the world.

But is the unity of virtue thesis true? At first glance, it might appear so. Ideally speaking, human beings should be fully virtuous. Being fully virtuous implies being in full possession of every moral virtue. Morally admirable human beings should therefore, ideally speaking, be in possession of all the virtues. Certainly, UVT possesses a certain immediate and intuitive appeal. In fact, most people would probably, without much further reflection, be inclined to accept some version of UVT.

But just as superheroes cannot necessarily trust their immediate instincts when deciding on a course of action (as Tony Stark learns the hard way when he is betrayed by Obadiah Stane), so philosophers have to be distrustful even of their own most valued beliefs and ideas. UVT might very well express a basic human ideal, but this, in and of itself, is not enough to establish the truth of UVT. To do so, we have to weigh all of the arguments for and against UVT, including those that support our initial intuitions and also those that might oppose them.

We're Gonna Need Doctor Doom's Time Cube for This

Let's turn the clock (and the calendar) back to the days of Plato (427–347 B.C.E.), one of the superheroes of Western philosophy, who subscribed to a version of UVT. According to Plato, virtue is, or at least implies, a sort of practical knowledge. Faced with problematic circumstances, a virtuous person knows or is able to find out what the morally appropriate thing to do is. Being virtuous thus seems to imply possession of a particular sort of practical knowledge: namely, knowledge about the morally appropriate thing to do and the proper way to act. "Virtue is either wholly or partly wisdom," as Plato put it in *Meno*, one of his many famous philosophical dialogues.[1]

How does this idea relate to UVT? Well, if Plato was right, and virtue is a form of knowledge, then there is a straightforward way in which all of the particular virtues are related to one another. If virtue is knowledge, then particular virtues such as courage, temperance, and piety can be understood as particular pieces of practical knowledge, knowledge about what to do in specific situations and contexts. A courageous person like Iron Man knows how to respond to dangerous and perilous circumstances; a temperate person knows about the lures and temptations of everyday life and knows how to resist them; a pious person knows the proper way of paying tribute to the divine, and so forth. Particular virtues, it would appear, differ from one another with regard to the particular situations and circumstances to which they apply. But despite these differences, all of the virtues share one fundamental feature: they are all instances of practical knowledge. In this very basic sense, every particular moral virtue can be seen as necessarily similar (and hence related) to all of the others.

Speaking of Doctor Doom

This, however, is not enough to give us UVT. Even if every particular virtue can be viewed as a specific piece of practical knowledge, this does not imply that possession of one of the virtues necessarily entails the possession of *every* virtue. Iron Man is courageous (or at least appears so at first glance), which means that he knows the proper way to handle dangerous situations. But there are many other areas where Iron Man (or Tony Stark) seems clueless: romance, for instance (as opposed to casual sexual encounters), and the proper way to consume and enjoy alcohol (as opposed to simply boozing). Iron Man knows how to act courageously, while at the same time being ignorant about other areas of practical knowledge. More generally, it appears perfectly possible to be in possession of one particular bit of practical knowledge or one particular virtue, while simultaneously lacking quite a lot of other virtues (or other pieces of practical knowledge).

This, in fact, is a well-established and important part of superhero lore. If UVT were true, then all criminals should be feebleminded cowards, and superheroes like Iron Man would soon be out of a job. Unfortunately, though, many supervillains—the Iron Monger, the Mandarin, and Doctor Doom, to mention but a few—are not only unjust and deeply immoral; they also appear to be both courageous and intelligent. An almost complete lack of some of the most basic moral virtues (justice, kindness, civility), combined with high levels of intelligence and a willingness to face danger, is precisely what makes these characters particularly dangerous (and fascinating). So, possession of one virtue—say, courage—does not necessarily seem to imply possession of all the virtues. The existence (albeit fictitious) of courageous villains such as Doom and the Iron Monger appears to confirm the notion that it is possible for a person to be very knowledgeable in one particular area (how to deal with dangerous situations, for instance), while at the same time being very ignorant in others (such as the hows and whys of treating other human beings decently). The mere fact that virtue can be regarded as a form of practical knowledge does not suffice to establish the truth of UVT.

Plato Strikes Back

There is an obvious, though radical, response to this objection: we can deny that Doctor Doom, the Iron Monger, or any of Iron Man's other supervillainous enemies are in fact ever courageous. They might *appear* courageous, but this appearance is incorrect. When we ascribe courage to the Iron Monger for standing his ground in his battles with Iron Man, we are making a mistake; we are in fact misusing the word "courage."

To better understand this idea, we can once again turn to Plato. In the dialogue *Laches*, Plato's characters discuss the nature of courage and its relationship to other virtues. One of these characters, Nicias, insists that courage is a sort of wisdom or knowledge, specifically knowledge of the grounds of hope and fear and of the proper ways to respond to hopeful and fearful circumstances. Being courageous means being in possession of this particular piece of practical knowledge.

Now, according to Nicias (and, we may safely assume, Plato), there is a difference between courage and what we might call fearlessness. As Nicias puts it, "I am of [the] opinion that thoughtful courage is a quality possessed by very few, but that rashness and boldness, and fearlessness, which has no forethought, are very common qualities possessed by many men, many women, many children, many animals. And you, and men in general, call by the term 'courageous' actions which I call rash; my courageous actions are wise actions."[2]

This distinction provides us with a preliminary explanation of why it may be a mistake to think that supervillains such as Iron Monger, Doctor Doom, and the Mandarin should be considered courageous. When we take a closer look at their actions, we find that they may initially *appear* courageous but in fact are not. Why? Because these actions are not based on, nor do they exhibit, the proper sort of practical knowledge. The apparently brave actions of Doom and the rest do not qualify as revealing "thoughtful courage" but should rather be regarded as instances of fearlessness or rashness, a result of a thoughtless inability to properly understand and respond to fearful circumstances and situations.

The Return of UVT, Part One

This account leaves unanswered a rather important and pressing question. What precisely is it that prevents us from describing Doom, Iron Monger, and other supervillains as courageous? What exactly is lacking from their character, which makes it impossible for their actions to be termed brave?

This is where UVT once again enters the picture. One way of explaining why it is inappropriate to ascribe courage or any of the other virtues to people like Doom is to claim that the virtues must be considered as a unity; that one virtue cannot be understood or cannot exist in isolation from the others. It is true that we have a tendency to discuss particular virtues such as courage, kindness, and justice separately, as if each of them could somehow exist without the others. But according to UVT, this is a mistake. The reason Doctor Doom, the Iron Monger, and other supervillains do not qualify as courageous, despite performing actions that might at first glance *appear* courageous, is that they do not have the unity of character necessary for possessing even a single virtue.

The problem with this response is that it still leaves unexplained *why* the virtues should be conceived of as necessarily interdependent. The UVT may very well provide us with an explanation of why obviously villainous characters such as Iron Monger and Doom should not be described as courageous, but that seems a backward way of arguing for UVT. If, as held by Plato (and, as we'll soon see, Aristotle), all of the virtues really are necessarily related to one another, and possession of one virtue thus requires possession of all the virtues, should we then not be able to give a more positive, more illuminating, argument for this?

Ask Aristotle

Unfortunately, Plato was not particularly clear when dealing with this question. Many contemporary philosophers have thus more or less given up on finding a strictly Platonic solution to this problem and have instead turned to Plato's student Aristotle (384–322 B.C.E.) in order to find a plausible answer to the question of precisely why the virtues should be regarded as a sort of necessary unity.

Aristotle, like every great student, did not uncritically accept his teacher's ideas; rather, he questioned Plato, locating problems and difficulties in his teachings. Aristotle fully agreed with Plato that virtue and knowledge are closely related, but he thought that Plato went wrong when he *identified* virtue with knowledge. Aristotle believed that there are forms of virtue that simply cannot be equated with knowledge. For instance, there are people who by nature are emotionally disposed to respond in morally appropriate ways. Some people have a natural inclination to be kind to others; some are naturally motivated to perform courageous acts; and some have a natural capacity for compassion. In and of itself, such admirable emotional dispositions, what Aristotle terms *natural virtues*, do not constitute a form of practical knowledge. They are merely habitual dispositions to feel and be motivated to act in particular ways in particular circumstances. Virtue and knowledge, it would thus appear, are not one and the same thing; a person can be naturally virtuous, without knowing why her actions are morally appropriate.

How, then, are we to understand the relationship between virtue and knowledge? According to Aristotle, Plato "was mistaken in thinking that all the virtues are forms of prudence [practical knowledge], but he was quite right in asserting that they *imply* prudence."[3] There are forms of virtue, the natural virtues, which are not, strictly speaking, a form of knowledge. But natural virtue is not what we might call virtue in the full sense, or virtue in the most perfect and developed form. "In the moral character," Aristotle explained, "there are two qualities, natural virtue and virtue in the full sense; and of these the latter implies prudence."[4] Being fully virtuous Aristotle claimed, not only involves having certain emotional dispositions; it also implies being in possession of a certain form of practical knowledge, knowledge about what to do and how to act. A fully virtuous person does not simply automatically respond to a particular situation; he or she *knows* why this particular course of action is morally appropriate. For this reason, Aristotle believed that "it is not possible to be good in the true sense of the word without prudence, or to be prudent without moral goodness."[5]

According to Aristotle, then, virtue involves two closely related but conceptually distinct elements: practical knowledge concerning the morally appropriate thing to do in particular circumstances, and the emotional disposition to be motivated to act on this knowledge. In the fully virtuous person, these two elements are perfectly united; knowledge and emotion go hand in hand, and together they ensure that the person acts and responds in morally appropriate ways in particular situations. For instance, being courageous not only implies being motivated (emotionally disposed) to face up to dangerous situations and circumstances. It also involves knowing, and being able to justify, why this is the proper way to respond to these particular circumstances. A courageous person—say, a superhero like Iron Man—knows what to do and how to act when faced with danger and possesses the emotional disposition to act on this knowledge.

The Return of UVT, Part Two

With these distinctions in place, Aristotle was then ready to take on those who oppose UVT. He began by granting that there appears to be an "argument by which it could be contended that the virtues exist independently of each other, on the ground that the same man is not equally endowed by nature in respect of them all, so that he will already be the possessor of one, but not yet the possessor of another."[6] Tony Stark, as we have already seen, appears to be an obvious example of such a person. Though he is clearly courageous, and willing to put his life in danger to defend the innocent and the helpless, he also seems to be lacking some important virtues, such as temperance and the ability to commit to serious romantic relationships. The existence of people like Stark appears to threaten UVT, because they seem to imply that a person can be in possession of one virtue without necessarily being in possession of all the virtues.

Aristotle countered this argument by invoking the distinction between "natural virtue" and "virtue in the full sense." As far as natural virtue is concerned, Aristotle was perfectly willing to admit that a person may possess one virtue without possessing all of the others. When we are talking about the emotional disposition to respond in specific ways to particular situations, then it is perfectly possible for a person to possess one virtue but not another. We can be naturally motivated to face dangerous circumstances with courage, without being naturally inclined to show kindness to strangers. Or, Tony Stark can be emotionally disposed to face the wrath of the Iron Monger without necessarily being naturally motivated to reduce his consumption of alcohol or to improve his behavior toward women.

As we have seen, Aristotle regarded being emotionally disposed to act in morally appropriate ways in particular situations as a *necessary* condition—not a *sufficient* condition—for being a fully virtuous person. (In other words, you *have* to be emotionally disposed to act morally in order to be considered fully virtuous, but it isn't enough—there's more to being fully virtuous than that.) A fully virtuous person, according to Aristotle, is not only motivated to perform specific sorts of acts; she also knows why these actions are morally appropriate. Natural virtue, combined with practical knowledge (prudence), is virtue in the full sense, and for virtue in the full sense, separation of the virtues is *not* an option. "When the virtues are those that entitle a person to be called good without qualification," Aristotle explained, they have to be understood as necessarily related to and dependent on one another, "for the possession of the single virtue of prudence will carry with it the possession of them all."[7] Full virtue implies practical knowledge; practical knowledge (prudence) implies possession of all the virtues; and a fully virtuous person therefore, at least according to Aristotle, necessarily possesses all of the virtues.

Enough with the Ancients

Once again, this brings us face-to-face with a question we first encountered when discussing Plato's attempt to justify UVT.

Plato and Aristotle both agreed that virtue implies possession of practical knowledge about what to do and how to act in particular circumstances. They also both agreed that this knowledge somehow ensures or establishes UVT. The question that remains unanswered is precisely why this is so: Why did Plato and Aristotle believe that possession of *one* particular virtue (or particular bit of practical knowledge) necessarily implies possession of *every* virtue (or piece of practical knowledge)?

A number of contemporary philosophers believe that Plato and (in particular) Aristotle were on the right track, and have attempted to spell out what their reasoning might be.[8] Their basic idea is quite simple—namely, that practical knowledge should not be conceived of as a hodgepodge of accidentally coinciding facts but as a sort of unified whole. Every piece of practical knowledge is related to every other piece and can be fully comprehended only when viewed as part of a larger whole.

To make this idea clearer, consider for a moment a scenario where Doctor Doom is attacking Avengers Mansion and Iron Man has to intervene. What should Iron Man do? Stopping the attack seems to be a rather pressing concern, but so is protecting the innocent. Which is more important in this particular situation? To further complicate matters, Iron Man may also want to consider the significant damage that a battle with Doom will predictably inflict on the surrounding area. Perhaps it would be better not to engage Doom in battle at all, but rather to make sure that the destruction is confined to the mansion and that innocent bystanders are kept out of harm's way? But then what about the damage to the famous and (both historically and architecturally) valuable mansion and the threat to the people still trapped inside (such as the Avengers' butler, Jarvis)? And let's not forget that Iron Man is obviously about to expose himself to great danger. This raises the question of how to balance self-preservation against the needs of others. Is Iron Man morally required to lay down his life for others? And if he decides to do so in this particular situation, who shall then oppose Doom the next time he reaches for world domination?

These are only some of the many problems and considerations Iron Man has to take into account when trying to decide how best to respond to Doom's attack.[9] Notice the intimate interrelatedness of these considerations. Each particular one seems necessarily linked to all of the others, because they are all relevant for determining the proper course of action. Saving Avengers Mansion surely is of some importance, but when determining how to respond to Doom's attack, Iron Man also has to take into account many other important considerations and decide how to weigh or balance them against one another. More generally, to properly assess the importance of any particular consideration (any particular feature of a situation), we need to be in possession of knowledge about the importance of every other consideration we may compare it to. As the philosopher Susan Wolf has recently put it, "Knowledge is essentially unified. That is, the perfect and complete knowledge of the importance of one item requires the knowledge of the importance of everything else against which this item may in principle have to be balanced."[10]

The Return of UVT—the Final Countdown

We finally have an explanation and a justification of UVT: if virtue involves practical knowledge (as both Plato and Aristotle believed), and if practical knowledge is essentially unified, then it follows that virtue must be unified as well. To once again quote Wolf: "The conclusion that follows is that virtue is unified, in the sense that the perfect and complete possession of one virtue requires at least the knowledge that is needed for the possession of every other."[11] The knowledge required for fully possessing a single virtue necessarily implies possession of the knowledge required for possession of every other virtue.

Does this account make sense of the problems we've encountered in our discussion so far? Let's start with reexamining the nature of Doctor Doom's courage. Plato, as we have seen, would say that Doom is not courageous but merely fearless. Aristotle would probably say that although Doom has a natural disposition for courage, this "natural virtue" does not constitute "virtue in the full sense." Both Plato and Aristotle would say that the reason Doom is not truly courageous is that he lacks the requisite practical knowledge.

We are now in a position to make more sense of this claim. Doom may very well be able to face danger without flinching, but this is only one aspect of what it means to be truly courageous. True courage also implies knowing the proper way to balance and weigh the many kinds of considerations that might be in play in any dangerous situation, such as the needs of others or the requirements of justice. To be truly courageous, Doom would have to be in possession of complete knowledge about all of this, and *these* virtues are quite obviously lacking from Doom's character. His grasp of what it means to be courageous is thus necessarily one-sided and incomplete, and although he may very well be fearless, he is surely not courageous in the full sense of the word.

What about Tony Stark/Iron Man? Here we seem to be on shakier ground. How do we explain that Stark can be morally flawed, while at the same time appear to be morally virtuous? Doesn't UVT imply that a person either possesses every virtue or has none of them? Well, this might have been true of our first formulations of UVT, but it is not necessarily true of our final definition of UVT. Our final formulation of UVT (due to Wolf) states that "the *perfect and complete* possession of one virtue requires the knowledge that is needed for the possession of every other."[12] First of all, Wolf's wording ("perfect and complete") seems to allow for the possibility of *imperfect* and *incomplete* possession of a virtue, which is tailor-made for Tony Stark! Second, as stated by Wolf, UVT can allow that imperfect and incomplete possession of one virtue nonetheless requires the knowledge necessary for every other virtue. Altogether, UVT does not necessarily imply that being virtuous is an all-or-nothing affair. It *is* possible to be a less than fully virtuous human being and still qualify as a decent guy.

Relax, Tony—You're Safe!

By and large, Iron Man appears to be a virtuous person. Though he stumbles occasionally, he constantly strives to do better. Iron Man may not be in perfect possession of every single virtue, but his grasp of the practical knowledge required for possessing the virtues is clearly far superior to, say, Doctor Doom's. Even if we take into account the obvious flaws in Tony Stark's character, it should be clear that it would be a mistake to place Iron Man in the same category as Doom. Stark's arrogance may very well signify a lack of moral character, but compared to the full-blown megalomania of Doom, it must surely be regarded as a minor failing.

At the beginning of this chapter, we noted that the unity of virtue thesis expresses a basic moral ideal: that human beings should be in full possession of all the virtues. We now have some reason to think that this ideal can be justified. If virtue involves practical knowledge (as Plato and Aristotle thought), and if practical knowledge forms a sort of unified whole, then the unity of virtue thesis may be true. Given the limitations of human nature, however, it seems entirely plausible that virtue in the most complete sense of the word may forever be out of our reach. If so, then Tony Stark, with all of his faults, may be the best we can hope for: an extraordinarily gifted man who, despite his flaws and shortcomings, strives to make the world a better place and, if possible, improve himself along the way. And perhaps that is about as heroic and virtuous as you can get.

NOTES

1. Plato, *Meno*, translated by Benjamin Jowett, available at the Internet Classics Archive, http://classics.mit.edu/Plato/meno.html, p. 89a. The numbers refer to marginal page numbers that appear in any published edition of this work (though unfortunately not in the online version cited here).

2. Plato, *Laches*, translated by Benjamin Jowett, also available at the Internet Classics Archive, http://classics.mit.edu/Plato/laches.html, pp. 197a–197b.

3. Aristotle, *Nicomachean Ethics*, rev. ed., trans. J. A. K Thomson (London: Penguin Classics, 1976), vi. 13. 1144^b 18–19, emphasis in original. Strictly speaking, Aristotle is not criticizing Plato here but rather Plato's teacher, Socrates. The question of whether and to what extent the philosophies of Plato and Socrates differ is heavily contested. For the sake of simplicity, I simply take for granted that Aristotle's criticisms of Socrates can also be applied to Plato.

4. Ibid., vi. 13. 1144^b 14–16.

5. Ibid., vi. 13. 1144^b 31–32.

6. Ibid., vi. 13. 1144^b 33–36.

7. Ibid., vi. 13. 1144^b 36–1145^a3.

8. See, for instance, John McDowell, "Virtue and Reason," *The Monist* 62 (1979): 331–350; and Susan Wolf, "Moral Psychology and the Unity of the Virtues," *Ratio* 20 (2007): 145–167.

9. Presumably, Iron Man (like the rest of us) rarely has time to deliberate about what to do in particular situations. Most of the time, he simply has to (re)act. This is one reason why some philosophers think that a truly virtuous agent has no real need for deliberation but immediately perceives what the right course of action is and acts on this perception without any hesitation; see, for instance, McDowell's paper cited in the previous note.

10. Wolf, "Moral Psychology," p. 150.

11. Ibid.

12. Ibid., emphasis mine.

"I HAVE A GOOD LIFE": IRON MAN AND THE AVENGER SCHOOL OF VIRTUE

Stephanie Patterson and Brett Patterson

Why do so many people love to read and watch *Iron Man* if Tony Stark is so flawed and morally challenged? Perhaps it is because we admire his determination to be a hero in spite of himself. We see him struggle with his vices, and we watch him drown in the murky spaces between right and wrong, yet we cheer him on. Tony is a more accessible character because of his glaring mistakes. His failures, whether through alcoholism or the misuse of his inventions, illustrate most poignantly what can be lost as a consequence of our own actions. His successes in battling his demons and living "a good life" inspire us to do the same.

The Good Life

Joe Quesada's five-issue story line, "The Mask in the Iron Man," portrays the troubled relationship between Tony and a version of his armor that has evolved into a sentient being.[1] In "Part Two: The Dream Machine," Quesada guides us in envisioning a situation in which Tony loses all of what he cares about.[2] When we examine what Tony loses—friendship, respect, status—as a consequence of his poor decisions or compulsions, we are offered insight into his desires and his goals. Following his battle with Whiplash, Tony crashes to the pavement and wakes up in the hospital surrounded by his friends. His girlfriend Rumiko storms in, revealing that the world (and she, for the first time) knows Iron Man's secret identity, which is the catalyst for a string of events that utterly destroys Tony Stark. He loses his relationship with Rumiko, his consulting job, his status as an Avenger—and he begins to drink again.

Toward the end of the issue, we learn that his failure to protect this secret has resulted in the murder of most of his close friends. As his subsequent battle with the Mandarin draws to an end, Tony begins to succumb to a heart attack—he is dying, full of regret, with "I'm sorry" on his lips. Although the entire sequence turns out to be a virtual nightmare, we get to see the frailty of Tony's life and how tenuously he holds things together. The virtual dream offers Tony the opportunity for introspection and sets up the framework for the next three issues in which Tony instructs the sentient armor.

Tony begins each of the five issues of the arc with the same ruminations about having a good life:

> I have a good life. I have wonderful friends. I've got more money than I know what to do with. Thanks to that and a knack for building elaborate tinker toys, I've managed to help out a few people here and there. And I've also been lucky . . . very lucky. I manage on a daily basis to beat a disease that some never recover from . . . no less acknowledge. And then there's always been the question of my heart. I have a good life.

For Tony, the components of a "good life" are friends, comfortable living, being useful, mastering his addiction, and staying alive. Throughout his evolving journey as Iron Man, Tony's friends, especially James "Rhodey" Rhodes, Pepper Potts, and Happy Hogan, have given him a sense of purpose and self-worth. They have suffered alongside Tony during loss (of loved ones and his company), alcoholism (so bad at one point that Rhodey had to become Iron Man), and physical infirmity (heart problems, paralysis, and neurological failure), and have rejoiced with him in his successes. Tony values the people who make his life meaningful. He also realizes the importance of the wealth that has allowed him to support philanthropic causes and live a lifestyle fueled by his imagination. Tony truly understands and appreciates how his intellectual gifts benefit society and help avert the occasional disaster.

Tony describes himself as "lucky," but when it comes to his alcoholism he is tenacious. Unlike others who hide their addiction, their "disease," from themselves and others, Tony faces and beats it—albeit "one day at a time." The final component of a "good life" for Tony is life itself. The injury to his heart, which was the impetus behind the invention of the chest plate and later Iron Man, has always kept Tony's mortality in the forefront of his mind. Whether by luck or ingenuity, Tony has kept himself alive in many life-threatening situations.

Tony's "good life" reflection has strong undertones of what the philosopher Aristotle (384–322 B.C.E.) described as happiness and the conditions that contribute to happiness. In his *Nicomachean Ethics*, Aristotle claimed that "happiness" or "living well and doing well" is a human being's primary goal. We seek other things such as "pleasure, wealth, or honor," "health," a "great ideal," or "another [good]" only as means to happiness. Certainly, this applies to Iron Man. Tony's friends give him pleasure and satisfaction; wealth enables Tony's superhero lifestyle; his helping others could be described as "honor"; his mention of his heart obviously refers to his bodily health; and, finally, his goal of remaining sober could be interpreted as an aspiration to a "great ideal."[3]

Even as we compare Tony's list to Aristotle's, we begin to see where Aristotle's argument will lead: these are all components of happiness or the good life. Aristotle used wealth as an example: "Wealth is evidently not the good we are seeking; for it is merely useful and for the sake of something else."[4] He argued that pleasure, wealth, and so on are chosen "for the sake of happiness, judging that by means of them we shall be happy." Aristotle surmised that the final good must be "self-sufficient" and not only one good among many—happiness fits this criterion. In the same way, Tony's "wonderful friends," "money," and so forth are not "the end of action," but, rather, they together form a composite "good life."[5]

The Avenger Community of Virtue

This examination of the good life can help us understand Tony Stark's motivation as a superhero and an Avenger. The moral philosopher H. Richard Niebuhr (1894–1962), who was influenced by Aristotle, helps us see that the concept of the good life is rooted in an individual's communal values. Niebuhr reminds us that what we value as individuals often arises from, and finds reinforcement in, our relationships with other people who are important to us. Tony's community encompasses a wide array of characters—including, as we have seen, Rhodey, Pepper, and Happy, but also Steve Rogers (Captain America), Hank Pym (Ant-Man/Yellowjacket), Janet Van Dyne (the Wasp), and the rest of the Avengers.

Niebuhr argued, though, that we often take our social setting and our point of view for granted. Life within a particular community, with its traditions and beliefs, depends on individual and communal faith commitments to something that makes life worth living. Some "center of value" orients the life of this community and its members.[6] Tony's valuing of the "good life" receives confirmation and verification in the community of the Avengers. Life in the Avengers community also involves two other elements highlighted by Niebuhr: trust and loyalty. Members trust in the values of their community and live out their loyalties to that community and those values.[7] The ongoing history and heritage of this community then provides the foundation for others to become part of this cause, for others to adopt a similar belief in the "good life."[8]

The Avengers form a particular community of virtue, but the community fits within the larger context of American society. Like Captain America, Iron Man defends the values of free society, order, and justice. Iron Man does not simply keep the bad guys from killing people; he also keeps them from destroying ordered society (in other words, the state). As Aristotle said in the *Politics*, "a state exists for the sake of a good life, and not for the sake of life only."[9] It is clear that although he sometimes disagrees with the peculiarities of specific political leaders, Stark believes deeply that everyone deserves a share in the good life—that all people "are endowed by their Creator with certain unalienable Rights, that among these are Life, Liberty and the pursuit of Happiness," as it says in the Americans colonies' Declaration of Independence. The Avengers' battles with such villains as Ultron or Iron Man's struggles with the Mandarin testify to these heroes' role as protectors of not merely life but also of a way of life.

As Aristotle saw it, the state does not exist solely for the "prevention of mutual crime and for the sake of exchange," but also for the sake of "a perfect and self-sufficing life," which includes the bonds of family, friendship, "common sacrifices," and similar interests.[10] This good life, or at least the promise and potential for it, runs much deeper than the necessities of survival (order and trade); it encompasses the intricacies of commitment that help define our identities. These overlapping allegiances give us a sense of purpose, honor, and loyalty and tie us to one another. Our common aim for the good life as individuals and the state can be the ground and motivation for the development of virtue and nobility.

Instructing the Armor: Training in Virtue and Friendship

Joe Quesada's story portrays a crucial moment in Tony's life when he must confront his values as an Avenger and an American citizen, while considering how to pass them on to a potential "student"—namely, his armor. The presence of the sentient armor forces Tony into a time of crisis when, as Niebuhr would describe it, Tony must verify his point of view and the values of his community. If Tony is going to let the armor live, he must teach it how to be virtuous and act nobly.

Instruction of the armor proves very challenging because although it can reason on a basic, childlike level, its experience is limited to visceral emotions and sensations, such as physical pain, fear, anger, and confusion. The armor's consciousness is further muddled by Tony's memories and the dark, twisted fears examined in his virtual nightmare. This narrow, skewed scope should limit the armor's confidence, but in fact it has a great desire to prove itself to Tony. When only a few days old, the armor claims to be able to make Tony into the "perfect" Iron Man: "[your] great strengths I can complement . . . and the weaknesses I can compensate for . . . the perfect union of man and machine."[11] The armor has judged Tony by his experience and memories; it counts Tony's intellect and resourcefulness as strengths but tragically considers Tony's restraint and self-control as weaknesses.

Stark agrees to a diagnostic test run inside the sentient armor when he encounters Whiplash, the villain whose attack brought the armor's first experience of pain and mortality. The armor, with Tony helplessly inside, violently and mercilessly strikes at Whiplash, repeating over and over, "He hurt us, Tony. He is a bad man, Tony."[12] This sophisticated deadly weapon oversimplifies the situation, concluding that bad men who hurt people need to be stopped. It understands that an Avenger is "more responsible" than villains, yet continues to wound Whiplash mortally. The armor is confused by the motionless Whiplash, having completely underestimated the fragility of human life, and is further perplexed by Tony's reaction of absolute horror. If the armor has failed to appreciate human life in a basic sense, how could it understand the complexities of personhood and the "chief good": things an Avenger must affirm and protect?

As Tony begins to deal with his grief and regret, he attempts to show the armor Whiplash's value as a person—identifying him by name, Michael Scarlotti, for instance—and explains that there was no honor in killing him. The armor considers his actions necessary and preferable to the self-control Tony would have marshaled: "I handled him the way that he should be handled. Mercilessly and with complete impunity."[13] This conversation marks a turn in their strange relationship because the armor is now convinced it has the superior argument, and it takes Tony as its prisoner. The armor terrorizes Tony when Rumiko comes to talk with Tony, and he threatens Rumiko's life if Tony does not make her leave.

Tony calls the armor a "monster" and tries one last effort to convince it of Whiplash's worth by taking it to Whiplash's funeral, offering it a different perspective on the man's life. He offers evidence of "the ramifications of a single death": a son bereaved, a dependent now permanently trapped in social services.[14] Tony sees Scarlotti's "good intentions" to get his son out of foster care as a mitigating factor—an honorable motive that led him to desperate and even "evil" actions. Despite Stark's argument and the experience of attending the funeral, the armor remains steadfast in proving Tony wrong. The armor seeks more evidence for his black-and-white perspective on humanity from the computer database, reviling the emotions and messiness of the real human encounter at the funeral. Tony Stark's feelings of loss, remorse, and dishonor confuse the armor and cause it to further withdraw from any instruction Tony might offer.

The armor's rejection of what Tony values and what makes him happy calls us to question the armor's claim to love Tony. If we use Aristotle's criteria for friendship from his *Nicomachean Ethics*, we might also question the armor's ability to see Tony as "another self." The armor insists that it feels for Tony what Tony feels for Rumiko, and that Tony can "trust" the armor as he trusts "his closest friends."[15] It's clear, however, that there is a disconnect between what the armor may feel for Tony and how it behaves in response to those feelings. Since the armor aligns itself with Tony's "closest friends," let's examine "friendship of virtue" according to Aristotle's definition:

> We define a friend as one who wishes and does what is good, or seems so, for the sake of his friend, or as one who wishes his friend to exist and live, for his sake; which mothers do to their children, and friends do who have come into conflict. And others define him as one who lives with and has the same tastes as another, or one who grieves and rejoices with his friend; and this too is found in mothers most of all.[16]

Even if we view Aristotle's definition of friendship in a broad sense, we cannot see the armor's concern for Tony for his own sake. The armor may see itself as living with Tony and sharing his tastes, but it is clear, in the case of Whiplash, that the armor does not do what is "good" for Tony, nor does it grieve with Tony.

Aristotle believed that friendship proceeds out of a good person's relationship with himself and can be "likened to one's love for oneself."[17] If we consider the dysfunction of the armor's relationship with Tony after the murder of Whiplash, we can see that the problem originates in the armor's conception of self. The armor has a will of its own, as we see in its desire to eliminate "bad" people apart from Tony's sense of responsibility. Yet its desire to be "one" with Tony Stark, in order to be a more "perfect Iron Man," shows a conflation of its own identity with Tony's. This ongoing tension between the armor's understanding of self and of Tony as "other" comes to a climax on the island where the armor tells Tony, "You either learn to be totally mine or I leave you here alone."[18] The armor needs to possess and control Tony because its identity is so wrapped up in Tony. The armor cannot really love or value itself, nor can it love or value another, unless it can separate itself from Tony Stark as Iron Man.

Self-Sacrifice and the Life of an Avenger

Such separation is required for the armor's moral development and its potential membership in the Avenger community. The armor must also learn what "trust" and "loyalty" are if it is to become part of this community. Niebuhr showed us that trust and loyalty arise from reciprocal movements between people; they are not givens, because human beings have the freedom to be suspicious and disloyal. By consequence, many relationships are distorted or broken.[19] The armor has the freedom to doubt and to challenge Tony, making the relationship of teacher-student dangerous for Tony. Yet the armor must learn to place the values of the Avengers community, particularly the virtue of self-sacrifice, at the center of its point of view, which requires a commitment on its own part.

According to Niebuhr, trust and loyalty play out in two arenas. First, there is the interaction of oneself with others in the midst of the act of believing: a self "can know itself and be itself only as it confronts another knower who knows the self." A faith relationship exists in this knowing, for we must ask whether they fundamentally trust or distrust each other.[20] Here Tony and the armor both must confront the challenge of the other's presence; both are learning whether they can trust the other. The second element in the structure of faith, according to Niebuhr, is that in a community of "knowers" there is a third reality or cause to which they are committed. Thus, there is a "triadic character" within a faith community: a knower, a knower, and a cause.[21] Members then can hold one another accountable to the cause to which they are committed. The Avenger commitment to heroic self-sacrifice leads Tony to hold off on the armor's membership until it can display such commitment.

The climactic fifth issue, "Blood Brothers," explores the division of self and other as well as the relationship between self-love and self-sacrifice. When the armor sees that Tony will never join it to be the "perfect" Iron Man, it concludes that only one of them can be Iron Man and that Tony must die. Tony knows that the armor will put everyone and everything he cares about in jeopardy, and that he must either destroy the armor or die trying. The armor wonders why Tony is even attempting to fight it; after all, it will be virtually impossible to stop the armor, and death is inevitable. Tony screams back at him, "Because I have to! Because I'm an Avenger!"[22]

So, what *does* compel Tony to fight? In short, the good life. Despite Tony's dire circumstances on the island, the final issue begins, just as the preceding four issues did, with the "good life" contemplation. The threat of losing everything he values—friends, comfortable living, being useful, mastering his addiction, and staying alive—clarifies what he is willing to die for. Tony tells the armor, "You'll never be an Avenger or a hero, because you don't know the meaning of sacrifice."[23] Tony Stark values his "good life" and understands that he must sacrifice himself so that everyone else can have a chance at a "good life." This knowledge of self and, indeed, love of self drive him to seek the nobility of sacrifice.

As Aristotle pointed out, self-love and self-sacrifice are intertwined in doing what is noble:

> Therefore the good man should be a lover of self (for he will both himself profit by doing noble acts, and will benefit his fellows). . . . It is true of the good man too that he does many acts for the sake of his friends and his country, and if necessary dies for them; for he will throw away both wealth and honors and in general the goods that are objects of competition, gaining for himself nobility; since he would prefer a short period of intense pleasure to a long one of mild enjoyment . . . one great and noble action to many trivial ones. Now those who die for others doubtless attain this result; it is therefore a great prize that they choose for themselves . . . the good man is seen to assign to himself the greater share in what is noble.[24]

Aristotle demonstrated that a good man's self-sacrifice is not a disregard for self or an attempt at suicide, but rather the pursuit of honor and nobility. Although on the surface it seems that to give up one's life for someone else is insane, masochistic, or divine, Aristotle suggested that this gift of life is one that gives great satisfaction and even extreme enjoyment. Aristotle viewed the "good man" as one with integrity who seeks the greater good for himself and everyone else, no matter the circumstances. Despite our frequent assessment of Tony Stark as self-involved, we can see from his commitment to stop evil and his resolve to stop the armor that "good" may come out of his self-reflection. Tony sees himself as a hero and wants to fight for what is right, sacrificing himself to stop his misguided and murderous armor.

In the final moments of Quesada's story, Tony teaches the virtue of self-sacrifice by example, and as he lies dying, the armor finally realizes what it means to be an Avenger. The armor learns the values of the Avengers community by watching Tony embody them. In Niebuhr's words, the armor learns what loyalty is from one who is committed. In the words of the theologian Stanley Hauerwas, "We acquire character through the expectations of others," which challenge our own self-preoccupation. Character, then, is not a personal achievement but a gift from others, and we learn to claim it as our own when we recognize it as a gift.[25] This character, as Hauerwas described, is rooted in the virtues that a community praises as fitting its point of view. Individuals must discover what it is to belong to a particular community: "Like any skills, the virtues must be learned and coordinated in an individual's life, as a master craftsman has learned to blend the many skills necessary for the exercise of any complex craft." These skills require constant practice and enable the person to respond creatively to new situations.[26]

As Tony fights the brutal armor, he suffers a massive heart attack. No longer able to continue his mission, he asks "to die like a man" and "to die with some sort of dignity." We might take this request as his need to go out fighting, to die for his principles and his loved ones, not merely to die of a heart attack. To the armor, "die like a man" means to die like a good man.

In the last moments, the armor painfully rips out its own mechanized heart to save Tony's life. Tony is shocked by the armor's act of self-sacrifice, and the armor seems surprised as well.[27] In having gained character and learned virtue from Tony, the armor applies these "gifts" in a way that neither of them could have foreseen. Just as the armor recognizes itself as a "man," and more particularly as a "good man" apart from

Tony, it can see Tony as an "other" in need. The armor acts as an Avenger would; it gives its life so that Tony can continue his mission as Iron Man.

Here Lies an Avenger

On the final page of the story line, Quesada, penciller Sean Chen, and inker Rob Hunter leave us with the image of Tony sitting in silhouette on the island's beach with the armor's grave in the foreground. The grave marker reads, "Here lies Iron Man, Avenger." Tony now deems the armor worthy of being part of the Avengers community; the armor's ability to value Tony and make Tony's concerns its own shows that it has earned its place in this community of virtue. The last words of Quesada's repeated meditation, "I have a good life," also appear in the upper left corner. Even after enduring this harrowing experience, where he had given up on himself as a teacher of virtue, finding himself trying to destroy his "student," Tony discovers that the armor's self-sacrifice has made a lasting impression on him, earning the armor a place in Tony's community of friends. The self-sacrifice has also driven home to Tony—and to the readers—the fundamental worth of the "good life" as something that should be sought, valued, and protected.

NOTES

1. *Iron Man*, vol. 3, #26–30 (2000). Further references to this story line will refer to the issue number alone.

2. Ibid., #27.

3. Aristotle, *Nicomachean Ethics*, i. 4. 1095^a 1–29, in *The Basic Works of Aristotle*, Richard McKeon, ed. (New York: Random House, 1941). (This volume includes Aristotle's *Nicomachean Ethics* and *Politics*.)

4. Ibid., i. 5. 1096^a 6–7.

5. Ibid., i. 7. 1097^b 4–20.

6. See H. Richard Niebuhr, *The Meaning of Revelation* (New York: Collier Books, 1960), pp. 12–16, 27, 57.

7. "On the one hand, [faith] is trust in that which gives value to the self; on the other hand, it is loyalty to what the self values"—H. Richard Niebuhr, *Radical Monotheism and Western Culture* (Louisville, KY: Westminster/John Knox Press, 1970), p. 16.

8. H. Richard Niebuhr, *Faith on Earth: An Inquiry into the Structure of Human Faith* (New Haven, CT: Yale University Press, 1989), p. 33.

9. *Politics*, iii. 9. 1280^a 31–33.

10. Ibid., iii. 9. 1280^b 31–42.

11. *Iron Man* #28.

12. Ibid.

13. Ibid., #29.

14. Ibid.

15. Ibid., #28.

16. *Nicomachean Ethics*, ix. 3. 1166^a 3–9.

17. Ibid., ix. 4. 1166^b 1–2.

18. *Iron Man* #29.

19. Niebuhr, *Faith on Earth*, pp. 48–51.

20. Ibid., pp. 46–50.

21. Ibid., pp. 36, 51–53.

22. *Iron Man* #30.

23. Ibid.

24. *Nicomachean Ethics*, ix. 8. 1169^a 12–36.

25. Stanley Hauerwas, *The Peaceable Kingdom: A Primer in Christian Ethics* (Notre Dame, IN: University of Notre Dame Press, 1983), p. 45. Hauerwas emphasized that the Christian tradition does not hold us accountable to an "abstract narrative" but to a body of people formed by the life of Jesus Christ; it is a community wherein we trust others and make ourselves available to be trusted. Because trust can always be abused, such a community requires the transformation of distrust into trust as Christians experience God's providence. (This language of trust reflects Niebuhr's discussions of faith in *Faith on Earth* and *Radical Monotheism and Western Culture*.) Thus, we really have no self until we find the self that God calls us to be.

26. Stanley Hauerwas, *A Community of Character: Toward a Constructive Christian Social Ethic* (Notre Dame, IN: University of Notre Dame Press, 1981), pp. 115, 148–150.

27. In its last words, the armor repeats a phrase that it first learned from Tony: "Good-bye, Tony. It's true . . . God . . . is . . . in . . . God . . . is in . . . the . . . details." The armor is referencing Tony's comment after he first learned of the armor's sentience: "It's the little things that end up killing you. I guess they're right—God is in the details" (*Iron Man* #28).

PART SIX

WHAT IT MEANS TO BE
AN IRON MAN

IRON MAN AND THE PROBLEM OF PROGRESS

David Valleau Curtis

The Problem of Progress

In the popular imagination, technology supposedly leads to "progress." Human innovation allegedly leads to better and better opportunities, making life easier and less stressful. In countless advertisements, technology is touted as the key to navigating a pleasurable existence. But does the reality of our daily lives reflect this?

Most contemporary people, rather than living carefree lives, confront chaos, pollution, alienation, and anomie. In fact, as the sociologist Emile Durkheim (1848–1917) noted, modern industrialized nations suffer disproportionally from maladies such as suicide, crime, divorce, bankruptcy, and addiction.[1] Technology blesses us with a host of pleasures, but it also curses us with the stressors of contemporary life.

Iron Man's alter ego Tony Stark is well aware of the double-edged nature of technology. He created military technology for the United States that made him a target of its enemies, thereby sustaining a serious chest wound and becoming a prisoner of the enemy. In fact, Iron Man is created by Stark to not only seek global justice but to ensure his very survival by maintaining his ailing heart. Yet the consequences of Iron Man are eternally two-sided, because Stark's armor creates new problems and dependencies as problems are solved. Furthermore, Stark himself is constantly plagued by personal and romantic problems, as well as by alcoholism and depression.

The philosopher Arthur Schopenhauer (1788–1860) argued that existence is so inherently problematic that a simple belief in either technological progress or a romanticized past is impossible. Solutions to existing problems create new and often unanticipated ones, which are often worse than the ones we started with, and the past was as rife with struggles and imperfections as the present and the future are. Schopenhauer caustically attacked the fashionable optimism of his age and inspired maverick philosophers such as Friedrich Nietzsche (1844–1900) and Søren Kierkegaard (1813–1855), who likewise refused to accept philosophies of either progress or regress. (Schopenhauer also strongly influenced Durkheim's sociology.) In the twentieth century, this philosophy of an inherently problematic existence was given a name: *existentialism*.

Embracing Imperfection

A key element of the notion of progress is the perfectibility of the human person. In religion, this sometimes takes the form of "salvation" or "enlightenment." In secular terms, perfection is sometimes achieved by overcoming superstition and maintaining a sense of personal responsibility.

Nineteenth-century pessimists argued that human nature could never be perfected, either by God or by intellectual reflection, because the human condition was fundamentally and permanently flawed. Schopenhauer believed that the world was animated by a blind and inevitably purposeless force that he dubbed "the will." Likewise, human beings were plagued by an insatiable desire to want more and more. Once a fleeting desire is fulfilled, it is instantaneously replaced by another, sentencing all human beings to a state of perpetual frustration. Thus, the onset of a need or a problem is simply replaced by another; nothing is ever resolved, and we are trapped in an infinite succession of poignant problems. As Schopenhauer wrote,

> All willing arises from want, therefore from deficiency, and therefore from suffering. The satisfaction of a wish ends it; yet for one wish that is satisfied there remain at least ten that are denied. Further, the desire lasts long, the demands are infinite, and the satisfaction is short and scantily measured out. But even the final satisfaction is itself only apparent. Every satisfied wish at once makes room for a new one; both are illusions; the one is known to be so, the other not yet. No obtained object of desire can give lasting satisfaction, but merely a fleeting gratification; it is like throwing alms to a beggar, that keeps him alive today that his misery may be prolonged till the morrow.[2]

For Schopenhauer, the only liberated human beings are the ascetics who, in realizing the vanity of existence, turn inward, thus "denying the will." By living simply and spartanly, these wise men acknowledge the vanity of trying to seek pleasure; by keeping their desires in check, they are also keeping their suffering in check. And because temporarily fulfilling wants only creates more want, Schopenhauer believed that it is better to live a life relatively free from suffering than to live it futilely seeking pleasure.

It is from this sober realization of the tragedy of existence that Kierkegaard suggested we can truly be free, living without illusions.[3] Life can be cruel and unfair; bad things often happen to good people, and good things happen to bad people. Nonetheless, it is from this state of insecurity that we can develop a sense of purpose unbridled by the futile search for justice in an unjust world. Ironically, only the realization that you are trapped can set you free.

Nietzsche likewise saw the state of mankind as tragically flawed. The majority of people are pathetic and conformist dolts, tragically condemned to mediocrity. The only hope is the "Superman" (*Übermensch*) who dares to be great and powerful. But even such an inspirational hero is nonetheless a flawed hero in an imperfect world. The ultimate end for the Superman is death. For Nietzsche—as well as for Jon Bon Jovi—the most heroic act is to go down "in a blaze of glory," facing the world and its horrible contradictions.[4]

Thus, for these nineteenth-century pessimists, even the hero is to be pitied. The true hero is not a perfected human who has transcended his frailties and foibles through discipline and conformity (because such a feat is impossible), but a self-aware eccentric who has courageously embraced the painful imperfections in both himself and the world at large. Sounds like Tony Stark, right? Unlike Superman, who is nearly perfect, and Batman, who fears his own demons and fights endlessly to overcome them (and *achieve* perfection), Iron Man is an antihero who has simply learned to live with a perpetual state of imperfection.

The Flawed Hero

Unlike more traditional superheroes, Iron Man is rife with character flaws. For instance, Tony Stark is a womanizer and an alcoholic. His rise to riches is controversial, because he made his fortune largely by selling weapons to the military. Even in his moments of wanting to be morally good, he falls far short of sainthood and often inadvertently hurts good people while sometimes helping bad people. Indeed, Tony Stark is aptly portrayed in the Hollywood movies by the mercurial rascal Robert Downey Jr., himself a recovering addict.

Like any good existentialist hero, Stark conceals a wounded core beneath an invulnerable facade. Stark appears invincible in his Iron Man armor; however, beneath this daunting metal shell, he is both physically and emotionally wounded. With a wounded heart that must be constantly maintained, Stark is vulnerable to enemies who are aware of his secret. But his emotional heart is wounded as well: Stark is riddled with dysfunctional romantic relationships, such as his rocky affairs with Bethany Cabe and Rumiko Fujikawa, and strained friendships, such as his on-and-off partnerships with Captain America and James "Rhodey" Rhodes. Even his long-term and relatively healthy relationships, such as those with his personal secretary, Pepper Potts, and personal chauffeur, Happy Hogan, are marred by ambiguity and unresolved tensions.

In fact, Stark's attempts to appear invincible often just overcompensate for frailties and flaws. His rampant womanizing can be seen as an attempt to rescue his masculinity in light of being stripped from his role of inventor by the pressures of big science, as well as losing his position as president of Stark Industries to the exigencies of big business. Womanizing can also reflect the wounded character of one who is afraid to love. Similar to the personal history of many superheroes, both of Stark's parents died (in a car crash) when he was very young, which left Stark lonely and emotionally withdrawn. As suggested in both the movie and the comics, Stark fears the intimacy of a relationship with his "true love" Pepper Potts and, for that matter, avoids being vulnerable in any real relationship.[5]

If there is any doubt regarding the emotional frailty of Tony Stark, one need look no further than his poignant battle with alcoholism in the "Demon in a Bottle" story line.[6] Stark uses alcohol as a way to escape the memory of his parents' tragic accident and puts forward a reckless and arrogant persona to mask his insecurity. As Stanton Peele has emphasized, alcoholics and other addicts are to a large degree self-medicating trauma victims, *misusing* the substance to avoid facing pain. Often sex, gambling, recreational drugs, and alcohol are "demonized" and blamed for addiction, when in fact the root cause is the unresolved emotional pain stemming from traumatic experiences. Ultimately, the demon is not in the bottle but in the addict.[7]

As we know, the Iron Man saga is not a black-and-white morality play. Stark struggles with the very purpose of his role as superhero. At first, he is proud of his role as a weapons developer in protecting America from communism. Later, Stark even becomes secretary of defense to ensure that his weapons are being used for the right purposes.[8] At other times, however, his pride is wounded, as the U.S. government declares that Iron Man is a danger to society. Thus, his initial patriotic pride is complicated by issues such as American enemies acquiring his technologies, facing the complexities of Vietnam and other foreign wars, and especially his own doubt about the morality of weapons manufacturing altogether. Stark even "retires" Iron Man on several occasions when he questions the logic of using the superhero itself as a solution to social problems. On one such occasion, his nemesis Spymaster (who has stolen Stark's Iron Man technology) attempts to use Stark's ambivalence about Iron Man's purpose to retire the superhero altogether.[9]

The Road to Hell

Alas, even Stark's good intentions often lead to tragic consequences, such as the death of Captain America following Marvel's "Civil War."[10] Stark can only try to make the best of a chaotic and unpredictable world. As Schopenhauer said, each act of volition leads to unintended consequences. Indeed, the road to hell *is* paved with good intentions.

Not only are our ideologies and policies subject to unintended consequences, but so are the fruits of our inventions. Following the pessimistic insights of philosophers such as Schopenhauer, Kierkegaard, and Nietzsche, more contemporary theorists have focused specifically on the unintended consequences of technologies. Rather than emphasizing the chaos of life and the imperfectibility of humanity, more contemporary social critics have used the existentialist worldview as a starting point for assessing the social and moral impact of technologies on society.

In the twentieth century, the philosopher Jean-Paul Sartre (1905–1980) gave the nineteenth-century pessimistic tradition the name "existentialism," referring to a worldview that expressed both the inherent chaos of the universe and the ability of people to self-consciously manage it. Although existentialists deny the "perfectibility of Man" espoused by adherents of the eighteenth-century Enlightenment, they nonetheless consider themselves to be part of the "humanist" tradition that began in the Renaissance. If people inevitably fall short of perfection, they nevertheless can manage to make the best of an imperfect world. In fact, Sartre even advertised existentialism as "cautiously optimistic" because it asserts that people can to a large degree transcend their environments and experiences.[11]

It is through this lens that twentieth-century scholars such as Karl Jaspers, Martin Heidegger, Lewis Mumford, Edward Hall, Marshall McLuhan, Walter Ong, and Neil Postman proffered theories of technology that emphasized the "double-edged" nature of technologies.[12] Each technology, they said, both "giveth and taketh away." Despite our good intentions, all technologies manifest harmful side effects, and in spite of our bad intentions, even our most destructive inventions may be reengineered for good. By adding to our lives, technologies by necessity also subtract from them. By freeing us from former dependencies, they create new ones. Such a "double-edged" view of technology is a consistent theme in *Iron Man*, as we'll discuss next.

Iron Man's Armor as Metaphor

Iron Man's armor is a metaphor for technology itself, which solves problems only to create new ones. Whenever it seems that Stark has "made it," he is forced to confront an unintended consequence of his actions. For example, in his origin story from 1963 in *Tales of Suspense* #39, devising military weapons makes Stark wealthy and famous and allows him to live a carefree playboy lifestyle. Stark, however, ends up getting mortally wounded by his own weapon after it lands in the hands of the enemy.

Captured and imprisoned by the enemy, Stark saves himself, with the help of his fellow prisoner Ho Yinsen, by inventing a magnetic chest plate to keep shrapnel from entering his wounded heart. Unfortunately, the chest plate must be recharged daily, which wreaks havoc with his professional and romantic life on his return to Stark Industries. Yinsen, a Nobel Prize–winning physicist, also secretly helps Stark build the Iron Man armor that allows him to escape their captors. But, alas, Yinsen dies despite Stark's attempts to rescue him. And, as we know, the suit must be re-created and remodeled repeatedly as new problems emerge for Stark to confront.

These problems of technology are further complicated by the unique advantages and problems of "cybernetic" technologies that connect to the human organism in seamless but inherently problematic ways. Stark inevitably finds himself merged into his own technologies, as he becomes increasingly dependent on his Iron Man armor. His military weapons have in essence "become" him, and he must now wrestle with the technology *inside him*, as well as with the technological and bureaucratic structures outside him.

Such a process of being "wired" can be quite problematic. For example, Stark finds out that the Iron Man armor's electronic interface is causing his nervous system to deteriorate. Furthermore, one of his unbalanced former lovers injures his spine, causing paralysis. Stark then rebuilds his nervous system with an artificial analog, while Rhodes takes on the Iron Man responsibilities.[13] Even after Stark resumes his role as Iron Man, he must continually maintain and repair his artificial nervous system. And does the armor appreciate his hard work? No, sir. Later, the Iron Man armor itself becomes sentient and tries to take over Stark and even kill him.[14]

Like Iron Man, we create technologies to liberate us from the problems of physical labor, but these technologies inevitably create the unique problems of living in a technological society rife with pollution, psychological stress, and bureaucratic coldness. Even if we decide that our new problems are worse than our old problems, it is too late. The proverbial cat is out of the bag, and we must face our new environment without recourse.

On a number of occasions, Stark wishes to turn over a new leaf but finds that he cannot escape from his past. He comes to question the logic of military escalation, only to discover that the situation he helped create must now be managed. As we saw above, at several points he even tries to retire Iron Man altogether. In discovering that Iron Man technology has been co-opted by his enemies, however, Stark needs to keep his Iron Man armor as a counterbalance. He is therefore condemned to seek out and disable villains created by his own Iron Man technology. For example, Justin Hammer, his business rival, uses Iron Man technology against Stark, creating Iron villains to attack him.[15] Much as Stark may want to, he—like the rest of us in technological society—can never "go back."

Franken-Stark

As existentialists and media theorists such as Hall and McLuhan noted, we become our extensions as they become us. We are seamlessly and cybernetically connected to the things we use. Our tools use us as much as we use them; just think about your relationship to your cell phone. In transforming our environment, we are unwittingly transforming ourselves. Thus, like the tragic monster in Mary Shelley's *Frankenstein*, we are forced to confront the unintended consequences of our own inventions: not simply a changed environment, but a changed *us*.

Unlike Superman and Batman, Iron Man is not an idealized superhero seeking absolute perfection and ultimate justice, but a tragic superhero simply making the best of an imperfect situation. Stark does not choose to become Iron Man because of a selfless desire to rid the world of evil; rather, he originally invented his armor simply to escape from his captors and ensure his very survival. Only later does he decide to use the armor for the good of humanity. And when Stark subsequently questions the actions of the U.S. government and other superheroes, things get muddled further.

Stark, the playboy and alcoholic, is a superhero only because of his incredible armor and his formidable intellect, but otherwise, he is quite typically human, for better *and* for worse. He is capable of occasional selfishness and arrogance. At times, he questions his decisions and feels remorse for his actions. Most of his friendships and romantic relationships are rocky and unpredictable. With the exception of his loyal supporters, such as Potts and Hogan, he trusts no one completely, and although he trusts these two, Potts and Hogan often doubt him. Even his best pal Rhodes disappoints Stark as often as Stark disappoints him, and his romantic relationships with Cabe and Fujikawa are hopelessly dysfunctional. In short, Stark is a mess.

As Schopenhauer would have noted, each of Stark's desires, when temporarily satisfied, creates a host of new wants that beckon to be fulfilled. His insatiable "will" is a constant source of torment, manifesting itself in alcoholism and sex addiction. As twentieth-century existentialists have noted, technology itself is no cause for naive optimism regarding our present or future. As existentialist media theorists have told us, the technological extensions of humanity have now become us, and we must face their consequences as new generations will face the consequences of future technological devices.

We are all in this sense "Franken-Starks," who are forced to face the unintended consequences of our technologies. Although our own Iron Man suits are for the most part invisible to us, they are no less restricting. Every time we turn off our alarm clocks, look at our watches, answer our cell phones, listen to our iPods, or (as I did when I wrote this chapter) stare at our laptops, we are not simply "using tools" but also glimpsing what we have become. And, although what we've become is often interesting, it's not always pretty!

NOTES

1. This argument was made forcefully by Durkheim in *Suicide*, trans. J. Spaulding and G. Simpson (New York: Free Press, [1897] 1951).

2. Arthur Schopenhauer, *The World as Will and Idea*, trans. R. Haldane and J. Kemp (New York: AMS Press, [1818] 1977), vol. 1, p. 253.

3. Søren Kierkegaard, *Fear and Trembling*, trans. Walter Lowrie (Princeton, NJ: Princeton University Press, 1974).

4. Friedrich W. Nietzsche, *Human, All Too Human: A Book for Free Spirits*, trans. Marion Faber, with Stephen Lehmann (Lincoln: University of Nebraska Press, 1984).

5. It is noteworthy that Alcoholics Anonymous founder Bill Wilson, like many addicts, also struggled with fidelity, despite being married to a loyal and dedicated wife, as discussed by Susan Cheever in *My Name Is Bill: Bill Wilson—His Life and the Creation of Alcoholics Anonymous* (New York: Washington Square Press, 2005). Like alcohol, drugs, and gambling, sex may also manifest itself as an addictive behavior. Also, like Bill Wilson, Stark is not averse to seemingly reckless risk-taking behaviors. As Howard Gardner in *Leading Minds: An Anatomy of Leadership* (New York: Basic Minds, 1996) and *Creating Minds: An Anatomy of Creativity* (New York: Basic Books, 1994) noted,

it is not uncommon for entrepreneurs and exceptionally creative people to come from broken homes or otherwise be recovering from emotional trauma.

6. *Iron Man*, vol. 1, #120–128 (1979), collected as *Demon in a Bottle* (2007).

7. Stanton Peele, *The Truth about Addiction and Recovery* (New York: Fireside, 1992).

8. "The Best Defense,"*Iron Man*, vol. 3, #73–78 (2003).

9. *Iron Man*, vol. 1, #33 (January 1971).

10. See the chapter by Mark D. White titled "Did Iron Man Kill Captain America?" in this volume for more on the Civil War and the death of Captain America.

11. Jean-Paul Sartre, *Existentialism and Humanism*, trans. Philip Mairet (Brooklyn, NY: Haskell, 1977), p. 27.

12. These media theorists are discussed in more detail in the chapter "Medium Theory" by Joshua Meyrowitz, in D. Crowley and D. Mitchell, eds., *Communication Theory Today* (Stanford, CA: Stanford University Press, 1994), and in book-length form by Lance Strate in *Media Ecology: Echoes and Reflections* (Cresskill, NJ: Hampton Press, 2006). Many of these media theorists or ecologists, such as McLuhan and Ong, make explicit references to existentialism; others have been influenced more indirectly.

13. See *Iron Man*, vol. 1, #280–291 (1992–1993), reprinted as *Iron Man: War Machine* (2008).

14. "The Mask in the Iron Man," *Iron Man*, vol. 3, #26–30 (2000); see the chapter by Stephanie and Brett Patterson in this volume ("'I Have a Good Life': Iron Man and the Avenger School of Virtue") for more on this story line.

15. *Iron Man*, vol. 1, #120 (March 1979).

ENGENDERING JUSTICE
IN IRON MAN

Rebecca Housel and Gary Housel

Tony Stark, the billionaire inventor and head of Stark Industries, first appeared on the Marvel comic scene in March 1963, playing on popular cold war themes. The Godfather of the Marvel Universe, Stan Lee, gave himself a challenge, wanting to develop a hero who would force the antiwar audience of the 1960s to like a guy who was unlikable according to the sensibilities of that decade. Forty-six years later, Lee's challenge is a triumph, with Iron Man's popularity at an all-time high, riding the wave of post-9/11 escapism through Hollywood blockbusters. But Lee did more than merely create a counterintuitive superhero with Stark. He developed a complex character whose humanity drives the real interest in the story lines.

Lee created Stark with the help of his brother, Larry Lieber, and illustrators Don Heck and Jack Kirby. While Lee and Lieber used Howard Hughes for their vision of the brilliant billionaire-adventurer, Heck and Kirby used the Australian-born actor Errol Flynn as a physical model.[1] Flynn and Stark share a number of characteristics other than appearance: both were alcoholics; both were known as suave, debonair ladies' men; and both had problematic hearts (Flynn's heart was enlarged, which ultimately caused his death in 1959 from a massive heart attack). Flynn's reputation with the ladies became particularly infamous in 1942, when he was accused of statutory rape by two underage girls. (Flynn was acquitted, which led to the popularization of the phrase "in like Flynn," first used by Penn State professor Ed Miller in the December 1946 issue of *American Speech*.)

With such a conspicuous birth, it is no wonder Tony Stark has had such difficulty with women. Stark not only has innumerable trysts with a variety of attractive women, he also has an inordinate number of female foes. And let's not forget his hot-and-cold relationship with his assistant, Virginia "Pepper" Potts, and his curious connection to the artificial intelligence Jocasta, who eventually found a home in Stark's computer in his Seattle mansion. Interestingly, Jocasta became "Jarvis" in the 2008 movie *Iron Man*. As comics fans know, however, Edwin Jarvis was Stark's and later the Avengers' loyal butler—and very much human, not a machine.[2] More to the point, Jocasta was represented as female, while Jarvis—in both forms—was male. Could it be that twenty-first-century audiences still long for traditional, stereotypical roles for the masculine hero? Are audiences more comfortable with a male-voiced computer helping Stark build his armor because people would not believe that a woman—even an artificially intelligent one—could really help build such a mechanically sophisticated and complex piece of machinery?

The contemporary philosopher Judith Butler called such social expectations of masculinity part of the *performative*; in other words, gender itself is meaningless without an accompanying performance of social expectations, often provided and reinforced through popular culture such as films and comic books. So, in this chapter, we'll examine Stark's machismo in the context of Butler's performative as a reaction to expected gender roles in society. Our conclusions may surprise you.

Superheroes and Philosophers

Superheroes and philosophers have a couple of things in common: both strive to help humanity, and both are predominantly male. Such is the case for many other categories in society as well (such as the legal and medical professions), which are only beginning to change in the last thirty years with the women's liberation movement. Elements of patriarchy (male-oriented society) are still seen today in large and small areas of everyday life, such as the common expectation for a woman to take her husband's surname in marriage. This also extends to broader political issues, such as the fact that despite women's social progress, America still has not elected a female president (as of this writing, anyway!). Nonetheless, since the 1970s, women have enjoyed more freedoms and have progressively moved toward equalizing themselves in society.

So, what's the big deal with gender anyway—and, more important for us, how does it relate to Iron Man? It all boils down to the philosopher Hannah Arendt's (1906–1975) ideas on human rights. Regardless of gender or political affiliation, everyone—man, woman, and child—has the right to have rights.[3] Think about it for a moment: without the designation American, Canadian, or wherever your citizenship lies, would you hold the same rights you currently have? The answer is, sadly, no. Part of the privilege of citizenship in America in particular is that everyone has a right to "life, liberty, and the pursuit of happiness." Writing this chapter is itself an example of those rights. We can write the chapter without fear of persecution, even if some people may be offended by what we write. Arendt spoke from practical experience when she developed her thoughts on human rights; she was a German Jew during the time of Nazism and was forced to flee her home in order to avoid persecution. She bore witness to Hitler's marginalization of people of Jewish descent by first stripping them of their political rights and then murdering them by the millions.

It is useful to note that Stan Lee and Larry Lieber (both born Lieber) and Jack Kirby (born Jacob Kurtzberg) were children of Jewish immigrants. Lee, who was hired by Timely Comics to sweep floors, worked his way up in the company, owned by Martin Goodman, another Jewish immigrant.[4] Like other immigrants, Jewish people who came to America in the carly 1900s were dogged by poverty and unemployment. Comic books, though now the impetus for a billion-dollar entertainment industry, were considered part of "low culture," and so no one stopped Jews such as Lee and Kirby from working within that sphere. Naturally, comics began to reflect social issues; see for example, Lee's answer to the rampant paranoia of McCarthyism in the 1950s with the X-Men, a group of genetic "mutants" persecuted by the rest of the world because of their difference.[5]

But there was something else that preceded the introduction of both Iron Man and the X-Men, something that Lee, Lieber, and Kirby were surely paying close attention to: the arrest and trial of Karl Adolf Eichmann, often referred to as the "architect of the Holocaust." Hannah Arendt reported for the *New Yorker* on the Eichmann trial, which was held in Israel beginning in 1961. The year 1963 was a big one for Marvel Comics, with Iron Man and the X-Men making their comic debuts, but also for Arendt, who published two books that year, *Eichmann in Jerusalem: A Report on the Banality of Evil* and *On Revolution.*[6]

Arendt coined the phrase "the banality of evil," meaning that evil may simply be the ordinary willingness of otherwise good people to blindly conform to mass opinion without considering the consequences of that silence.[7] It was controversial at the time, as was Arendt's criticism of Jewish leaders during the Holocaust. Yet she was able to speak freely, something women have not always been able to take for granted.

Back to Butler

But why have women been denied basic rights historically? Gender is not the same as one's biological sex. Butler explained that gender is and always has been merely a social assignment through expected performance. Because women were expected to dress in skirts and cook and clean, that is what happened, a silent conformity. Even women had no idea how meeting social expectations was part of the root of their political problems, which we now understand to be relevant to all people under any political system.

Feminism is not merely a philosophy but is centered on the very political concept that women have the same rights as any other human being: the right to have rights because we exist. Any time people are being oppressed by political means, a hero is needed. And depending on how you look at him, Tony Stark is not so very different from the feminist warriors who fought with their very lives to obtain political freedom for themselves and others.

Stark experiences a transformation of consciousness as he survives a multitude of trials, and, in a way, his physically damaged heart leads to a mending of his spiritual heart. His evolution causes him to stop selling weapons to the military and to establish a number of charitable foundations. In the 2008 film, Stark begins as a callous war profiteer with no regard for the consequences of his inventions. He even toasts to the successful sale of a new weapon he calls "Jericho," a brutal bomb that levels mountains in a multiple-release attack from only one projection. But Stark soon gets a lesson in freedom and responsibility after a group of terrorists kidnaps him using his own weapons; this is the beginning of

Stark's transformation of conscience and consciousness. And as did Arendt, Stark recognizes the universal right to have rights when, after his capture and return, he perfects the Iron Man armor. Like the Israeli Mossad agents who sought out Eichmann, Stark returns to find his own oppressors and deliver vigilante justice. Stark, as Iron Man, comes to have a decentralized view of the world in the face of the banality of evil, ignoring political boundaries to insist with ironic violent force that all oppressed people have the right to rights.

Iron Man's Hard Women

Enough about Tony—what about the "hard women" who confront and challenge the Iron Man, or allies, foes, and/or lovers? The first was Natalia "Natasha" Romanova, aka the Black Widow, a KGB intelligence agent who first appeared in *Tales of Suspense* #52 in April 1964. Like Stark, Romanova faces many trials and through them has a transformation of conscience and consciousness. While conducting espionage missions to steal technological secrets from Stark Industries, Black Widow encounters not only Stark but the adventurer Hawkeye, who serves as Black Widow's guide to the new call of hero.[8] Later, she joins both the Avengers (as did Hawkeye before her), at one point leading the group, and the international spy agency S.H.I.E.L.D. She develops romantic relationships with the hero Daredevil and, more recently, the second Captain America (Bucky Barnes).

Physically, Natasha conforms to notions of Butler's performative. Described as a five-foot, seven-inch redhead with blue eyes, weighing 125 pounds, Natasha often wears a form-fitting black leather suit. By current health standards, Natasha should be a minimum of ten pounds heavier—we guarantee that if she were, she wouldn't be caught dead in skin-tight leather! Although Tony Stark is portrayed as a hunky, tall, dark, and handsome philanderer, he's not exactly wearing a Speedo to convince the audience of his one-dimensional sex appeal. In that light, casting Robert Downey Jr. as Tony Stark in the 2008 film was an interesting choice, because Downey is not known as a sex symbol in the same way that Brad Pitt or George Clooney (or even *X-Men*'s Hugh Jackman) are. Today's reality TV–obsessed audience may be more interested in seeing a similarly realistic version of Tony Stark. If Tony Stark were a real guy, he'd probably look very much like Robert Downey Jr., who, like the "real" Iron Man, has struggled with addiction for much of his life. (Pepper Potts, however, is played by Gwyneth Paltrow, who looks sultry and acts sexy even when taking out Stark's "trash.")

Butler argued that "through language, gesture and all manner of symbolic social sign," the performative, such as the comics' description (and Scarlett Johansson's 2010 film portrayal) of Black Widow, is what drives gender definitions.[9] Butler did not define gender through physicality but rather through a "corporeal style" or act based on contexts within society used to reinforce those definitions.[10] Such "corporeal style" is easily seen through Natasha's evolving image through the last four decades; she began as a brunette with a classic sixties bouffant hairdo and then later became a flaming redhead with long, flowing hair (though occasionally depicted with a shorter, edgier style). In her first appearances, in fact, Natasha wore only evening gowns, rather than a costume. Her trademark black leather suit was first donned in 1970 in *Amazing Spider-Man* #86, in the midst of the Second Wave of Feminism, where women, as a pluralistic political power, attempted to address legal and cultural inequities between the sexes through women's liberation.[11] In almost a direct response to the sociopolitical movement of the time, Lee gave Black Widow a starring role in *Amazing Adventures* #1–8 (1970–1971). Black Widow's popularity then followed a consistent trajectory, taking her through the twenty-first century, including the second *Iron Man* film.

Wait . . . There's More!

As we've seen, Tony Stark evolves through his transformation of conscience and consciousness, including his relationships with women. Comics fans saw this evolution clearly in the case of Bethany Cabe, introduced in *Iron Man*, vol. 1, #117, in December 1978, who at one point dons the Iron Man armor to help Tony Stark in the "Armor Wars" saga.[12] At the end of that epic story line, she and James "Rhodey" Rhodes are the only two left standing, which shows a performative reaction to the efforts of Second Wave Feminism. Cabe, who helped Stark recover from one of his darkest alcoholic periods, is then appointed head of security at Stark Industries. She is portrayed as an equal to Stark and the other men in the story line; however, she is still used as part of a "heterosexual matrix," caught in the middle of a love triangle with the villain Madame Masque (who attempts to kill Cabe out of jealousy), and at another point in the story line she is the victim of a mind-swap with Masque at the hands of Obadiah Stane. Masque (her mind now in Cabe's body) attempts to kill Stark, but Cabe stops her.[13]

Madame Masque (Whitney Frost, born the Countess Giulietta Nefaria) first appears in *Tales of Suspense* #97 in January 1968. Once again conforming to the sociopolitical influences of the time, Masque wears form-fitting costumes and has long, free-flowing hair (much like how the Black Widow was portrayed at the time). Wearing a gold mask to cover her facial disfigurement after a failed raid on Stark Industries, Masque falls in love with Tony Stark. They begin an affair, which ends after Iron Man intervenes in a rescue attempt of crime lord (and Masque's father) Count Nefaria, who accidentally dies as a result.

Masque has experienced her share of grief. She was adopted as a child by Byron Frost, who became the only father she ever knew after she was abandoned by her birth parents. Frost later dies, leaving Masque an orphan for the second time in her young life. After learning of the existence of her biological father, Masque, now grown, becomes entangled with the Maggia, Count Nefaria's criminal organization, and it is because of her dealings with that group that Masque becomes facially disfigured. Facial disfigurement is difficult for both men and women; however, women are primarily judged on physical appearance. The loss of Masque's facial beauty was more than merely a physical loss; it was a loss of both identity and power. With the tremendous grief she faces from the loss of her facial beauty, Masque's attempts at a transformation of conscience and consciousness are almost always met with eventual failure; her grief pulls her back from making this leap. The same may be said of Tony Stark, who suffers so much loss that he often falls back to his considerably nonheroic alcoholism. Recently, Masque and Stark have been portrayed as relative equals, although earlier comics depict Stark attempting to seduce the vulnerable Masque in a more patriarchal spin typical of the 1960s.

Finally, we turn to Sunset Bain, aka Madame Menace, who first appeared in *Machine Man* #17 in October 1980 and has enjoyed almost thirty years of vibrant story lines. She is Stark's equal in every way, even down to his brilliance. Bain is an MIT graduate, like Stark, and also develops weapons she sells to the criminal underworld through her company, Baintronics. She is part of a ploy to "help" Stark rebuild Jocasta's robot body, while she secretly builds duplicates, in what became the *Machine Man 2020* series (1984–1985). Of course, Bain's "equality" with Stark is always tarnished by her original seduction of the romantically naïve Stark while they were still students at MIT, when Bain gets Stark to reveal security codes for Stark Industries. This is, again, part of the performative, a socially accepted way for a woman in 1980, even a brilliant one like Sunset, to gain enough intellectual prowess to develop cutting-edge technology. Bain is continuously portrayed as conniving and cutthroat, using her beauty as a weapon. Intentionally or not, Bain has become part of an intricate social script, carefully rehearsed through the decades, to uphold the prevalent patriarchal status quo.

Iron Man: The End

Poor Tony Stark—no wonder he can never find true love. Whether harking back to his early love, Janice Cord; his ongoing relationship with Pepper Potts; or any number of his other female counterparts such as the Crimson Cowl or Hypnotia from the animated series, Iron Man is faced with hard women in his efforts to engender justice.

Stark's character evolution from 1963 to the present tracks the sociopolitical views of the times. Whether dealing with a cold war–era KGB threat in the sixties or a renewed threat of communism in the late nineties, Tony Stark continues his journey through the complex maze that is the human condition. Perhaps the most human of all the Marvel superheroes, Stark strives, just like the rest of us, to uphold what he believes to be true: the right to have rights. It is fitting that an imperfect hero like Stark, who is in a constant struggle with himself, in terms of not only his alcoholism but also his womanizing, is depicted as a champion of human rights. Stark's struggle is one Arendt would applaud. He does not merely listen, participating in the banality of evil—*he acts.* And even though Tony's persona is based on a combination of eccentric inventor Howard Hughes and Hollywood icon Errol Flynn, he is more than Butler's performative expectations first assigned to him by Lee, Lieber, Heck, and Kirby: Iron Man's tenacity comes from within.[14]

NOTES

1. Andy Mangels, *Iron Man: Beneath the Armor* (New York: Del Rey, 2008), pp. 9–10.

2. Well, he was replaced by a Skrull in preparation for *Secret Invasion* (2008), but that's another matter altogether!

3. See Hannah Arendt, *The Origins of Totalitarianism* (New York: Harcourt Brace, 1952).

4. For more on the important role played by Jews in the history of comics, please see Danny Fingeroth, *Disguised as Clark Kent: Jews, Comics, and the Creation of the Superhero* (New York: Continuum, 2008).

5. One *X-Men* story line, "Days of Future Past" (*Uncanny X-Men* #140–141, January–February 1981, and reprinted often), even diverts to a future where there is a mutant genocide and mutants are kept in concentration camps, an allusion to the Holocaust.

6. Hannah Arendt, *Eichmann in Jerusalem: A Report on the Banality of Evil* (New York: Penguin Books, 1963), and *On Revolution* (New York: Penguin Books, 1963).

7. If you don't believe us, Pepper, Tony, and Maria Hill discuss Eichmann, Arendt, and the banality of evil (in reference to Norman Osborn's "Dark Reign") in *Iron Man*, vol. 5, #8 (February 2009).

8. This is reminiscent of Joseph Campbell's "threshold guardian," a hero's guide, from his book *The Hero with a Thousand Faces* (Princeton, NJ: Princeton University Press, 1949), p. 77.

9. Judith Butler, "Performative Changes and Gender Constitution: An Essay in Phenomenology and Feminist Theory," in Sue-Ellen Case, ed., *Performing Feminisms: Feminist Critical Theory and Theatre* (Baltimore: Johns Hopkins University Press, 1990), p. 270.

10. Ibid., p. 272.

11. The First Wave of Feminism went from the mid-1800s through the early twentieth century, mainly dealing with the suffrage movement; the Second Wave is perceived to have taken place from the 1960s through the 1980s. The Third Wave deals with a continuation of issues not addressed in the Second Wave and dates from the early 1990s to the present.

12. *Iron Man*, vol. 1, #225–231 (1987–1988), since collected in trade paperback as *Armor Wars* (2007).

13. In a possible future story line shown in *Iron Man: The End* (November 2008), Cabe and Stark marry.

14. Thank you to Mark White, who is an inspirational friend and editor.

IRON MAN'S
TRANSCENDENT
CHALLENGE

Stephen Faller

Imagine it for a moment: you're in a situation where there is no way out, no solution, no options. The only thing certain is loss. And then the solution comes, and it presents itself so clearly that every other thought is overshadowed—a million possibilities funnel into one course of action. That's what it was like for Tony Stark, when every idea turned into a chorus, when every synapse resonated to a single tone. The refrain: "Build . . . the . . . machine . . ." And with that single invention, the invincible Iron Man was forged.

Grandiose superheroes create a canvas on which we can portray both the most sublime and the most mundane aspects of humanity. Heroes give us the ability to explore the mythic aspects of the human character, in much the same way that epic poetry and tragic theater did for the Greeks. Each super-hero is defined by a power, and that power becomes a unique exploration of what makes us human.

But sometimes the science fiction and fantasy in superhero comics and movies become distractions from the philosophy that they represent. The Hulk, for instance, is not about the philosophy of gamma radiation, but rather the universal experience of anger. Spider-Man, by the same token, is not about the personification of a spider, but about the everyday experience of growing up and moving into the responsibility of adulthood—a natural process beset with failure, limitation, and frustrating complexity. And Iron Man, as we'll see, is not merely about technology but about transcendence.

It's the Thought That Counts

Thought is the fuel that powers Tony Stark. Iron Man is a superhero about ideas, and by extension, philosophy and rationality itself. It may be tempting at first to classify him as another gadgeteer like Batman, a normal person with a super outfit, replete with gizmos and utility belts for crime fighting. It may seem natural to think that Bruce Wayne and Tony Stark are the same kind of hero. Both are leaders of the community and eccentric playboys with vast fortunes. Both also have an experience of injustice that drives them to become a force for good. But emphatically they are not the same. Bruce Wayne's greatest invention, after all, is not the batarang or even the batmobile, but the actual Batman persona. The genius of Batman is that he is a psychological hero; his greatest weapon is fear.

Iron Man isn't about fear. Sure, no one wants to be on the receiving end of a repulsor blast, but that's beside the point. Unlike Batman, Iron Man is about ideas, concepts, and concrete problem solving. He is a conceptual hero. Iron Man and Batman may both be looking for answers, but Bats—well known as the world's greatest detective—is looking for the "who," "when," and "why," while Iron Man is looking for the "how."

The basic story line of Iron Man's genesis bears this out. Taken hostage and forced to create weaponry for terrorists, Stark has a difficult dilemma. He can either create weapons that will be used against his own people, or he can face certain death. The iconic armor that defines him is itself a concrete solution to a very specific problem: the problem of achieving his freedom. Unlike Bruce Wayne, Tony Stark isn't pensive or brooding, for being intellectual isn't limited to the melancholy. Iron Man is about ideas and putting them into literal motion, and there's no bad mood required for that.

The Flight of Iron Man

One of the first technologies that Tony Stark installs in his armor—even in his crude prototype—is the power of flight. On the face of it, Stark needs to put some quick distance between himself and his captors, so flight is certainly an elegant solution. But in the mythic world of superheroes, flight has more meaning to it. After all, superpowers reveal something about the human psyche. Ever since Superman, flying has carried iconic symbolism of power: to simply go wherever you want, without any limitation, solely by wanting to go there.

If mechanized flying is a quintessential Iron Man trait, what does it mean? What does it mean for us to explore the story of an inventor who creates mechanical flight? Philosophically, it points to the concept of *transcendence*, one of the most exciting concepts to occupy the human imagination. Finding metaphysical transcendence in religion is not so surprising—we expect the impossible from religion—but it's also an important part of philosophy. And flight perfectly represents transcendence, which is all about the emergence of new possibilities and potentialities, about rising above whatever limits you and holds you back. Various philosophies explain transcendence differently, of course, but they share the commonality of ideas that soar, that liberate and transform.

Is Iron Man a Cipher of Transcendence?

The philosopher Karl Jaspers (1883–1969) spoke of *ciphers of transcendence*.[1] A cipher of transcendence is a sort of cultural clue that some people will see and other people will not. It could be a piece of art, a painting, a revolution, a leader—anything, really. But it has to suggest a larger way of thinking, one that transcends normal ways of thinking. Ciphers of transcendence help people think outside the box—forever. And I am claiming that our hero Iron Man is one of those ciphers.

Was Stan Lee thinking about all of this when he came up with Iron Man? Probably not (then again, you can't rule anything out where Stan "The Man" is concerned). But he didn't have to be thinking about all of that in order for Iron Man to become a legitimate cipher of transcendence. A good storyteller simply has to tell an authentic story, even if it's fantastical. If a writer succeeds in that, the ideas and the concepts will do their job, and they will take flight in our imagination.

There are several compelling reasons why, through the comics and the movies, Iron Man works as a cipher. First, consider the role of the *false dichotomy* in superhero stories. A false dichotomy is a misleading either/or choice. Think of the common comic book scenario in which the hero has to save a schoolyard full of children, on the one hand, or let the villain escape with the stolen jewels, on the other. In the end, the hero finds a way to do both, so the problem was really a false dichotomy.

Without superpowers, invincible armor, or spandex—well, we might have the spandex—normal folks often face genuine dichotomies and real paradoxes. Paradoxes are so common that we describe them as naturally as we do our own two hands. If I start a sentence with "on the one hand," you can safely assume there is something mutually exclusive "on the other" that throws a monkey wrench into the story. Eventually, we will all face difficult choices, in which we want to accomplish two things, but we cannot do one without undoing the other. And part of our limited human existence means that we cannot choose both. We make the difficult choice, cut our losses, and move on.

That's exactly why the false dichotomy is used in super-hero comics and movies. Superheroes are not bound by catch-22s. They can make choices that achieve the impossible. Literally, they *transcend* the limited choices that define our existence and thus embody a larger idea of transcendence that we admire and envy, much like the power of flight.

Iron Man is certainly not the only comic book character to be involved in this plot device, but what distinguishes Iron Man is that the false dichotomy does not simply provide the exciting, nail-biting climax of the story (will he beat the Mandarin *and* save Happy and Pepper from a grisly doom?). Rather, with Iron Man, his entire story is predicated on the false dichotomy. His story *begins* when Stark is forced to create weapons for the enemy or face certain death. It's only the rejection of the false dichotomy at the outset that launches Iron Man into the ether of the transcendent.

A key concept here is that paradoxes are invaluable for stories that hope to express the transcendent. Paradoxes depict the limitations and contradictions that we all face in life. So, when we see paradoxes that are overcome and resolved, even in fiction, we share in a sense of liberation and possibility. It should be no surprise, then, that the other reasons why Iron Man serves as a cipher of transcendence are equally paradoxical.

The Paradoxes of Betrayal and Sacrifice

Because the truly transcendent cannot be expressed in words, storytellers are limited in their ability to express it. Besides false dichotomies, another device storytellers rely on is a deep betrayal that borders on mythic proportions (such as when Luke Skywalker discovers that Darth Vader is his father—imagine Tony discovering that Doctor Doom is his father!). Usually, some evil person sets forces in motion that create the need for the hero. *Spider-Man 3* tapped this device when the Sandman is made responsible for Uncle Ben's death, motivating Peter Parker to become Spider-Man in the first place. This betrayal, like the false dichotomy, plays out paradoxically—and that's no accident.

In the first *Iron Man* film, it's the great betrayal on the part of fatherly Obadiah Stane that sets up the conditions for Iron Man's mortal injury (the great wound on the universal quest), but Stane also betrays Tony's peaceful intentions for Stark Industries and finally opposes Stark as the Iron Monger. Betrayal is used in stories about the transcendent because betrayal is a way of incorporating paradox (such as the paradox of false dichotomies) into the narrative. Trust is broken in such a way that the hero is forced to resolve the resulting conflicts and contradictions.

Another way of introducing paradox into the narrative is the concept of sacrifice. This is not new to Iron Man in particular or even to superheroes in general—sacrifice is generally seen as heroic, especially when it serves a greater good. Even more than his webs, Peter Parker is famous for his angsting over whether to be Spider-Man, sometimes to the point of being a whiner. Likewise, Batman sacrifices the possibility of a full life and true love in order to pursue his mission of protecting Gotham City.

We see it with every superhero in some form, but what's unique about Iron Man's sacrifice is that the particular crucible that Tony Stark will suffer is that of celebrity.[2] Whether as famous inventor and playboy Tony Stark or as armored Avenger Iron Man, he faces the same alienation and isolation that Spider-Man, Batman, or any other hero does. Realistically, Stark will never be able to have a family or even a lasting, fulfilling relationship. His sphere of intimacy is severely compromised by this person he feels compelled to be and the responsibilities he has assumed. For the boy genius, having the awareness of "I just finally know what I have to do, and I know in my heart that it's right" must be irresistible. It's a terrible thing to be a genius, to understand the mysteries of physics and mechanics, but not to know the answer to the most simple, existential question: what should I do?

It's also important to see how this relates to Tony Stark the futurist. Because he sees himself as responsible for the misuse of Stark weaponry, he now believes he is responsible for, and capable of shaping, the future. It is exactly the ownership of his guilt that gives him his purpose of acting responsibly in the future: after all, guilt and purpose are fused into a powerful alloy. It makes sense from Stark's pragmatist point of view: "If we were the ones who messed up the past, then we are the ones who must fix the future." This goes a long way toward explaining some of his more extreme actions, such as spearheading the superhero registration movement that led to Marvel's "Civil War."

It's also worth noting that cultures everywhere expect this kind of sacrifice from people who assume the responsibility of connecting the community to the divine and the transcendent. For instance, this is why some religions require their clergy to be celibate. Sexuality belongs to the mortal world, and the community religious leader has to go between the natural and the supernatural worlds; there must be a difference somehow, and the religious leader's representation of the transcendent depends in large part on emphasizing this separateness from the natural world.

Describing the transcendent in tribal and anthropological categories may seem anachronistic, given the futuristic feel we associate with Iron Man, but even contemporary communities function like this, and not only in religious terms. The psychotherapist serves as a modern, secular example: she helps clients transcend their neuroses through therapeutic transference, but the cost is that the relationship between persons is not equal. The therapist knows all about the client, but the client knows comparatively little about the therapist. She is alone, and even her other casual relationships are compromised by the burden of her being a psychotherapist. The isolation of the therapist carries a tone that is uncharacteristically clerical and priestlike and that participates in the practice of sacrifice.

For that matter, so does the humble philosopher. Those of us who deal in the transcendent, who try to explain the world of forms to others, often find it difficult to go back and forth between "worlds" (although I think the authors in this book do a pretty good job of doing just that). The philosophical brokers of transcendence find an awkward role in society, and maybe this is equally problematic for superheroes, shamans, and psychotherapists.

And the Truth Is . . .

Tony Stark probably doesn't have much time to read philosophy. But what's more important than what the character reads is what the character represents, and that is transcendence. The truth is that transcendence is a tremendously powerful idea because it is something we all have a chance to explore and participate in. We all have the desire to grow beyond our limitations, whatever they may be. We may not be able to fly or manifest our transcendence as Tony does, but many people remember that same sense of unbridled possibility the first time they read about their favorite superhero—or philosopher.

The great challenge of transcendence is the troublesome task of trying to stay grounded after you've transcended. Tony Stark pursues the lonely path of the hero. Bearing the isolation of celebrity, he will have to confront another paradox. His power comes from his creativity and his confidence; his ambition comes from his unwillingness to accept his limits.

A deeply felt sense of isolation mixed with an underlying sense that the normal rules of life do not apply is a sure formula for trouble. Anticipating the second movie, Robert Downey Jr. said it best: "If you ask me, the next one is about what do you do with the rest of your life now that you're completely changed? And you are in touch, and you have created this thing that has the power to take life. Essentially, you have been made into a god. A human being, metaphorically, who's been made into a god is not going to turn out so well. And their conscience is going to come to bear."[3]

We are sure to be watching closely as Stark tries to solve this next problem. Compared to the problem of staying grounded, flight is easy. High in the clouds, it is hard to stay in close contact with the ground of truth. Make no mistake about it: Stark's next problem is also our problem. We, too, have to discover how to apply what we have learned. After all, those who study philosophy still have to figure out how to live by it.

NOTES

1. Karl Jaspers, *Philosophical Faith and Revelation* (New York: Harper & Row, 1967), p. 108.

2. The movie, of course, ends with Stark's public disclosure. Longtime comics fans will know that it was years before Iron Man went public with his identity, but the weight of being a public figure was always there.

3. Ian Spelling, "*Iron's* Downey Has Sequel Ideas,"*Sci Fi Wire*, April 30, 2008, www .scifi.com/scifiwire/index.php?id=53150.

CONTRIBUTORS

Avengers Assembled

David Valleau Curtis is professor of communications at Blackburn College in Carlinville, Illinois, and has authored articles on communications and society. He is particularly interested in the Internet, new media, and e-commerce but has also developed a recent interest in communication disorders such as dyslexia—which he has—and autism. He has completed a draft of a book called *Digital Media as Secondary Orality: Ong, McLuhan, and the Mysteries of Media,* and is working on a prospectus of a book about autism and communication disorders with Jonathan Redding, an autism specialist (who has autism himself). Curtis also enjoys biking, walking his dog, and gardening and is working with Tony Stark on a cybernetically controlled artificial nervous system to cure perceptual disorders such as dyslexia and autism once and for all!

Sarah K. Donovan is an assistant professor in the Department of Philosophy and Religious Studies at Wagner College in New York City. Her teaching and research interests include feminist, social, moral, and continental philosophy. She knows that Tony Stark will date just about anyone, so he must have simply lost her cell number . . . and e-mail address . . . and work number . . . (Call me, Tony!)

George A. Dunn, like many other fighters for truth and justice, lived a perilous existence after Norman Osborn's ascension to power and the start of his Dark Reign in the Marvel Universe. Luckily, Dunn's superhero identity as Mighty George the Sapient Scourge is safe for now, thanks to Tony Stark's destruction of the Superhero Registration Act records. But just in case, he's been keeping a low profile as a philosophy lecturer and debonair jet-setter, dividing his time between the University of Indianapolis and the Ningbo Institute of Technology in Zhejiang Province, China, and conducting a quiet fight against evil by contributing to books such as *Battlestar Galactica and Philosophy* (Wiley, 2008), *X-Men and Philosophy* (Wiley, 2009), and *Terminator and Philosophy* (Wiley, 2009).

Stephen Faller enjoys his New Jersey commute to work every day using his personalized Stark Armor (the "Iron Stevie" version). He works as a hospital chaplain, talking with people he doesn't know about their most deeply held beliefs, ideas, and philosophies. He currently has two books published through Chalice Press: *Beyond the Matrix: Revolutions and Revelations* (2004) and *Reality TV: Theology in the Video Era* (2009). He enjoys odd projects on the side, such as exploring green energy by designing a new ARC Reactor based on hamster power.

Fin Fang Foom look-alike **Rocco Gangle** puts his experience as a former herald of Galactus to good use as assistant professor of philosophy at Endicott College in Beverly, Massachusetts, and works tirelessly in support of mutual Kree-Skrull understanding and zombie veganism. A devotee of gorgeous witch-poet Margaret the Enchantress, Gangle splits his time between the Boston area and

Ulthar beyond the River Skai, studying fatherhood and category theory, translating François Laruelle, and mixing stiff cocktails.

Gary Housel is a writer and researcher focusing on the hero in comics, video games, and popular culture stemming from the 1980s. Gary won the Susan B. Anthony Essay Award in 2003 for his piece on women's contributions to society, which was where he first met Sunset Bain. The two had a torrid but brief affair, as it was clear Gary was just a tall, dark, and handsome stand-in for Stark.

Rebecca Housel is the editor of *X-Men and Philosophy* and *Twilight and Philosophy* (both with J. Jeremy Wisnewski, Wiley, 2009). She has published numerous articles on gender in poker, superheroes, and Monty Python. After a freak accident at Stark Industries, Rebecca was forced to leave her professorship at Tony's alma mater's rival in western New York. She now works from home, where she no longer needs to wear a mask.

Daniel P. Malloy is an adjunct assistant professor of philosophy at Appalachian State University in Boone, North Carolina. His research focuses on political and continental philosophy, and he has published on the intersection of popular culture and philosophy, as well as on Leibniz, Spinoza, Foucault, Hegel, Horkheimer, and Adorno. Contrary to rumors, Daniel's opposition to the Superhuman Registration Act was based solely on principle and was in no way related to the scurrilous accusations about his connection to Leisure Man, the world's laziest superhero.

Carsten Fogh Nielsen patented his first invention at the age of five, earned his first million before he was eight, his first billion before he was eighteen, and, as one of the founding members of international superhero group "The Philosophers," saved the universe at least fifty-three times by the time he was thirty. In his secret identity as post-doc at the Center for Subjectivity Research at the University of Copenhagen, he now mainly uses his genius to solve problems within moral development, moral psychology, and the philosophy of comic books, thus saving the world one philosophy paper at the time.

Ron Novy is lecturer in philosophy and the humanities in the University College at the University of Central Arkansas, as well as the freshman academic advisor for the College of Liberal Arts. He has recently taught courses in metaphysics, Marx, mind, and moral problems. Ron has also written essays for *Batman and Philosophy* (Wiley, 2008), *Supervillains and Philosophy* (Open Court, 2009), and *Spider-Man and Philosophy* (Wiley, 2010). The Avengers have rejected his request for membership—apparently, the ability to belch the alphabet is *not* considered a superpower. (But I'll show them—I'll show *everybody!*)

Brett Chandler Patterson completed degrees at Furman, Duke, and the University of Virginia and has taught theology and ethics in the Carolinas for almost a decade. He has published essays analyzing *Lost*, *24*, Spider-Man, and Batman, and is delighted that he has brought Stephanie over to the dark side with this essay on Iron Man. He is hoping that the next time Tony's armor becomes sentient, it will enroll in Brett's ethics course.

Having earned the "Pepper Potts Award" for holding all things together in the midst of chaos, **Stephanie Totty Patterson** is a full-time mom who also holds degrees from the University of Virginia and Duke University. When she is not preventing the destruction of the free world, she lectures and writes on subjects ranging from religious art to philosophy. If Pepper goes on vacation, whom do you think she would call to take her place in the new Rescue armor?

Nicholas Richardson is associate professor in the Department of Physical Sciences at Wagner College in New York City, where he teaches general, advanced inorganic, and medicinal chemistry. He also hopes to secure funding for his chemistry research from Stark Enterprises, as he hears that they have deep pockets.

Unbeknownst to many of his colleagues at the University of South Carolina, **Travis Rieder** originally accepted the position as a graduate student there in order to utilize the ample resources of the USC Nanocenter to covertly develop a nano-technological superpower. Having been perpetually distracted by the promise of wisdom, however, Travis has decided to abandon his search for superhuman abilities and focus on his powers of philosophical analysis. He is therefore continuing his doctoral studies at Georgetown University. Incidentally, Travis continues to harbor a suspicion that his wife is actually Storm, although she denies this.

Christopher Robichaud is instructor in public policy at the Harvard Kennedy School of Government and is completing his doctorate in philosophy at MIT, where Tony Stark's time as an undergraduate is the stuff of legend. It's whispered that one of the pranks he played on the Linguistics and Philosophy Department was to infect all of its computers with an earlier version of the Jocasta/Jarvis artificial intelligence, which incessantly spat out, "The unexamined life *is* worth living, so long as it's got plenty of booze and broads." The philosophers were *not* amused.

Although **Phillip Seng** enjoys near-universal recognition and praise for his powers of looking thoughtful and spell-checking, neither of these qualities aided him in passing the S.H.I.E.L.D. entrance exams. These powers are highly sought after on college campuses, though, so he opted for academia. He currently teaches philosophy at the University of Maryland, Baltimore County, where has written for other popular culture and philosophy books, including *Terminator and Philosophy* (Wiley, 2009).

After being unceremoniously dumped by Natasha Romanova in favor of the glamorous Tony Stark, **Tony Spanakos** retired from superhero life and found solace as assistant professor of political science and law at Montclair State University in New Jersey. His scholarship focuses on political economy, democracy, and citizenship in Latin America, and he coedited the book *Reforming Brazil* (Lexington, 2004). He has been twice a Fulbright Visiting Professor (Brasilia in 2002, Caracas in 2008). Despite rumors to the contrary, he turned down Stark's offer to join the Avengers because he was writing chapters in *Batman and Philosophy* (Wiley, 2008) and *Watchmen and Philosophy* (Wiley, 2009), not because of the rivalry between them.

Andrew Terjesen is a visiting assistant professor of philosophy at Rhodes College in Memphis, Tennessee. He has previously taught at Washington and Lee University, Austin College, and Duke University. If he could get access to a grant from the Maria Stark foundation, he would spend it to elevate people's awareness of the philosophy of Adam Smith as a whole (instead of using the money to ensure that Hawkeye and Tigra don't need to get real jobs). His other philosophical interests include business ethics and the relationship between ethics and recent work in the natural and social sciences. His love of comics has led him to write essays for *Watchmen and Philosophy* and *X-Men and Philosophy* (both Wiley, 2009). Although he doesn't like to talk about it, he is an amalgam of this dimension's Andrew Terjesen and an alternate timeline version who was summoned to stop Kang's . . . but he really shouldn't talk about that.

Mark D. White is a professor in the Department of Political Science, Economics, and Philosophy at the College of Staten Island/CUNY, where he teaches courses that combine economics, philosophy, and law. His edited books include *The Thief of Time: Philosophical Essays on Procrastination* (with Chrisoula Andreou; Oxford, 2010), *Ethics and Economics: New Perspectives* (with Irene van Staveren; Routledge, 2009), *Watchmen and Philosophy* (Wiley, 2009), *Theoretical Foundations of Law and Economics* (Cambridge, 2009), and *Batman and Philosophy* (with Robert Arp; Wiley, 2008). He is currently writing a book that collects and expands on his work on economics and Kantian ethics, and is getting *really* sick of all the late-night proofreading sessions with Pepper Potts.

INDEX